THE PROUD
PEOPLE
Agaar "Dinka"

William Mayom Maker

A Note from the Publisher

The publisher wishes to acknowledge and thank Dr Douglas H. Johnson for his invaluable help and support for Africa World Books and its mission of preserving and promoting African cultural and literary traditions and history. Dr Johnson and fellow historians have been instrumental in ensuring that African people remain connected to their past and their identity. Africa World Books is proud to carry on this mission.

© William Mayom Maker, 2020

ISBN: 978-0-6489698-1-5

Design and typesetting: Africa World Books

Contents

SUBSISTENCE STRATEGIES

TRADITIONAL DANCES AND GAMES

Preface

THE IDEA OF WRITING THIS BOOK came about when I visited South Sudan in 2016. Having been away from home for over three decades, I found that our culture had changed. At first, I thought I was just suffering from reverse culture shock that usually occurs after a significant lapse of time. But as I stayed longer in my hometown, Rumbek, it became apparent to me our culture had considerably changed for the worse.

The Second Civil War (1983-2005) between the central Sudanese government and the Sudan People's Liberation Army had impacted the Agaar socio-cultural systems, forcing the people to abandon cultural pursuits and focus on survival and security. Boys begged or pick-pocketed in the streets. Youths, including traditional warriors, the *apärä̈puö̈öl*, drank alcohol and did all other culturally unacceptable things. Girls and women ran here and there with bleached skins and toxic wigs on their heads. Men played cards all day, watched football in poorly ventilated clubs, or boozed in local bars. The Agaar culture I knew was no longer visible, and everything appeared alien to me, including the way people dressed, talked, and acted. Subsequently, I felt lost and isolated as I missed the familiar symbols, customs, and attitudes, which once defined the proudest people of Agaar.

What was even surprising to me was that people had become comfortably numb to the chronic chaos. In Rumbek, killing, revenge-killing, robbing, cattle-rustling, and many other inhumane activities had become a part of people's daily lives. Overwhelmed by the immensity of the change, cultural values had been forsaken and no one had attempted to revive them even after the war was over. Even elders, who were supposed to be the custodians of wisdom and cultural values, seemed to have given up hope of restoring the lost culture and traditions.

Two days after arriving in Rumbek, I met a group of young men sitting under a mango tree in the market. They were three young men aged between 16 and 20. They sat on a bench made from poorly arranged bamboo poles. What I saw confirmed what I already knew: the culture had changed. The young men were wearing saggy pants and big chains around their necks—a hip hop style I did not expect to find in that part of the world. Also, they were smoking cigarettes. And when I approached, they smelled as if they had just emerged from a nearby bar. They were talking and laughing as they passed a lit cigarette around.

On the east side of the tree was a group of four elderly men sitting on plastic chairs. One man, with a big belly, wore a dark-brown shirt and black trousers. Sitting on a stool directly behind the big-bellied man was a young soldier wearing a green uniform with an AK47 on his lap. The big-bellied man was a high-ranking government official, perhaps a general in the national army, and the solider was his bodyguard. The other two men wore loose jalabia-robes and were probably relatives who had visited from rural villages. They were all talking and laughing absent-mindedly while drinking tea, not even paying attention to the young men who were doing culturally unacceptable things right before their eyes.

My mind flashed back to the time when Agaar's cultural values were stable. Back then, when an adult saw a child misbehaving, the adult had a moral obligation to advise the child to behave appropriately, even if they were not related. Children were the responsibility of the entire community as expressed by the phrase, "A child belongs to all the community." I could not believe these elders could share the tree with intoxicated youths who were smoking and wearing saggy pants.

I ignored the elders and approached the young men. "*Kudual!*" I said, "Greeting!"

"*Acin kerac,*" they said in unison, "nothing bad; all is good."

The oldest of them, who was probably around 20 years old, threw the filter on the sandy floor and stepped on it before shaking my hand. He wore skinny-legged jeans and a half-buttoned criss-cross shirt. He appeared more talkative and articulate than his friends.

I arranged the loose bamboo poles on the bench to support me as I sat down and leaned against the mango trunk. Near the tree was a small shop with a verandah where a young woman was cooking tea in a soot-coated kettle. On the far side, I could see Rumbek's busy main road, where cars and people mingled in the spiraling dust.

"Where are you coming from?" I asked the young men.

"We live in here in Rumbek," the young man with an unbuttoned shirt said—I later discovered his name was Jima.

I realized I had not been specific in my question. What I wanted to know was their clan, not where they lived. It was typical for an Agaar elder to approach subordinates by trying to know their parents and sub-clans. Nevertheless, I wanted the conversation to continue. I intended to build rapport with them, to understand what they were up to. In other words, I wanted to know why they smoked, drank, and dressed like that.

Surprisingly, I learned they were decent students from Rumbek Secondary School, who were just hanging out and having a good time on the weekend; the saggy pants, chains, smoking, and drinking were typical styles many youths had recently accommodated, because of media influence.

"Your time was different," Jima playfully remarked after I told them I was not allowed to smoke or drink when I was their age. "Things have changed now."

Having built up a rapport with the young men, I lectured them about the importance of our cultural values and keeping their culture as the primary foundation, with education and modernity to strengthen the original foundation. They respectfully agreed, and were even interested to hear more, especially when they learned I came from Canada. Jima even promised to quit smoking and drinking after I told them about the side effects of smoking and drinking, including addiction, a shortened life span, and interpersonal and respiratory problems.

"I've never heard such advice from a well-informed gentleman before," Jima said, in English. "I'm glad that educated individuals like you have come from abroad to teach us." He switched to Agaar language. "Like the fox said, 'the reason I defecate on the road is that no one tells me it is a bad habit.' Now that I know how bad smoking and drinking are, I'm quitting."

The other young men kept nodding in agreement without saying much.

Soon they excused themselves, saying they were heading to watch a soccer match in Medan Horiya, (the Freedom Field), the main soccer field in Rumbek. The tea woman came over and asked me if I need a cup of tea. I asked for a bottle of water instead, but she said she only sold tea. She went to the other side to collect cups. The big-bellied man reached into his back pocket and extracted two notes of a hundred South Sudanese pounds, which he pressed into the woman's hand.

As I was about to leave, I heard a voice say, "Let me ask you something first. Have you come here with those lies of yours?"

I looked around to see who was speaking. It was the big-bellied man. He looked at me with a combination of a chuckle and a smirk. I did not understand what he meant by that.

"What lies?" I asked.

"The lies you people from abroad bring to us," he said. "Like what you were telling those boys."

I knew I had to be extremely careful here. There was nothing more threatening to an illiterate, influential leader than a young, educated individual coming from abroad. Unaware that I had fought in the liberation of South Sudan before resettling to Canada, they assumed we had run away during the war and had now returned to take their jobs. If he felt like I disrespected him, he could arrest me himself. Even worse, he could send an unknown gunman to take care of me. Many educated young men from the USA, Canada, and Australia were harassed, arrested or even gunned down in Juba and other towns and cities by unknown gunmen. Besides, I was in the Sudan People's Liberation Army (SPLA) before, so I knew the system better. A high-ranking government official could put anyone to prison without charges. So, I had to play smart with this big-bellied general, or else I would not return to Canada.

"I was not telling lies, Comrade," I said. "I was just trying to instill our cultural values in those young men—"

Many South Sudanese leaders like to be addressed as "honorable", but I strategically used the term "comrade", the term SPLA fighters used, trying to demonstrate to him that I had fought in the liberation of South Sudan before moving to Canada. But the Big Belly didn't buy it.

"Nonsense," he barked. "If we, who have lived here our entire life, can't do it, do you think you can? Here in Rumbek, most boys and even girls are drinking. Even in rural villages and cattle camps, the *apäräpuööl* (traditional youth) mix alcohol with *makuanga* (groundnut paste). Are you going to talk to all of them? You are wasting your time if that is why you leave your comfortable life in Canada and come here."

I knew I had to deescalate the situation. Trying to reason with such an individual was not a wise idea. It's like trying to reason with a grumpy buffalo; you end up in its sharp horns.

While contemplating on what to do, a pickup Toyota arrived, and the Big Belly with his associates focused their attention on the vehicle.

Two men got out of the car. The four men rose to their feet to greet the two men. The guard gave his chair to one man and yelled to the tea woman to bring more chairs and three more cups of tea.

I looked at my Casio watch on my wrist; it was 5:12 pm, Wednesday, January 4, 2017. I had 48 minutes to get home before the sun went down. My mother had warned me to return home before sunset to avoid being robbed or even killed by criminals. It was the time when unknown shooters randomly killed people in Rumbek. Coming from Canada with a smartphone, watch, expensive boots, and clothes, I was a high target for criminals. But before worrying about the criminals, I had to get away from the Big Belly.

When they were preoccupied, I figured this was the best opportunity for me to leave while the Big Belly and his associates were distracted. I got up and walked away like a gazelle that has just escaped from the lion's paws.

On the way home, I played the entire episode over in my head. The chuckle and smirk, coupled with the way he looked at me as he made that remark, told me the Big-Belly was mocking me. The implication was that if the cultural change was so immense that the influential leaders in Rumbek could do nothing about it, what could an immature man who came from Canada do?

But the Big Belly's behavior, not to mention his associates who didn't intervene, was pure ignorance at its best. I thought the elders like them would appreciate my courage and effort of confronting those young men. But that was not the case. It became apparent to me why our cultural values had deteriorated. Because if such influential leaders of our community were this ignorant, who could blame the youths?

The behavior of the big-bellied general with his associates reminded me of this story of a hummingbird, narrated by a Kenyan professor and a Noble Peace Prize winner, Wangari Maathai:

One day, Dr. Maathai said, a devastating fire broke out in a forest. Frightened, all the animals came out of the woods and stood at a safe distance as they watched their livelihoods destroyed by the raging fire. The animals were disheartened and overwhelmed, and they felt there was nothing they could do to stop the fire.

A little bird called a hummingbird, the smallest of all the animals, gathered enough courage and said she wanted to do something about the fire. So she flew to a nearby river, picked up a water drop with her tiny beak, flew back, and poured the water onto the fire. Then she dashed back to the river. The hummingbird repeated this action, every time bringing a drop of water and dumping it on the fire. Even though her effort was insignificant, the hummingbird was committed, determined, and persistent.

Meanwhile, all the other animals and birds, including the elephant, giraffe, rhino, and lion, were standing there watching helplessly as their livelihoods destroyed. Instead of running to the steam to draw water to try to put out the fire, the other animals mocked and discouraged the hummingbird: 'Look at this little bird!' the elephant said. 'What are you doing? You are too little for that fire. You can't even bring enough water because your beak is too small. Do you think you can put out the fire which has overwhelmed us, the big animals? Forget it!'

Think about that for a moment. The elephant, the most significant animal, with the biggest trunk that could carry gallons of water, did not just stand there and watch helplessly, but shamelessly mocked, discouraged, and sabotaged the hummingbird that was working hard trying to save their livelihoods. Now, think back to my encounter with the general and his associates. Being both the leaders and elders, they had more power and influence than anyone to change things in our community. But instead of using his status to change the mindsets of those culturally incompetent youths, the general discouraged and sabotaged me by saying I was wasting my time, without even acknowledging my effort, courage, and determination; just like the elephant who disapproved the hummingbird's effort, forgetting he had the biggest trunk that could carry much more water to put out the fire.

Do you know what the hummingbird said when the elephant discouraged her? She said, 'Irrespective of how insignificant my effort looks to you, I'm doing the best I can.' So, to the big-bellied general who thought I was wasting my time lecturing to the intoxicated young men: irrespective of how insignificant my effort looked to him, I was doing the best I could to save our deteriorating cultural values.

When I returned to Canada on January 18, 2017, I met another culturally incompetent 20-year-old man at a McDonald's restaurant in New Westminster, British Columbia. I lived in a city where meeting another black person, let alone a South Sudanese, was a rare treat. There was a massive lineup, so I queued up, and the young man stood right behind me. We nodded our heads in acknowledgment. He was wearing saggy blue jeans, a white football jersey, and a cap turned backward. His physical appearance (dark, thin, and tall with cropped hair) told me he was a South Sudanese. But I was not cocksure.

"Are you a South Sudanese by any chance?" I asked.

The elderly Canadian man wearing shorts and big framed eyeglasses who was ahead of me, looked back, thinking I was talking to him. He realized I was not talking to him, so he refocused his attention to the cashier who had just yelled, "Next person in line!"

"Yes," the young man replied, sounding like he was not sure about his answer.

He did not have a South Sudanese accent, so I gathered he was born in Canada.

I did not want to approach him the same way I approached those young men in Rumbek by asking his names and where he came from. Instead, I approached him in the typical Canadian style: "My name is Mayom," I said as I extended my right hand, which he shook.

"I'm Doubt," he said.

"Doubt?" I said.

"I mean, it's not my real name; it's my nickname, but I prefer it."

"Well, nice to meet you, Mr. Doubt."

He did not want to reveal his identity to a total stranger, which I understood. So I did not press on asking his real name. But I was dying to know what tribe he belonged to. If he told me his name, I would know whether he was from the Dinka, Nuer, Equatoria, etc. Not that I indorsed tribalism, but that's the typical way South Sudanese elders approach juniors.

"So . . . Mr. Doubt," I said, "do you know what part of South Sudan you are from? I hope you don't mind me asking."

"I'm not sure exactly," he said. "I mean, I was born here in Canada."

"Fair enough," I said.

I realized he seemed more comfortable talking about Canada than South Sudan, so I stayed on the subject for a while, not wanting to spook him. We were the only black people in the queue, but that did not stop us from carrying on the conversation. He said he was born in Calgary, Alberta, and then moved to Ontario with his mother, and now had come to Vancouver to visit his girlfriend. I was not interested in all of that, but I just wanted to make him feel comfortable enough to keep the conversation flowing. I wanted to know what part of South Sudan he was from.

After talking about Canada for a while, I changed the subject and asked whether he had ever heard from his parents what part of South Sudan they're from.

He thought for a moment. Then he said, "Dinka Rumbek? I mean, I always hear my mother saying we are from Dinka Rumbek."

I wanted to laugh when he said Dinka Rumbek in that typical Canadian accent, but I didn't want to embarrass him. My mind flashed back to the young men whom I'd met under that mango tree in Rumbek Town. At least those young fellows knew where they came from, and they spoke Dinka fluently. This Canadian-born son of Agaar, who called himself 'Dinka Rumbek,' was indeed a lost sheep.

"You mean to say you are from Dinka Agaar?" I said, trying to correct him.

"I don't know what that means," he said.

"Never mind then," I said. "I'm from Dinka Rumbek, too!"

"Are you serious?" Mr. Doubt said, enthusiastically. "What a coincidence!"

All the other Canadians in the line were listening, but I didn't care. We were the only ones talking. I kept asking question after question, and he answered them to the best of his ability. He was a very outspoken young fellow.

"Next person in line please!" the cashier said. Our turn came to place our orders. Mr. Doubt ordered a Big Mac with coke and French fries. I also ordered the same things, and then I told the cashier to add up both bills and I would pay.

"Why would you do that?" Mr. Doubt said. "I will pay mine. I have the money."

"I know you have money," I said. "But that's how we do it in Dinka Rumbek. Whenever you meet an uncle in a restaurant, the uncle usually pays."

"But how do you know we are even related?" he asked, trying to give me that typical Canadian smartness. "We've just met."

"In Dinka Rumbek's culture," I said, "any older person you meet is considered your uncle or aunt. So, I'm your uncle."

"So, what happens if the uncle does not have money?" Mr. Doubt countered.

"If the uncle doesn't have money, then he doesn't have to offer to pay," I replied. "The reason an uncle gives something to a junior is not that the uncle is rich," I continued, "Instead, it is just a gesture so that the junior can do the same thing to another person younger than them."

The Canadian old man wearing big framed eyeglasses who was now waiting for his order had heard enough: "Tell me where Dinka Rumbek is," he interjected, as those in the line roared in laughter. "I want to move there!"

Another young Canadian man wearing a baseball cap and a Douglas College sweater looked at another middle-aged man standing behind him and said, "I guess you are my uncle."

"I guess so," the middle-aged man said, "but I'm not paying for your shit. I want to move to Dinka Rumbek myself."

Everyone in the line laughed, and we found ourselves in the center of attention, as they completely interrupted our conversation. After getting our meals, we went and sat at the same table to continue talking. While we were eating and talking, my phone rang, and I excused myself to talk on the phone in Dinka. The fact I switched from English to Dinka fascinated him. "It's incredible how you just switched from English to another language in seconds," he said after I had finished talking on the phone. I told him I was fluent in both English and Dinka Rumbek, which he thought I was "super cool."

Surprisingly, Mr. Doubt asked me to teach him a few Dinka Rumbek words. He wanted to impress his mother when he returned to Ontario. I was like, "Okay, I can help you with that."

We started with the items on the menu which he wrote down on a napkin. Nouns: meat = *ring*; water = *piu*; milk = *ca*; tea = *cäi*. Verbs: eat = *cam*; drink = *dek*. Pronouns: you = *yïn*; I, me = *yɛn*; him, her, or it = *yien*.

After memorizing the Dinka vocabulary, I got carried away and ventured deeper into Dinka grammar. I explained to him that English uses one (drink) verb to describe the intakes of all liquids, such as water, tea, milk, alcohol, or soup. But Dinka uses three different verbs: *dëk* is the intake of water and alcohol; *ruëth* is the intake of milk; and *yöp* is for hot beverages, such as soup, tea, or broth. The same thing applies to different foods: the eating of food is *cääm*, but the consumption of meat is *cuët*; eating of crunchy or hard food is *rëm*; and consumption of powdery food is *mok*.

"But that doesn't make sense," Mr. Doubt protested.

"Look, man," I said, "English doesn't make sense either, but we just follow the rule and learn the language anyway. For example, your nickname, Doubt, is spelled with the letter b, but the letter b is not in the pronunciation. Now, if you want to learn Dinka, just follow the damn rules!"

After spending over one hour talking and laughing, I parted from Mr. Doubt. I gave him $100 and told him to go and take his girlfriend out. He thanked me profusely, saying, "You are the coolest Dinka Rumbek I have ever met." But the most important thing I heard from Mr. Doubt was when he said "I will visit Rumbek one day."

I left the restaurant that day knowing I had changed the perspective of that young fellow, Mr. Doubt, not mentioning the Canadians who were eavesdropping, by showing him a piece of our culture. Not that many Canadian-born African children talk about visiting home because of the misleading images they see on television about the starving African children who are too weak to even swat flies away from their faces. People think the entire continent of Africa is like that. But the fact Mr. Doubt talked about visiting Rumbek one day meant I had changed his attitude.

However, I knew my effort was not enough to change the views of all South Sudanese children born in Canada, let alone the other Western countries, but I was doing the best I could, just like the hummingbird.

Shortly after returning to Canada from South Sudan, I created a social media page where I wrote and shared culturally significant stories. I intended to educate young South Sudanese who were born abroad, just like Mr. Doubt. These stories received positive reactions from a wide variety of readers, including non-South Sudanese readers. In 2016, my first piece, titled *Kawaja*, was published in an anthology book, *Pearls 35*, at Douglas College in British Columbia, Canada, where I obtained a bachelor's degree in Financial Services and Administration. I also wrote several short stories I posted on social media, to give today's generation a glimpse of how things were before South Sudan's Civil War. These stories generated lots of enthusiasm among young people, both at home and abroad. South Sudanese news media picked up and published some of these stories in *Gurtong Trust, PaanLuel Wel Media*, and others. Thousands of followers, mostly South Sudanese, including politicians and generals in the army, followed me on social media. I received numerous phone calls, emails, and text messages from the followers, including top-ranking South Sudanese government officials, who thanked me for the stories, encouraged me to continue writing about our culture, or asked me to write a book about our cultural values. The following are some comments I received on my Facebook wall:

On May 7, 2019, at 12:45 am, Agel Machar, the spokesperson of the First Vice President of the Republic of South Sudan, General Taban Deng Gai, wrote:

General Taban Deng Gai, the First VP of the Republic of South Sudan, had read this [article], and he liked it very much. He was laughing nonstop as he read [because of the humor in your writing]. Keep writing, Comrade Willy Mayom Maker.

On December 20, 2018, at 6:04 am, Telar Deng, former ambassador to Russia, wrote:

Willy Mayom Maker, your stories exemplify the difficulties we had faced during the liberation struggle of our country [...]. We are all encouraging you to continue writing our stories for the next generations to learn how this country came about.

On December 12, 2019, at 5:35 pm, Jokmagai Dengdit wrote:

What a beautiful story! It's so full of our cultural flavors [...] Thank you, William Mayom Maker, for teaching us, the city-dwellers, some of our forgotten traditions.

On December 13, 2019, at 9:26 am, Deng'Kur Mading wrote:

There is one Africa that is trouble when it travels beyond the seas of the ocean. There is yet another, which makes you feel the pride of being a native. Your posts glue us to our historical past. I can, however, conclude that you are a great narrator, Mr. William Mayom Maker.

On September 22, 1019, at 10:19 pm, Jacob Dior Macueng commented:

I am a die-hard fan of your writings, Willy Mayom Maker. Thank you for all of these posts. I hope one day, you will compile them into a book because these stories could change someone else's life.

On July 20, 2019, at 7:29 pm, Darwin Matur Bol wrote:

Magnificent indeed! Thank God that traditionally incompetence (individual) like me will learn from this great mind. You are the best writer of our cultural vibrant I have even known. Willy Mayom Maker, we are benefiting from your writings. I want to say thank you, William Mayom Maker, for these great posts full of cultural references.

On May 03, 2020, at 7:05 am, Kur Wel Kur wrote:

I settled down few minutes ago to read this story. The story is rich. There is a kind of mannerism you display in your writing—the calmness in the storytelling, the one that only belongs to expert (our grand fathers and mothers).

On September 25, 2018, my niece, Mary Nyibol Maker wrote:

Nënër [maternal uncle], the stories you write are inspirational to us. Keep them coming. You make me so proud!

On September 13, 2020, after I posted the introduction of the book on Facebook, I received a gracious call from Eng Chol Tong, the current ambassador to Russia and former governor of the Lake States:

I want to thank you for such a wonderful work. I have read your piece on social media and it's captivating. Your knowledge on the subject, and well as your writing skills, are exceptional. Our culture is deteriorating, and I'm glad young people like you are trying to do something about it. This book will serve generations to come.

After gaining online popularity, I seized the opportunity and wrote several letters to South Sudanese government officials. After achieving independence in 2011, the South Sudanese struggled to govern themselves for the first time. With a country where over 80 percent of the population was illiterate, former rebel commanders, who had minimum or no education at all, were automatically installed as governors. As they struggled to rule the country, we in the Western countries, who had achieved certain proficiency levels, tried our best to help our people and our newly formed nation. Some returned home to assist in the development, and others sent material support in terms of money or advice. So, I wrote several letters, loaded with cultural references and metaphors, to South Sudanese politicians, especially those from my state, Western Lakes State.

In 2018, I wrote the first letter to Governor Matur Chut. I talked about the violence, corruption, and culture of impunity that had plagued the state. The message was too long to include here, but you can find its theme throughout this book, especially in the introduction. Here are the introductory paragraphs of the letter:

Mr. Governor,
The dinosaurs were like the Agaar people. The dinosaurs were big and powerful compared to all other animals, but they always fought. And while they were busy fighting and killing each other, all the other animals were adapting and readapting to the changing environment. When great destruction struck the land, it wiped all the dinosaurs out from the face of the earth; meanwhile, the other animals survived.

The Agaar people are in a similar situation. Rumbek was powerful. Giants like Wuol Aruai, Ayuol Nhial, and others who defeated the Turko-Egyptians and the British, hailed from Agaar. The Sudan government used to dispatch Agaar chiefs, like Chut Dhuol, Majok Derder and others, throughout the country to solve tribal court cases other leaders could not answer. Additionally, Rumbek Secondary School was the envy of the country, where anyone who did not attend felt like he was not well educated. The school incubated all South Sudanese revolutionaries, intellectuals and leaders including: Dr. John Garang, Joseph Oduho, Abel Alier, William Deng Nhial, Samuel Aru Bol, Peter Cirilo, Joseph

Lagu, Isaiah Kulang, Dr. Justin Yach Arop, Professor Martin Marial Takpiny, Peter Gatkuoth, Dr. Marial Benjamin, Dr. James Wani Igga, John Luk Jok, Dr. Martin Majier Gai, Dr. Riek Machar Teny, Samuel Gai Tut, Lawrence Lual Lual, Dhol Acuil, etc. No doubt, Rumbek was a land of the giants.

However, the Agaar started to fight each other, just like the dinosaurs. And while they were busy fighting and killing each other, the other tribes in South Sudan adapted and readapted to the changing environment. The great destructions have arrived in the form of civil wars, guns, strange religions, and laws; the other people seem to be coping well, and the Agaar people seem to be heading in the same direction the dinosaurs went.

Although we may not become extinct physically, like the dinosaurs, our cultures, values, and norms are indeed dying. Anyone who has no cultural values is as good as dead because culture is the only thing that defines anyone's humanness. The disappearance of Agaar cultural values is the main reason we are in such a mess. People are dying every day in Rumbek. Boys are loitering on the streets, both at home and abroad, begging or pick-pocketing. Women are running up and down with altered skin, hair, or even private parts. The divorce rate is at its peak. Youngsters don't respect or listen to parents or other elders. Apäräpuööl youths in rural areas are rustling cattle and killing innocent people. Our cultural values are vanishing, and so is our dignity. These are symptoms of a society heading down the drain.

In 2019, I also wrote another letter to General Deng Mamer, who replaced Governor Matur Chut. Before General Deng even took the oath of the office, I seized the opportunity to write him a letter. The following is an abstract of the message:

Dear General Deng Mamer,
As a newly appointed governor, you've just been given spearheads alone without the shafts. You have to find your shafts. As a newly elected governor, you've been given powers and authorities (spearheads), and you have to find members of your administration (shafts).

We know that the quality of its shaft determines the usefulness or accuracy of a spear. If you attach a poorly made or useless rod to your spear, you may miss your intended target. A fisher who fastens a bent shaft to his fishing spear may accidentally spear his foot. Similarly, members of your cabinet can determine the effectiveness and efficiency of your governing. If you surround yourself with unqualified or uneducated members, then things will never get done, and your leadership will fail. Furthermore, if you surround yourself with family members, friends, and relatives, irrespective of their qualifications, like most politicians do nowadays, then your leadership will be a complete disaster. Hence, you've speared your own foot. But if you want to succeed, you have to surround yourself with highly educated individuals who will guide you to the goal, just as a right shaft guides the spear to the target.

And when looking for his shafts, an experienced warrior often avoids big branches that are difficult to bend or straighten. A mature tree branch either breaks or remains crooked. Instead, he looks for a delicate, flexible, and still growing tree that shapes and reshapes accordingly. Likewise, when selecting members of your administration, stay away from old folks with tribal mindsets, for they are the reason why we are in such a mess in the first place. Instead, find young and educated individuals who have the time and flexibility, and of course, the twenty-first-century knowledge and skills to adapt and readapt according to the environment while getting things done.

Lastly, you must thoroughly diversify your governing team. I'm talking about employment equity. A good warrior usually has a bundle of spears, comprising different spears and fishing spears, barbed and not barbed, all in different shapes, sizes, and forms for various functions. Therefore, it's crucial to engage in proactive employment practices to increase the representation of the following six designated groups: women, youths, seniors, disabled persons, visible minorities, and veterans. Diversifying your team is the best way to develop our state politically, socially, and economically.

You can therefore see from my encounters with the youths to the stories posted on social media and the letters I sent to the governors, my intention had always been clear: I wanted to restore our cultural values. *The Proud People* is my contribution towards the process of our aesthetic, cultural restoration. This contribution may be insignificant, but I'm doing the best I can. You can do the best you can too. Don't be a spectator. Don't be like the other animals that watched helplessly as their livelihoods were destroyed. We should all be like the hummingbird. Together, we can restore our culture, history, and identity—the vital elements which define our humanness.

Introduction

It is crucial to bring back our culture or *cieng (ciɛŋ)*. *Cieng,* by definition, is the accumulated lessons from our ancestors—lessons that define who we are and where we come from. These lessons include our language, history, spirituality, values, artistic expressions, customs, and practices. As the main components of *cieng*, these lessons provide us with a better understanding of our history and identity; they link us to the past, present, and future. Therefore, without *cieng* and its vital components, we lose our identity as a distinguished people. Every *Muonyjang* (Dinka) must know this indisputable truth.

Since foreigners arrived in our beloved country, Sudan, centuries ago, our culture and history have been stained with blood, pain, and suffering that multigenerational colonization and Arabization have caused. This has created enormous destruction of our land, our people, and our way of life—the *cieng*. Our ancestors called these devastating effects of oppression the "ruin of the earth" (*riäk* ë piny). Indeed, our land was ruined because the foreigners brought their alien cultures such as guns, religions, laws, and regulations, which they imposed on us. These cultures, especially the guns and religions, appeared toxic, and they ultimately poisoned our pure and natural ways of life—the critical components which defined our humanness. Subsequently, the proudest people of Jieng, particularly the Agaar, were turned upside-down and inside-out until they no longer recognized themselves, their lived environment, and their creator—*Nhialic* God.

Our land was ruined because, even after we liberated ourselves from the oppressors and created the Republic of South Sudan where the Jieng are the ruling majority, our societies were messier than ever before. Our culture was ruined and legacies of oppression still exist in our political, social, and economic system. Corruption, nepotism, and a culture of impunity have plagued every government system; our leaders shamelessly accumulate wealth to develop themselves instead of the society or country, and the prerequisite to landing a job, scholarship, or contract today is having your uncle or aunt as the boss. Our land is wracked with violence and crime, which have crippled the cities, towns, and rural areas; and when prominent tribes or sub-tribes, armed and equipped by their crooked politicians, obliterate smaller ones.

The ruin of our land and culture can't just be measured by political, social, and economic deterioration. We have also lost common sense and decency. Some South Sudanese believe our separation from the North was a "mistake." Others even called it a "curse." How could you fight for over 50 years and then call it a mistake or a curse after achieving the objective? That makes no sense. Obviously, we are making the same mistake the children of Israel made when they complained and whined after God had delivered them from bondage. We know what happened to the Israelites. They wandered for 40 years without enjoying the Promised Land. For nearly ten years now, since our independence in 2011, South Sudanese have been whining, complaining, and fighting each other; nearly one million people are languishing in displacement camps and neighboring countries. If we don't reverse this situation, we will be like the children of Israel wandered for 40 years, eating quail and manna.

The truth is our separation from the North was not a mistake. It was the freedom and right of self-determination, which cost nearly five million lives in several wars: the Anya-nya One and Anya-nya II movements, and finally, the Sudan people's Liberation Army (SPLA), with its political wing, Sudan People's Liberation Movement (the SPLM). The separation was not a curse either; it was a blessing from our land, ancestors, and creator—Nhialic God.

Therefore, the main reason we are in such a mess after our independence is because we have ignored our culture and embraced foreign culture—the very cultures that led us into this mess. To enjoy our freedom and blessing in our land and put our society in its rightful place, we must restore our God-given cultures, morals, and institutions, which governed our people for generations. We must bring back the *cieng* and its components—the sacred lessons from our ancestors, lessons which teach us of the correct ways of doing things.

Think about how pure and decent our societies used to be before foreign influences arrived. Before guns came, violence and crime did not exist in our land. We did not even have a designated term for a crime. We called it *jerima*, which is an Arabic term for crime—evidence that crime did not exist before the Arabs came to Sudan.

In the late 1980s, people closed their homes with nothing but grass doors called *athin* and went to cattle camps or fishing grounds in the Toc Swamp for months. No one stole or vandalized their belongings in their absence. In other words, theft, robbery or looting, which is prevalent today, did not exist before. In all the villages I lived in the Agarland, I never saw or heard of murderers, thieves, or rapists. Crimes were foreign concepts, only heard of in distant places where cultural values did not exist.

Before the advent of guns, traditional warriors carried spears, shields, and clubs. These weapons were considered sacred and were rarely used. You couldn't even point a spear at someone, let alone spear him. If an individual accidentally or intentionally killed another person in a fight, which was rare, the killer often reported the killing to elders or authorities, even if no one had witnessed the murder, so that proper measures were taken to compensate for and purify the loss of life.

Now that people are heavily armed with automatic assault rifles, killing, cattle-rustling, robbing, looting, stealing, and raping have become a part of people's daily lives. The *Gelwong* youths who bring guns to fistfights are killing each other mercilessly and making both rural and urban areas ungovernable. In town cities, unknown gunmen kill people like flies regularly.

When we worshipped God in our way, we lived in peace and harmony. We even knew how to protect and preserve the environment and its bounty before foreign spiritualities arrived. The Jieng society, especially the Agaar, used to place an extremely high value on protecting and preserving the environment and the resources considered essential to them. Our wise ancestors believed they were part of the natural world, and that everything on Earth was connected and you could not destroy one part without touching the other. So, our ancestors created environmental protection and conservation measures, which they embedded in their cultural practices.

One of these practices was the concept of using totems to demonstrate the relationship (*ruäi*) between humans, animals, and the environment. So the Agaar people were sectioned into sub-sections. Members of each section were "related" to plant or animal, or both in this *ruai*-totemic system. It was then the duty of individuals within the clan to protect and defend their totems, which were also considered spiritual relatives. This obligation ranged from not harming the animal or plant to actively feeding, rescuing, and caring for it. The following are the Agaar clans, based on this *ruai*-totemic system:

Pacuer ("people relating to the lion"); Palou ("people relating to the bamboo"), Pathoth ("people relating to the fire"); Patiop ("people relating to the fox"), Pawen, ("people relating to the hippo"); Pathian, ("people relating to the snake") Padiangboor, ("people relating to the moon"); Paloong, ("people relating to the sun"); Panol, ("people relating to the kite"); Paderek, ("people relating to the cow"); Pagong, ("people relating to the tortoise"); Pathian, ("people relating to the frog"); Pamel, ("people relating to the sheep"); Paloth, ("people relating to the bell"); Pabuongkuach, ("people relating to the leopard"); Pacoor, ("people relating to the eagle"); paloi, ("people relating to the wind/weather"); Pabuong, ("people relating to the gourd"); Payibek, ("people relating to the apac grass"); Anet, ("people relating to sausage tree"); pamaany, ("people relating to the python"); Pajiel, ("people relating to the palm tree"); Pador, ("people relating to the tamarind"); Panyangciek, ("people relating to the dog"); and so on and so forth.

As you can see, both living and non-living things were protected in this *ruai*-totemic system. And because of these protective measures, animals or plants did not become extinct. Today, with the planet in peril and some animals and plants increasingly heading to extinction, people can understand or even appreciate the wisdom embedded in our culture to protect and preserve the environment.

Unfortunately, this *ruai*-totemic system ended when Christian missionaries arrived and told people it was devilish. Remember, our ancestors did not worship animals, plants, or objects; they worshipped Nhialic. Yet, they were forced to abandon their traditional rules for protecting and preserving the environment. Subsequently, the new converts, who rejected the ruai-totemic system, neither respected each other nor the environment. Armed with the Bible and guns, they started killing each other over the resources. The newly converted Jieng extensively hunted the animals and cleared the forests. With tanks roaming the land and gunships in the sky, the environment (animals, plants, soil, water, and air) was polluted and destroyed. The Jieng people, who were once proud custodians of their environment, were reduced to the perpetual trespassers and violators of the Earth's delicate ecosystem. This was the basis of the spoil and ruin of the Earth.

In conclusion, all the foreign cultures, including the religions and guns, which we have incorporated into our contemporary culture, are the major contributors of the chaos. Honestly, Christianity was not the religion of our choice. It was our fierce resistance to Islam that forced us into Christianity. I'm not saying Christianity is a bad religion, but the first missionaries who came to spread Christianity were nothing but conmen and women who used religion to bamboozle people and exploit their resources. Currently, over 95 percent of the South Sudanese are Christians, and people pray in churches and under trees in towns, rural villages, and cattle camps. But are we righteous? Hell no! Our communities are heavily armed with automatic assault rifles. But are we safe? Certainly not! Therefore, these foreign cultures are doing more harm than good to us.

Enough is enough! We must bring back our *cieng* and start a new memory of culture in our children's minds. *Cieng*, with its components, is a fundamental pillar for the reconstruction of our social fabric. Therefore, we must restore our *cieng* in its entirety, being intangible cultural heritage, such as oral traditions, performing arts, local knowledge, and traditional skills, including songs, music, craft, and festivals; or tangible cultural heritage, such as conventional tools, buildings, artworks, landscapes, and biodiversity. These vital components of our culture—the lessons from our ancestors—must be restored, safeguarded, and passed on to the next generations.

We don't want our children to inherit these toxic foreign cultures, which poisoned our political, social, and economic system for centuries. We want our children to inherit pure and cultural heritage; the correct way of living. When an Agaar child was born, the first phrase the child heard when it made its first cry after the delivery was *bai aceng*, meaning "welcome, the people are at home." Remember, the word *aceng* comes from the word *cieng*—the accumulated lessons from ancestors. Therefore, *bai aceng* symbolizes the availability of all components of *cieng*, which the child would live by and pass on to the next generations.

The same love for one's cultural heritage was in the phrase, *kön dëël du* ("hold on tight to your stump or foundation")—a phrase used when a child sneezed. *Dëël* is a foundation or stump that withstands floods in the Toc Swamp. So the implication of the phrase was that culture is the stump or foundation—the *dëël* that would withstand disasters. So, the child was reminded to hold tight to his culture to avoid being carried away and getting lost in this dangerous world.

I am a living testimony of how culture guides people. I left my mother in 1987 when I was eleven years old and joined the SPLA rebels. For six years, I lived in the bushes holding a gun which was almost taller than me as a child soldier. In 1992, when I was sixteen year old, I came to Kakuma Refugee Camp, where I languished for eight years as an unaccompanied minor. In 2000, when I was twenty four years old, I resettled in Canada, where I suffered from an incredible culture shock. Throughout these long journeys, several of my friends succumbed in one way or another. Some abused substances and others ended up in prisons or cemeteries. But because cultural values were instilled in me when I was little, I stayed clean as a proud son of Agaar. Even though many of my friends who started these journeys with me (from Sudan, to Ethiopia, Kenya and finally to North America) had resorted to substance abuse, I have never tasted alcohol, not to mention drugs, since I was born. In Agaar culture, young people did not drink alcohol. You could be eligible to drink when you were mature enough, and all your children had grown. Even so, you could not decide to drink on your own. The oldest persons in the community would introduce you to alcohol. However, since I grew up outside the Agarland without the oldest person to introduce me to drinking, I have not tasted alcoholic beverages. If it wasn't because of my strong cultural values, I would have been a substance abuser.

The world is getting smaller. Now that children are sent to study abroad, those who lack strong cultural values may not return to their respective communities. They will try to learn a different culture out there, but the reason they drop their own culture will enable them to drop any culture they encounter. Currently, there are many Agaar children languishing on the street or in the jails of Western countries, especially in Australia and America, because they have no culture to hold on to. Culture is the only freeway that will lead you home, no matter how far you have gone. It is therefore crucial to bring back our cultural values and traditions.

In addition to culture, it is also crucial to know our history. Both history and culture go hand in hand. Culture guides you to identify between wrong and right, and connects you to your family, community, and the environment. On the other hand, history links you to political, social, and economic functions. Whether you live in cities, towns, or villages, lands, boundaries, ownership, and regulatory rights to cattle camps, fishing grounds, grazing, and farming lands are inherited through historical facts. Without detailed genealogical history linking you to such locations, you have no origin in this world; you are just a trespasser. And without culture harmonizing you with other human beings, plants, animals, and the environment, you are a violator of the Nhialic-God's creation. Therefore, culture and history are crucial, and they must be reclaimed and passed on to our children.

It is also important to note we should not embrace our culture and ignore the modern world. Instead, we must drop the old parts of our culture, which do not fit in the contemporary world, and maintain the most valuable parts of it as the central pillar, and then add the modern world, such as advanced education, on top of the existing foundation. By blending culture with advanced education, we recapture our proud selves, redefine our rich cultural heritage, and reinvent our true identity.

The Proud People starts with the general history of the Jieng people, but narrowed down to the Agaar people. Even so, the book does not describe everything in Agaar culture and traditions. Instead, it offers a general description of material and non-material cultures. The book will help readers understand some essential elements that sincerely defined Muonyjang and the Agaar from how they conceptualized the world to the impact of their worldviews, ways, myths, livelihoods, and relationships. Therefore, the book focuses on day-to-day activities such as eating, dancing, occupation, education (non-formal), visiting, courtship, marriage, beliefs (festivals and liturgies), naming and burial ceremonies, entertaining friends and guests, greetings, and spirituality.

This book is not a research paper or an essay. Instead, it is a recollection of memories and stories recorded, archived, and shared orally from generation to generation. While writing this book, I had to reach back to the teaching of my parents, grandparents, great grandparents, and wise village elders. I have stated all the facts to the best of my ability, and as honestly as possible. In every sentence, I pictured myself sitting under a tree in a big circle of elders and children. As I spoke, I was mindful of these two audiences. I was cognizant the elders would serve as my peer review, so I did not delve into subject matters that would be questionable, or else it would hurt my credibility. Also, I was mindful of the children, as I was the link between them and our ancestors; a chain no one in his right mind would want to jeopardize. Therefore, I have narrated the valid accounts of these events, the same way previous generations passed them on to me.

However, when writing this book, I did not think about the "experts" who have studied the Jieng people. I'm aware there are many books non-Jieng experts have written. I do not need any validation from these non-Jieng experts who have written books and research papers about our histories and stories. Because no matter how much you have studied me and my culture and history, you can never be more of an expert than me. If you have not received stories and tales directly from your parents, and you cannot even speak the language, you may see things from an outsider's perspective, and your views may not reflect the events, issues, and priorities of my community.

This book, *The Proud People*, is a direct translation of oral histories and traditions received directly from my parents and grandparents. I do not doubt the authenticity of their accounts. My main concern was that authenticity might have been lost in the translation as it was not easy to translate such rich culture into a foreign language. From the external experts, therefore, I may need validation in the language the book is written, but not the content. This is my history. This is my culture. As one African writer said, I am the expert, historian, and anthropologist of my history and culture.

I am a Muonyjang, from the Agaar section of Bhar el Ghazal region. I have lived in three different worlds. First, I was born in an Agaar village, where oral traditions were the only ways wisdom and knowledge were reproduced, preserved, and conveyed from generation to generation. And because I grew up with older generations with lifestyles that foreign cultures had not significantly influenced, I acquired pure historical facts from my parents, grandparents, and other wisest men and women in the land. Second, as a young person, I joined the SPLA/M movement in the fight against the Khartoum Islamic regime. So I learned all the necessary political, social, and historical facts of our people and country from the leaders of the movement. Third, I have lived and studied historical facts about our history in Canadian schools and libraries. Based on this diverse background, I am in a better position to provide accurate historical facts about the Jieng people and the Agaar. Being the son of Agaar, I acknowledge I am in a position of authority concerning narration, interpretation, and dissemination of information concerning the history of our people.

History

Background

THE AGAAR (plural, Agar) are a part of the "Dinka" people—the largest and most influential group in the Republic of South Sudan on the continent of Africa. However, the name Dinka, to which these indigenous South Sudanese are affectionately known worldwide, is not their original name. Most people, especially those who live in rural areas, do not even know the name exists. Only educated individuals and urban dwellers know and accept it when referred to as Dinka. Their original name is Muonyjang (plural, Muonyjieng) or simply Jieng— meaning "the people."

When the prefix *muony-* is added to Jieng to form *Muony-jang*, it denotes masculinity. Muonyjang, by definition, is a male individual who belongs to the Jieng people or tribe. The femininity is formed by adding the prefix *nyan-* to create *nyan-jieng*. But as a patriarchal society, Muonyjang is often used as a gender-neutral name.

Sometimes, the word Muonyjang (spelled with u) is confused with mony-jang (without u). The latter, mony-jang (pronounced *mony ë jäŋ*), which means "husband of other people" is an offensive term used against non-Jieng groups. The name was invented a long time ago when Jieng came into contact with the outsiders. As conflicts and political discourses intensified, Jieng warriors called themselves "husband of other people (*mony ë jäŋ*)"—intending to insult or insert superiority over non-Jieng groups. It was this offensive name that people modified, perhaps for political correctness' sake, to translate as "men of the men," "men among men," or "people of the people"—none of which applies to the original name or meaning. Irrespective of these speculations, the original name is Muonyjang or Jieng. Period!

With this background, it is prudent to say the name Dinka has no historical and cultural roots. We do not know its meaning, where it originated from, or who named us. Some speculated that the name might have come from the first explorers who found it difficult to pronoun the tongue-twisting word Muonyjieng, so they had to rename them. Others said they were named after a chief named Ding Kak, which the foreigners mispronounced as Dinka. Perhaps the oppressors, who ruled the Jieng people, were aware of the offensive name, *mony-jäng* (husband of the people), which was used against them, so they had to rename them. These are mere speculations. The origin of the name is unknown. All we know is that the name Dinka has stuck.

We have incorporated the name Dinka into our contemporary culture, just as we have adopted Arabic and English as our official languages. In a sense, people use the name Dinka as a translation of the original name into English or Arabic. It is easy for someone to introduce themselves as Dinka when speaking in English or Arabic and Muonyjang or Jieng when speaking in Thuongjang (Jieng language). By assuming Dinka is the translation of Jieng in other languages, the educated Jieng have learned to cope with this strange and mysterious name.

However, I find it extremely difficult to cope with the name Dinka. What irritates me the most is that nobody knows where the name originates from, who named us, or what it means. The name could be an insult. In the old days, political correctness was not practiced, so the names provided during the first contact with other groups were extremely offensive. For example, "nigger" was offensive term used against the black people, "whitey" against the white people, or "chink" against the Asians. Most prominently, identifying ourselves by a strange name, a name that has no cultural significance or historical roots, is utterly disrespectful to our cultural heritage; it is a mockery to our ancestors, and our Creator. For these reasons, I cannot cope with the name Dinka, which is why I put it in quotation marks on the book cover. So, I will use the original name Muonyjang or Jieng throughout this book.

Name aside; I also don't accept the history outsiders have written on our behalf. Many modern historians and researchers often concluded that "little is known" about Jieng history or origin. But the question is by who is little known? Such a conclusion illustrates that the knowledge of our history comes from non-Jieng narrators, who often view our accounts from an outsider perspective. When a stranger comes to cultivate your piece of land, it means that he is satisfying his hunger, not yours. The outsiders who came to our land and wrote our history and culture had their own agendas and interests in mind. I'm not surprised their narratives often reflect the values and priorities of the outsiders— not ours. They cultivated our land to satisfy their needs.

While some modern historians said little is known about the Jieng, others tried to link us to the north, west, or east of African. Someone claimed the Jieng must have come from West Africa because their name Dinka is similar to the Mandinka people of western Africa. Another said they must have come from North Africa because of their slave-like devotion to their cattle, just like the ancient Egyptians. These claims show those who wrote our histories and stories know nothing about us. So, they were right to say "little is known about the Dinka" because it is them who know little or nothing about us.

But it shouldn't be this complicated. If you find a group of people living in an area, and you can't trace their origin elsewhere, common sense will dictate there is an excellent likelihood these people are the original inhabitants of that particular land. Irrespective of the outsiders' claims, we know our origin in this world. Ask any elder in the village, and he will tell you we have inhabited this land since the dawn of time. Chief Rok Reec, for example, one of the oldest Agaar chiefs, used to say, "We have lived here since the creation of the Earth. This is the land of our ancestors."

Oral history indicates that, for thousands of years, before foreigners (Europeans and Arabs) arrived in Sudan, successive generations of Jieng people had lived on their land. Each group marked their territory, protected it, and named all the animals, plants, and rivers in it. They used the *ruai*-totemic system for the environment and engaged in an economy that respected the land and its bounty—from animals to plants, forests, and water bodies. The Jieng people were peaceful and well organized socially and even politically. They had their own rules and regulations that governed their families, clans, and tribes, and their lived environment. The communities where these rules and regulations were pertinent knew of and conformed to them. These traditional laws and regulations, along with stories, histories, and all other facts of life, were orally recorded, shared, and archived from generation to generation.

When the foreigners arrived, they could not find a written language and historical record of the Jieng societies. There were no rocks, stones, mountains, or caves which preserved historical data in the Jiengland. Oral narratives existed, but the foreigners didn't have access to these sacred facts. It's unclear whether the foreigners ignored the oral history or the Jieng didn't provide true historical records to strangers. Whatever the case, the foreigners were left with nothing but an assumption "little is known about the Dinka." In other words, the Jieng were people without history. Subsequently, the foreigners wrote our history based on their interpretations, observations, and understandings.

Today, our history is still being portrayed based on these misleading observations and assumptions that foreigners made a long time ago. In simplest terms, our history is grossly being misrepresented. This is why the facts don't match our history and culture.

Although the narrated accounts were stubbornly unsatisfactory, the Jieng could not provide accurate reports of their history for several reasons. As mentioned earlier, the Jieng people relied on the oral transmission of stories, tales, and all other events of life to maintain historical records and sustain cultural identities. They considered these historical facts too sacred to be openly shared with outsiders. Besides, the first foreigners who visited our land were there for the exploitation of resources, so they were not trusted. And since the foreigners arrived, the Jieng and other indigenous people of South Sudan have been fighting for freedom and the right of self-determination, so they didn't have time to share different aspects of life with the outside world. Last but not least, most Jieng were illiterate, so there was no way of disputing the misrepresented history and sharing their accurate account with the outside world. Because of these factors, the outsiders could write and rewrite the Jieng history based on their understandings and interpretations, which often fit their narratives.

Now the Jieng and other South Sudanese have liberated themselves from the North and created their country, the Republic of South Sudan. And unlike before, when most people were illiterate, many Jieng are now well educated. Therefore, concrete historical events that were orally recorded, shared, and archived are now emerging. This book is one of them.

Chief Rok Reec

In the Agaarland, elders occupied a particular position in the society, for they had painstakingly accumulated a reservoir of personal experience, knowledge, and wisdom, and they freely offered this wisdom to living generations of their people to help them connect harmoniously with the past, present, and future. In other words, Agaar parents passed spoken words of wisdom and history down to their children and their children's children. Each generation passed what their parents had given them through rote memorization. The memorization started at a very young age, whereby children cited their lineage by name, starting with their father back to twenty or more generations. By the time I was three years old, I could recite both my parents' lineages up to 15 generations back. I did not do this for fun; however, this was a complete identity. Jieng people didn't have surnames; the total tally of ancestors defined one's personality. This practice made the children extremely interested in historical facts gathering, as they would consider any piece of information coming from adults to be vitally intriguing, exciting, and attention-grabbing. Like any other Jieng child, I orally acquired these historical facts I now share with you from elders.

In the late 1970s, when I was a small boy in a small village called Pachong, about 10 miles away from Rumbek, the capital city of the Lakes State, I had the opportunity of learning the historical facts firsthand from the oldest and wisest men in the land. His name was Rok Reec.

Rokdit (Rok the Great), as we used to call him, was not just an ordinary elder; he was the highest chief of the entire Agaar people during the colonization era. Before he died in the early 1980s when he was over 100 years old, Rokdit bestowed his wisdom upon his people. This was the wisdom which attracted the colonizers to put him in charge of one of the most significant sections of the Jieng: the Agaar people.

Chief Rok Reec was born in 1896 in the Agarland[1]. In 1902, as a young boy of less than ten, British forces captured him as a slave and took him to the North. In the North he grew up in the care of a North Sudanese soldier named Abdalla. In the North, they forced Rok

---

1   Kuyok A, Kuyok, South Sudan, The Notable Firsts, Bloomington: Author House, 2015

into Islam, and they renamed him Rizig[2], which means luck. Abdalla thought he was lucky to have a slave to work for free. But you are not lucky when you have an Agaar as your slave. In fact, it was Rok who was lucky. He utilized the opportunity to learn Arabic and eventually joined the army and police forces. Later he became a police in Wau, the capital city of Bhar el Ghazal.

After gaining popularity, Rok left the army and police force and returned to the Agarland to lead his people. In 1921, the British authorities appointed Rok Reec as paramount chief of all the Agaar people. As the first government paramount chief of Agaar, Chief Rok Reec established three court centers namely, Luel, Akot and Pacong.

But Chief Rok was not happy with the way the British were running the country, and it didn't take long for him to fallout with them. Subsequently, the British authority exiled him for three years. But the Agaar people pressured the British authority who permitted Rok to return to the Agarland to resume his duties as the paramount chief of the Agaar tribe.

When he was around 90 years old or so, Rokdit used to go to Pacong Primary School to teach both teachers and students oral history. When he was not in school, he would sit on a recliner chair under a mango tree, narrating stories and tales of the Jieng people to both children and adults. Our homestead was about 10 minutes walk from Rokdit's homestead. His great grandsons, Mayiei Marial and Dok Marial Dongrin, who later became the chief of Panyar section, were my childhood friends, and we spent free time, along with other village boys, at Rokdit's homestead, sitting with him, listening to, and participating in the accounts of past deeds, beliefs, taboos, and myths. From Rokdit, I learned not only about the arrival of strangers (Egyptians, Turks, and British) in our land, but also the migration and dispersal of the Jieng people.

Rokdit told us stories about how the entire Jieng speaking groups used to live in what is now known today as the Bhar el Ghazal region around Lakes State territory. From there, they grew in numbers and expanded, migrating into three groups: the first group, according to Rokdit, emigrated in the direction of the setting sun. The second group moved toward the rising sun. And the third remained in the middle where they just expanded, not moving much. The third group, which

---

2   Ibid

did not relocate, included the Agaar, Gok, Luach, Atuot, Ciec, and Aliab people who still inhabit the Lakes State region today.

The first groups who migrated in the direction of the setting sun (west) were Rek (Tonj, Gogrial, and Aweil) and Ngok. From there, they grew in numbers and expanded northward and westward, respectively. The Ngok moved northward. A group of hunters who had tracked a wounded buffalo led the Malual (Aweil) people to the far west near the border of Sudan and Chad. When they reached that territory, they found many animals, especially buffaloes, to hunt, and the fertile soil suitable for crop cultivation. So the hunters convinced the tribe to move and settle there. They became known as "Malual who is following the buffalo" (*Malual Buɔth Anyaar*).

The second group, composed of Bor, Twii, Hol, and so forth, had migrated in the direction of the rising sun (east). Following the Nile River, its tributaries, and the swamp, these Jieng groups, like all other Nilotic groups, traditionally made their livelihood as subsistence farmers, river fishers, and pastoralists.

The arrival of foreigners was a turning point for the Nilotic groups including the Jieng. Subsequently, the Jieng became well organized traditionally and well equipped with spears and shields. Stirred up by the foreign influences, many conflicts occurred among the Nilotic tribes (the Jieng, the Nuer, the Bari, and the Shilluk, etc.) as they raided each other for cattle. Eventually, most of the Nilotic groups abandoned the pastoral systems and converted to agro-pastoralism, hunting-gathering, and fishing. The Jieng, the Atuot, and the Nuer dominated the cattle keeping system, forcing the other groups to other avenues, such as farming, fishing, hunting and gathering.

Right after the expansion, each section established its rites of passage, such as scarification marks, to distinguish themselves from the other groups they encountered on the way. The groups who migrated to the west (Gok, Tonj, Twic, Malual, and others) established V-shaped scarification marks, running from the front to the back of the head. The groups who migrated to the east (from Yerul to Bor and Twii) adapted either fan-shaped or V-shaped forehead scars, which stopped just below the hairline. The Agaar who had remained in the center started their typical horizontal scarification marks on the forehead, running from ear to ear. Also, other Jieng groups, such as the Ngok, Luach, and Hol have horizontal forehead scarification marks running from ear to ear, just like the Agaar.

The Nuers, who also have horizontal forehead scarification marks, are the only non-Dinka group that shares the same characteristics with the Jieng. Also, the Nuer people are devoted cattle-keepers, just like the Jieng. Because of these similarities, the Nuer people are the single people exempted from being called foreigners (*juur, duor,* or *nyinyaam*)—all words used to describe non-Jieng persons.

Hundreds of years after the expansion, it was the coming of the first strangers to our land that brought the Jieng to the center of world history. According to a traditional historian named Madingdit, strangers came along the Nile River and anchored their strange-looking boat at Relngong. Madingdit could not specify the geographical location of Relngong. But relngong is an Agaar term for an island. Since there is only one island in Sudan, Relngong was assumed to be the junction where the Blue Nile and White Nile meet, which the Arab later called Jezira.

Relngong or Jezira was a territory owned by a warrior-chief named Marol Benykook, according to Madingdit. When the strangers arrived and docked at Relngong, Marol and his band of warriors, equipped with spears and shields, waded through the Nile to investigate the trespassing strangers. Upon reaching them, Marol observed men of strange physical appearances. He later described the strangers as having pale skins, as if they had come from a land where the sun did not shine. The strangers looked visibly exhausted, and they had no weapons, apart from sticks they were carrying, Marol and his band of warriors observed. So Marol did not attack the strangers, as it was beneath his dignity to attack vulnerable men who were not competent enough to carry spears and shields. (Later, Marol learned that the sticks were fire-breathing weapons or guns).

After the first contact, communication between the warrior-chief Marol and the strangers became very difficult. Marol could not understand what the strangers wanted. And the strangers did not know the name of the land they were in. Eventually, the strangers asked a question in a few Jieng vocabularies they had gathered. They wanted to know the name of the land. But instead of asking, "What is the name of this land?" they said, "Who is the owner of this land?" The warrior-chief Marol found this question insulting. It was known far and wide that the territory belonged to him, and yet these strangers had asked a dumb question. "*Kuc?*" Marol rhetorically said, "Don't you know [the owner of this land]?" The letter "c" as in *kuc,* is pronounced «sh» in the Jieng language. Thinking Marol had told them the name of the land, the strangers wrote down «Kush,» saying they had visited the land of Kush. That's how the term Kush came about. Madingdit concluded it was the region between Ethiopia and Egypt.

The news of the visit to the land of Kush must have spread quickly among the foreigners as many visitors poured into Jiengland. The Arabs traders began coming to our area, which they eventually named *Bilad el Sudan,* meaning "land of black people." The trade between the Jieng and the strangers flourished. The early traders focused on the northern region of Sudan and along the Nile River. However, they were held back from reaching deep into the southern part by *Toc* Swamp, the largest swamp in the world, which the Arab named *Sudd,* meaning "barrier" or "obstacle," which prevented them from going through. The Arab traders brought beads, ceramics, clothes, salt, and metal goods to trade for ivory, rhino horn, ostrich feather, lulu-oil, and cowry shell. The trade between the Arabs and the Jieng and other Nilotes expanded. Gradually, the Arabs established several trading stations in the region to benefit from flourishing businesses. Not long after, the Arab traders settled permanently in Sudan, and eventually ruling the country for centuries. During the colonization of Africa, the British took the power from the Arab and they ruled the country for decades. The British installed those of Rok Reec to help them rule the country until 1956 when Sudan achieved its independence.

In 1981, Chief Rokdit passed away when he was over hundred year old. I attended his funeral. Before his death, he was taken to Pacong Primary school and where he was placed in a small house where both students and teachers went inside one by one to say goodbye to the great man. Unable to even move his hand, his wife was sitting beside him swatting flies away from his face. But Rokdit opened his eyes when I entered the room. I'm not sure if he recognized me, but I knew he was about to join the spiritual world with our ancestors. Shortly after that he died, and people danced for ten days to celebrate his life. Politicians came from Rumbek. A Muslim clergy, a priest and a spear-master conducted different prayers. He was buried in Pacong.

Historical Invasions

Due to illiteracy, traditional historians could not pinpoint the exact dates the events took place. All they knew was that the Arabs traders established their settlements in Northern Sudan first. Driven by the need to extend the empire, acquire wealth, and spread Islam, they launched Arabization campaigns against the indigenous Africans. Their objective was to Arabize South Sudanese, and then they would penetrate deep into Kenya, Uganda, and Congo. Gradually, Darfur, Nuba, and Blue Nile regions were absorbed into the Arab culture and religion. But the largest Nilotic groups, the Jieng and the Nuers, rejected Islam and Arabic culture. "We didn't want a divinity, where people smell the ground," Madingdit said, referring to the way Muslims prayed.

In response to this rejection, the Arab sent troops from the Northern Islamic Kingdom to attack the Southerners. They raided and captured slaves in the South, mostly in the Jieng and the Nuer territories. The Jieng and the Nuer formed a confederation to fight the Arabs. At the same time, the Jieng moved from Relngong areas deep into the Toc Swamp areas where their children and cattle remained safe from the Arab raids. Meanwhile, most of the Nuer moved eastward to the Ethiopian border, while some formed alliances with the Jieng and the Shilluk to continue fighting against slave traders. This era marked the beginning of centuries of slave raids, insecurities, and instabilities in the region—the ruin and spoil of the Earth.

Due to the superiority of their military organization and sophistication of their weapons, the Arabs defeated the Africans, ruling the country for centuries. For the first time, the Jieng were ruled by foreign authorities with alien laws and regulations. The foreign authority in Agaar colloquial is *tueny*, literally peculiar power, ruler, or oppressor.

Although dates were not recorded because of illiteracy, the periods of the foreign rulers were distinctly marked. The foreign authorities who ruled Sudan were grouped into three: the Turko-Egyptian rulers (*Tueny Malual-thith*)), al Mahdist or Arab rulers (*Tueny Larab*)), and the English rulers (*Tueny Diŋlith*).

The Turko-Egyptian Rule: In 1820, Egypt conquered Sudan, bringing the Turkish Ottoman Empire to rule the entire country for four years (from 1820 to 1824).[3] Through conquests, the Turkish Ottoman intended to extend its empire to spread Islam and acquire wealth. Armed and well equipped with modern weapons, the Egyptians crossed the desert and penetrated from the north, defeating the African forces and reaching Khartoum in 1821. Khartoum, which was the principal trading station, became the Egyptian strategic point, where they controlled their military operations. A year later, they captured the entire country, and Khartoum became the capital city of Sudan in 1822. Although they did not reach Southern Sudan because they were held back by the Toc Swamp, the Turko-Egyptians benefited by controlling trade routes and imposing high taxes and tariffs. To the Agaar, this period marked the era of reddish men's authority (*run tueny ë Malual-thith*).

The El Mahdi Rule: In 1881, one year after the Turkish and Egypt had captured the country, a Sudanese Arab named Mohammad Abdullah (also known as Mahdi, the chosen one) revolted against Egypt and Ottomans[4]. Claiming to be Allah's chosen one; Mahdi mobilized the Arabs and indigenous Africans, including the Jieng, in the fight against Turko-Egyptian rulers. Acknowledging the fierceness of the Jieng warriors, who had fought the Egyptians and the Turks, Mahdi charmed the Jieng, according to Madingdit, to ally with him to defeat the Turko-Egyptian rulers. Mahdi wittingly identified himself with Garang, capitalizing on the fact that the Jieng believed they were the descendants of Garang and Abuk, the first couple, like Adam and Eve. So Mahdi's message to the Jieng was that Garang sent him—a message which resonated well with the Jieng people. Having suffered under the Turko-Egyptians rulers, the vulnerable Jieng wanted a savior to save them from bondage. Subsequently, they believed that Garang indeed sent Mahdi. They Jieng christened el Mahdi to Maadi Garang. Jieng warriors sang the following war-song, asking Maadi Garang to protect them in battle:

---

3   Werner R., Anderson W., & Wheeler A., *Day of Devastation, Day of Contentment*, Nairobi: Paulines Publication, 2000, p. 109

4   Ibid 148

Wëi aa ci liklik,
Duok kë raan tôk cɔk dɔŋ wei;
Maadi Garaŋ, duk ë raan tök cɔk dɔŋ wei!

Translation:
Lives are preciously rare,
Don't leave one person behind;
Mahdi Garang, don't leave one person behind!

The Jieng people joined forces with the Mahdist. "As early as 1883, the Dinka groups had begun to fly the Mahdi's flag and break out in serious rebellion. The Dinka interpreted the Mahdist as a man with great spiritual power, the power of some divinity, like their own [Spear-masters]."[5] Subsequently, the Jieng and the Mahdist forces defeated the Turko-Egyptian rulers.

After el Mahdi gained power, he acted just like his predecessors. He imposed the highest taxes and demanded payments in either slaves or cattle. It did not take long for the Jieng to realize Mahdi was just a conman full of deceits, not divinity. The Jieng waged war against Mahdi until he died, and another Arab named Khalifa Abdullah succeeded him and ruled the country for years. To the Agaar, this period was the era of Arabic authority (*run ë tueny Larab)*.

The Anglo-Egyptian Rule: In1882, the British invaded Egypt, and Sudan became a condominium of the United Kingdom and Egypt[6]. Slowly, the British and Egyptian forces re-conquered all of Sudan, including Southern Sudan. In 1889, the joint British-Egyptian forces, commanded by Charles Gordon, recaptured Sudan from Khalifa Abdullah[7]. Having suffered under Khalifa, the Jieng did not even attempt to join the Arabs in the fight against the British. As a result, British-Egyptian forces captured and killed Khalifa when the colonization of Africa was at its peak. Egypt ruled Sudan (North and South) under the British yoke. The British ruled Sudan until 1956 when Sudan first gained its independence.

---

5   Ibid 155
6   Ibid 152
7   Ibid 153

The Warriors of Ancient Rumbek

In 1840, a Turkish captain named Salim Qapunda successfully sailed along the Nile, reaching Southern Sudan[8]. He was the first to penetrate the Toc Swamp after many Egyptians and British had been turned back by it. After Salim had opened the way, Europeans and Arabs flocked south in search of productive resources, such as ivories, ostrich feathers, rhino horns, and cowry shells, which they traded with clothes, salt, irons, beads, and brasses. The foreign traders brought gifts to the Jieng tribal chiefs, so they were welcomed wholeheartedly. But soon the friendly relationship collapsed and was replaced with the wickedness of extreme economic interests. A slave trade ensued.

Slave traders used different methods to acquire slaves from Southern Sudan. First, they imposed Islamic laws, which the Jieng knew nothing about, and those who broke the laws were arrested. From prison, they were sold into slavery. Second, the Arabs introduced high taxes and dubious loans or businesses, and then they demanded payments in either slaves or cattle. Third, they raided villages and captured slaves.

Throughout the Jieng-land, especially in Bhar el Ghazal region, slave traders had built several stockade stations where they kept slaves whom they captured from nearby villages, before shipping them to the North. Rumbek, Tonj, and Wau were the leading slave trade stations with huge stockades which helped the slave masters and slaves against attacks. Because of these enclosures, the Jieng words for city or town are *kal, geu,* or *pen*—all meaning stockade, fence, or gate—referring to the time when such enclosures were erected in those places, which eventually turned into big cities and towns. For example, Tonj was known as Kal-Kuel, meaning "gate of the kuel tree". It was also known as *Geu* or *Gen Anyuon* ("gate or fence of the grass"). Similarly, Rumbek was a thick woodland inhabited by saddle-billed storks; hence, *rum-bek*. It became known as *Kal Rum-bek* (("gate or fence in the woodland of saddle-billed stork").

To older generations, the slave trade in Southern Sudan from the mid-1700s to the early 1900s had a devastating impact on them. One of these people was an older man called Majak Ater, or simply Majakdit. Majakdit was the direct descendant of warrior-chief Marol,

---

8   John Ryle, *Warriors of the White Nile,* Amsterdam: Time-Life Books, 1982, 24

who inhabited Relngong. To prove he was the descendant of Marol, Majak used to recite his lineage: Majak, Ater, Wantok, Nyac, Gerger, Maliet, Deng, and Marol. Majak, the eighth generation of the warrior chief who first encountered foreign explorers, always recounted the slave trade stories his father and grandfather told him.

They used to hunt us like wild games, recounted Majakdit. The slave traders comprised Sudanese Arabs, Egyptians, and Europeans, all armed with modern weapons, would come with enough troops to surround a village in the middle of the night. This made it harder for the Agaar warriors to put up a defense, making it easier for the slave traders to capture their targets. At dawn, they would go from homestead to homestead, shooting aparäpuööl warriors, taking all the people and cattle, and burning down the houses with everything in them.

The captured slaves walked in single lines between armed Arab guards, as they were taken northward. Anyone who tried to run away was invariably shot. Those who collapsed due to injury or exhaustion during the unbearable journey had their limbs broken and were left behind to die.

Rumbek was a slave trade station in the Agarland. Knowing they would be well protected in that dense woodland, the slave traders built a stockade station, where they kept all the slaves they had captured in nearby villages and cattle camps. The Agaar warriors overran Rumbek several times until the slave traders gave up. That was how the slave trade ended, recounted Majakdit.

The giants who fought in the Rumbek war were Wol Aruai, Ayuol Nhial, and other warriors who had consistently resisted the Arab and European conquests. Both Wol Aruai and Ayuol Nhial hailed from the Agaar. Wol Aruai was a warrior who rose to chiefdom status, a warrior-chief of the Pakam section of the Agaar. Apart from his legendary wisdom, with which he had handled tribal court cases diligently, Wol Aruai was also a strategist his adversaries feared. Ayuol Nhial was from the Thiyiith section of Athoi. Unlike Wol Aruai, Ayuol Nhial was a young warrior who had led Athoi warriors into numerous victorious battlefields. Both giants, Chief Wol and Ayuol rose to the task when the intruders arrived with their evil system of slavery.

At first, said Majakdit, the Maathäng-lual ("Red-cheeks") appeared to have no bad intentions. Most of them were merchants who bartered salt and clothing for ivory and hides. So, we welcomed the traders as kamaan (guests). Generally, the Agaar people are by far the most hospitable on Earth. We fed, sheltered, and even protected the Red-cheek from harm.

But don't let their hospitality fool you. The Agaar are also the most violent people in the country. You can't get away with it when you offend them. "Your mischief is enough (kudu acë ceŋ)"; they retaliate violently when their dignity is violated.

The Red-cheeks violated Wol Aruai' sand Ayuol Nhial's dignity and built an enormous stockade in Rumbek where they kept the slaves and cattle they captured from the surrounding villages. The Agaar warriors declared war against the Turks. A fight broke out. The Turks were adamant because they enjoyed their clear, overwhelming military advantage through the technological superiority of their machine guns, and their sophisticated military organization. But Chief Wol Aruai, a brilliant strategist, somehow penetrated the Turkish army and mounted successful attacks with a band of warriors armed with spears and shields.

Seeking reinforcement, Chief Wol Aruai also dispatched messengers to neighbor clans with the following message: "The Red-cheeks are hiding in Rumbek. Come and help me purge them out." Without any hesitation, the neighboring clans (Agaar, Luach, Gok, Atuot, and even Nuer) abandoned their festering suspicious of each other, their deep-rooted hatreds, jealousies, and rivalries, and came together as one force to fight against the occupiers. The coalition forces mounted numerous successful attacks, inflicting 'unspeakable' horror on the Arabs.

Led by their respective chiefs, the Agaar warriors fought wholeheartedly, knowing that the war "had reached among the children"—a courage-evoking expression used by the Agaar, meaning "no retreat, no surrender."

Every Agaar, especially the older ones, knows a warrior-ship of their sub-clan who fight with the foreign invaders. Wol Aruai led the Pakam section, Ayuol Nhial was with Thiyith, and other warrior-chiefs led their sub-sections. Ayuol Nhial, who was brave, agile, and sure-footed, conducted a preliminary reconnaissance of the fortifications of the enemy's fort with a band of warriors before the attack.

But the Arabs were more robust, and their weapons were more lethal compared to the spears. They killed many Agaar warriors. For five days, said Majakdit, the Agaar warriors could not overrun the station. Unable to capture Rumbek, the warriors' morale was lower day by day.

Then on the sixth day, said Majakdit, Ayuol Nhial, a brilliant thinker, came up with an idea which ultimately changed the face of the battle. He instructed his warriors to smear butter on the back of their shields, making them slippery. The slippery shields, according to Ayuol Nhial's theory, would deflect the incoming bullets. He also instructed his warriors to chant whenever they heard gun shots: "Ee lueth, Nhialic (That is just a lie, God)!" Nobody knew whether Ayuol believed that the invention would work, or he knew it was ineffective, but he did with the intention of deceiving his warriors to fight harder—psychological motivation.

Whatever the case was, the strategy worked. The Jieng warriors fought courageously and tenaciously, mounting relentless attacks. The enemy's guns were no match for their spears. Many Agaar warriors were killed. But they kept fighting. Also, the neighboring clans kept reinforcing the warriors. As the war progressed, the enemy ran out of bullets. After they ran out of bullets, the enemy used bayonets, to no avail. The bayonets were no match for the sharp spears thrown from distance. Eventually, the fort (Rumbek) was captured, and the Arab soldiers fled to Khartoum. Many were killed along the way by other tribes. That ended the establishment of the slave trade in Rumbek, which is now the capital city of Lakes State.

Successive Arm Struggles

In 1904, the British finally conquered all of Southern Sudan. It took the British 30 years to penetrate the Sudd and defeat the Nilotes, spearheaded by the Jieng, the largest Nilotic group. Knowing the Jieng were fierce fighters who had resisted the Arabs for centuries, the British aimed to use them to stop the spread of Islam from the North to South Sudan into other East African countries such as Kenya, Uganda, and

Congo. To do so, the British introduced English and Christianity in the South, marking the territory as theirs. Some believe the reason the British developed the North and left the South grossly underdeveloped was to discourage the Arabs from coming to Southern Sudan. This tactic created the in-balance which existed between the North and South.

But the British's effort did not discourage the Arabs from having an interest in Southern Sudan. The Arabs stepped up their game. They defined Sudan as an Arab state, Islam as its national religion, and Arabic as the official language. For Southerners, the prerequisite to getting higher education or landing a good job or contract was the possession of Arabic names or wearing hijabs—the head covering Muslim women wear in public. By this time, the Jieng sent their children to school, so they were being forced into Arab culture and religion, literally. With Sudan refined as an Arab state, Islam as the national religion, and Arabic as the national language, the Arabs turned their attention to the history of the country and made it fit their narrative to the exclusion of all indigenous Africans. In history books taught in schools, you didn't find a single Jieng warrior being mentioned; they were all Arab and European warriors, such as Gordon Basha, Osuman Abu Digin, and others. Even the history book titled, *Dukuul el Arab fi Sudan* ("*The Entrance of Arabs into Sudan*"), which talked about how the Arabs came into the country, was changed to *Dukuul el Naath fi Sudan* ("The Entrance of the People into Sudan"). To Southerners, this was an attempt not only to try cover their tracks but also to erase Southerners from their history. By changing the history, the Arabs didn't want to be viewed as immigrants who came from somewhere else. Or they tried to assume that everyone else was coming from somewhere. In other words, the Arabs believed that the coming generation would not know who were coming from somewhere, Jieng or Arabs because the history book generally talked about The Entrance of the People into Sudan.

But they were wrong. The Jieng children knew their history, which had been orally recorded, shared, and archived from generation to generation. They knew Sudan was their country, and the Arabs came from the Middle East. Furthermore, they knew they were not Arabs or Muslims, but the Jieng people who shared similar traditions with the Nuer, Shilluk, and other indigenous Africans. They also knew when the Arabs came into our land as salt traders and called our nation Bilad el Sudan, and when the first explorers called the land Kush when they mispronounced the word *Kuc*. Most importantly, the Jieng children knew that their great ancestors, including Ayuol Nhial, Wol Aruai, Ariath Makuei, Anok Nyingeer, and other giants, had fought against the foreigners. So, the new generation of indigenous South Sudanese knew they had to follow in their ancestors' footsteps, if need be, to fight for freedom and self-determination.

In 1956, Sudan achieved its independence, and the British left, leaving the Arabs in charge of the entire country. Southerners were left out during both the negotiation and handing over of the power and state. The Jieng, the Nuer, and all other indigenous tribes were just handed over between the authorities, along with their resources. When the South Sudanese demanded representation in the government, they were ignored, as usual, by both the British handing over the power, and the Arabs receiving it. The Southerners had reached boiling point.

In 1955, the First Civil War started. Southerners had fought several wars before separately, but they all united to fight the Khartoum regime. In just a few months before the independence, the Southerners formed a movement known as Anyanya One, named after snake venom. Under the leadership of Joseph Lagu, the guerilla movement launched a full-scale war intending to achieve an independent state in South Sudan.

In 1972, after 17 years of war, both the rebels and the government signed a peace agreement known as the Addis Ababa Agreement, which was negotiated and signed in Addis Ababa, the capital city of Ethiopia. Witnessed by both the World Council of Churches (WCC) and the All Africa Conference of Churches (AACC), the agreement allowed the South Sudanese to govern themselves autonomously within the Sudanese republic. Subsequently, the Anyanya rebels were encouraged to return to Khartoum.

When Joseph Lagu, William Deng, and the entire movement returned to Khartoum after the agreement, wise leaders, including Gordon Muortat, the typical son of Agaar, refused to return to Khartoum knowing this was just a trap. Instead, Gordon Muortat went into exile.

"You don't know the mentality of the Maathäng-lual," Gordon Muortat said, "They are luring us back to Khartoum to be murdered one by one. So I'm not returning to Sudan to share the country with the Maathäng-lual."

Gordon Muortat was right. After the Anyanya fighters put their weapons down and returned to Khartoum, it was not long before the Khartoum regime resumed business as usual. They started dismantling all the Addis Ababa agreement. The South Sudanese leaders who signed the Addis Ababa Agreement were eliminated one by one when they questioned the regime. William Deng Nhial was one of the first victims assassinated on the 9th May, 1968. After the South Sudanese leaders were killed, arrested, or quarantined, the government looted their resources openly. Southern Sudan was chunked up into three provinces, Bhar el Ghazal, Equatoria and Upper Nile, which were left under-developed. The North Sudan was given eight provinces which were thriving. Taxes, oil and all other natural resources were abstracted from the South and sent to the North, leaving the South grossly poor and under-developed. A humongous canal was dug in the south to guzzle the Nile waters to the North, leaving the Southerners and their animals with inadequate water sources. The Arabs had pushed Southerners to their limit once more.

In 1976, President Jaafar Nimeri survived a coup attempt by hardliner Islamists. To protect himself from future coup attempts, he allied with the Muslim Brotherhood, resulting in the imposition of Islamic law known as sharia in the entire country, which came into effect in 1983. In direct violation of the Addis Ababa agreement, Nimeri dissolved the South Sudanese government and divided the region into three provinces: Bhar el Ghazal, Equatoria, and Upper Nile. High-ranking Southern officers who agitated for fair treatment were forcefully transferred from South to North, where they would be arrested, quarantined, or killed. This opened up the old wound in the hearts of Anyanya One fighters as they mutinied, leading directly to the revival of Southern Sudanese liberation moment.

On May 16, 1983, the Southerners responded swiftly. Dr. Garang led them with the newly formed Sudan People's Liberation Army (the SPLA) with its political wing, Sudan People's Liberation Movement (the SPLM). The second Civil War erupted, the biggest of its kind, where even Muslim regions like Nuba Mountain and the Blue Nile eventually joined the Southerners in the fight against the Khartoum Islamic regime.

In 1985, while undergoing a medical examination in the United States of America, President Nimeri was overthrown in a bloodless coup which brought Abdel Rahman Swar Al-Dahab into power in 1985. In 1986 Sadiq Al Mahdi came into power. Sadiq continued to fight the SPLA forces, which were capturing towns and cities, mostly in Southern Sudan. In 1989, four years after he came to power, a coup overthrew Sadiq and brought in Umar al-Bashir, who ruled the country with an iron fist for 30 years until the Sudanese finally ousted and arrested him in 2019.

In 2005, after 22 years of war, Umar Bashir finally responded to the pressure from the persisting SPLA, which had gained the support of the international communities. As a result, the SPLA and the Khartoum regime signed a peace agreement known as the Comprehensive Peace Agreement in Nairobi, Kenya. Witnessed and mediated by the International Authority on the Development (IGAD) and other international bodies, the agreement was that South Sudanese would wait for six years before voting whether to remain as one country or breakaway.

While waiting for the referendum, Dr. Garang, the leader of the SPLA/M, died in a very suspicious helicopter crash in July 2005. Even though there was no proof, the Southerners knew who the killers were, as it was not the first time indigenous leaders had died in such a mysterious way. Nevertheless, another Jieng, General Salva Kiir Mayardit, led the movement during the interim period.

In 2011, 98.83 percent of Southerners voted in favor of breaking apart from the united Sudan and creating their own country. On July 9, 2011, the South Sudanese finally gained their independence under the name of the Republic of South Sudan, with General Kiir as the first president of the Republic of South Sudan.

Right after independence, the South Sudanese politicians debated the name of the country. Some said that it should be called Kush, and others said it should be South Sudan. Eventually, the newly created state was temporarily named South Sudan, but later might be changed to Kush. Remember, these are historical names that had been orally passed down from generation to generation, the same names which Chief Rok Reec, Majakdit, and Madingdit had archived and shared verbally for generations.

The People

Geography and Climate

FOR THOUSANDS OF YEARS, the homeland of the Agaar people, called Agarland (piny Agaar), has been geographically located in what is now known as Lakes State. Traditionally, the territory has been divided into four settlements: towns, villages, cattle camps, and fishing grounds.

Towns and villages are located in the woodland on the higher ground, where people build permanent houses, grow crops, and raise families. Cattle camps are located near the plains in the Toc Swamp, where the animals have plenty of water and grass. Between November and April, temporary settlements sprung up along the Naam River and Lake Akeu, where people conduct annual fishing festivals. All subsections of Agaar have their separate villages, cattle camps, and fishing grounds.

Towns are located along the main roads, connecting the Lakes State to other parts of South Sudan. Rumbek, the capital city of Lakes State and the biggest town in the Agarland, is located 308 kilometers (188 miles) away from Juba, the capital city of South Sudan via air or 377 km (234 miles) via road.

Before Sudan split into two countries (North and South), this territory was a part of Bhar el Ghazal, one of the three Southern Sudan provinces. After South Sudan achieved its independence in 2011, Lakes State was divided into three states: Eastern Lakes State, Gok state, and the Western Lakes States. But in 2020, when the country returned to ten states, the three states became one. The tribes which share the Lakes State with the Agaar include Atuot, Ciec, Gok, Aliab, and Jurbel.

Before the British arrived, the Agaar was divided into eight sections called *wuot* namely: Athoi, Duöör, Köök, Kuëi, Nyuɛɛi, Pakam, Panyar, and Rup. When the British arrived, however, they restructured the Agaar into five main subsections: Aliamtoc One and Two, Rup, Kuei, and Pakam.

Each of these five sections was further divided into several subdivisions. Aliamtoc One comprised Athoi, Kook; Aliamtoc Two comprised of Panyar, Duoor, and Nyuei. Rup had eight sections: Panyon, Bɛɛr, Böör, Jäth, Aliääp, Akök, Ajiɛɛk, and Tiɛk or Monytiik. Kuëth comprised Amoth-nhom, Tiɛk, Awan, Duor, and Yom. Pakam was divided into six sections: Manuer, Anïn, Niëlniël, Gääk, Akorkor, and Liɛth.

These sub-sections were further divided into smaller subsections. For example, Athoi had three smaller sub-divisions: Thiyith, Gony, and Dhiei. Panyar comprised of Apin and Muocoor; Duor comprised of Duor Ciek and Duor Bär, and so on. Remember, this was 1970s division and it is slightly different from today's division. I stay away from today's division because of politics involved.

The Agaar population is estimated to be less than one million. However, this estimation is far from accurate because no reliable censuses are conducted. Since independence in 2011, the country was embroiled in internal fighting; corruption and lack of infrastructure have made it impossible to do statistics. The UN had attempted several censuses, but they could not reach remote villages due to the impassable roads. So we are not sure about the exact population of the Agaar or any other tribes in South Sudan.

The climate is tropical, hot and wet. The wet season is hot and overcast and the dry season is sweltering and partly cloudy. The average temperature varies from 70 degrees 100 degrees Fahrenheit. This tropical climate has an abundance of vegetation and mango, Shea, and palm groves. It also has savannah forests inhabited by elephants, lions, leopards, hyenas, giraffes, buffalos, gazelles, baboons, and other animals found in the forests. Birdlife includes ostriches, cranes, storks, pelicans, guinea fowls, plovers, weavers, and shrikes. Reptiles include crocodiles and various lizards and geckos. Insect life is abundant: mosquitoes, flies, dragonflies, and Tsetse flies are typically found throughout the land. However, decades of wars and overhunting have decreased animal populations. But you can still find animals, including big games.

Living in Canada, what I miss the most is seeing animals in the forest, like I used to when I was in South Sudan. Once I went for a walk in a park in New Westminster, BC, and saw a sign that said, "Watch out for coyotes." I laughed to myself, saying, "Give me a break. I'm from Africa, so don't warn me about mere coyotes; warn me about lions, elephant, buffaloes and other big games. That will get my adrenaline going wild. But a coyote?! I have never been warned of coyotes since I was three years old. These Canadians have lost their damn minds. I'm sure of that!"

The amount of rainfall varies widely from year to year, a factor that causes extreme problems for agriculture and animal husbandry, the two significant sources of sustenance for the Agaar people. Typically, the area is prone to torrential rain from May through October, while November through April tends to be hot and dry. These two seasons (wet and dry) regulate the activities of the Agaar all year round. As proud farmers and cattle keepers, their permanent villages are located around the fringes of the Sudd—the world's largest swamp, fed and drained by the Nile River and its tributaries. Their seasonal cattle and fishing camps are in the Toc Swamp, along the Naam River and Lake Akeu. During the rainy season, from April to December, the Agaar people grow crops such as sorghum, millet, groundnut, sesame, beans, cassava, and yam. At this time, the cattle camps move to higher ground near villages when the swamp, rivers, and lakes overflow.

From November to the end of April, young men will move their cattle to Toc Swamp during the dry season where water and grass are plentiful. In this dry season, the people will catch catfish, tilapia, perch, and many other varieties in the Naam River and Lake Akeu.

General Characterizations

I know it sounds preposterous to attribute one peculiarity to an entire tribe, but it is safe to say the Agaar are the most hospitable people you will ever meet. When you visit an Agaar home, whether you are a stranger or local, you will be treated with utmost courtesy. To be a guest (*kaman*) means to be fed, sheltered, protected, and entertained during the entire visit. This hospitality is a deeply rooted value in their culture; it is an ethical obligation every community member practices.

Whether the host is poor or rich, a visitor is first welcomed with water upon arrival, whether he is thirsty or not, as a symbol of acceptance. And from the entry to departure, the guest is the priority: he must be given the best part or more significant portion of the food, and he sits or sleeps in the most comfortable place in the house. When there is a shortage of food, the hosts will fast to let the guests eat. When there is a shortage of sleeping mats, the host, usually the man of the house will sleep outside or next door. The guest must be entertained, and the entertainments, such as talks or jokes, must be appropriate, not insulting or disrespectful in tone. Even if there is a fight or quarrel in the family, it's always put off until the guest leaves.

Both locals and strangers are welcomed similarly. And there is no limit to the sacrifices the host makes for a visitor. An Agaar rarely kills an animal for food, but will not hesitate to kill a chicken, sheep or cow, depending on the number of visitors. The arrival of a visitor is an excuse to feast, as described in the phrase, "Why don't visitors come so we can be satisfied." Economizing the budget when a visit comes is not acceptable. The food must be offered to guests, even if there will be nothing to eat tomorrow. As Dr. Francis Mading Deng said, Jieng food doesn't last all year because of their lavish entertainment of guests.

This hospitality is universal among all the Jieng groups, and they are proud of it. The following song by Panchol Deng Ajang, describes their pride in hospitality:

> A visitor came and stood far away in front of my cattle.
> And he called, 'I need milk for sale!'
> I told him, 'Visitor, come and sit.
> The milk of Deng Wade's cows has never been bought by anyone (it's free).
> Even if you stay all wet and dry seasons, you'll leave on your own.
> It's the hair (life) that belongs to the owner of the cow,
> But the milk belongs to a guest like you.
> This is the land where people eat free of charge,
> So keep your money …

As mentioned in the song, you cannot ask the guests to leave, no matter how long they stay in your house. Doing so is impolite. It is also rude to ask a guest about the purpose of his visit before the end of the visit. Doing so implies you want the guest to leave. You must wait until the end of his visit.

When the guest declares his departure, formal speeches are often made by both the guest and the host, usually the head of the family. Right before the departure, if the guest does not voluntarily provide the purpose of his visit, the host will politely inquire. The term used when asking a visitor is so polite that it sounds vague and confusing: *Yi cath kadi?* Literally meaning, "How did you walk?" By this it means, "What is the purpose of your visit?"

On the other hand, it is impolite for a guest to take off without giving notice. The visitor should provide enough notice before leaving so a farewell meal may be prepared, especially if the visitor is coming from far away.

When the visitor leaves, he is always escorted. Sometimes, the host can even accompany the visitor until he is close to the visitor's home before returning. The purpose of the escort is to extend the time with the visitor as much as possible. Not escorting the guest implies you are not happy about their visit. The next time the guest may not visit again because he senses you are a rude person who hates visitors. And when friends or family members do not visit your home, you are an outcast, a rejected individual no one wants to be associated with.

Generally, giving is the key to the Agaar's social life. As a member of society, you are involved in a never-ending cycle of giving and receiving: you are obligated to give and accept. They believe, "Something you've given away is something you have invested or put away for the future." People acknowledge any kindness and consideration and will eventually repay favors, no matter how long it takes. A gift in the form of cows is not easily forgotten.

In most cases, gifts are carried down from generation to generation. A dying father may tell his sons to repay favors he has not paid yet. When I visited home after 30 years away, a distant cousin of mine approached me. "I will not forget what your father did to my father," he said. The man explained that when his father married his mother, my father had given him a bull as a bride price. When his father passed on, he told his son to repay the favor later on. This is what they mean by "a gift is a future investment."

The Agaar culture has adapted to an uncertain environment where it is necessary to build up a reciprocation network to survive. The term *duiit* (unwillingness to give), refers to someone who feels he or she has no obligation to share; a mean person who hoards and privatizes while his relatives and friends are in need. Such a person risks social isolation because no one would associate with him or her. "No one will rush to your house when you cry for help," they say.

In this group-oriented society, those who are perceived as individualistic are frowned upon in the community. Putting your own needs above family members, relatives, friends, and the entire society isolates you because no one will then help when you need a hand. Individual accomplishments are celebrated by all family members and relatives because generosity is emphasized. In other words, a person's success is expected to be shared with members of the immediate and extended families and even clan-men. When you are low on food supplies, you can always go to your family members or even neighbors, and they will be ready and willing to share with you. It is not uncommon for a person to take his relative to court, saying: "My children are starving, and my brother does not want to share."

However, while effective at the village level, the Agaar system can cause challenges in urban settings. For example, it is not uncommon for rural-dwellers to go to Rumbek or even Juba and expect relatives to support them, even if they don't have jobs. When hunger strikes, villagers travel to towns and cities and expect relatives with shops and stores to buy goods free of charge. Some villagers bring their children to relatives in town to be fed, sheltered, and educated. Many Agaar business people are unable to move ahead in Rumbek because of this obligated kindness and generosity.

Nevertheless, the Agaar people, like any other Jieng group, are always proud of this hospitality and generosity as part of their heritage. Typically, a person's allegiances extend toward the family first, and then, in descending order, to the nuclear family, extended family, relatives, sub-clan, and so on.

Language

The act of speaking in Jieng language is known as *jam* (speaking). But the act of speaking in other tongues is known as *guel* (*guɛl*), meaning "misspeaking". In other words, you are said to be logical and coherent when speaking in Jieng and incoherent (misspeaking) when talking in English, Arabic, or any other language. Therefore, I'm now misspeaking in English and you are just reading misspoken words.

The above statement illustrates the typical Jieng's worldview. Noticeably, the Jieng society loves every aspect of its culture and values its God-given tongue and will not forfeit it for anything in the world. Believing that their culture is the best, they are not afraid to impose their superiority over others through their language as shown above.

In the early 1980s, when I was a small boy in an isolated village called Biling Daldiar, I thought Thong Agaar (the dialect of Agaar) was the only language spoken worldwide. This was at a time when there were no schools, hospitals, televisions, or telephones. One day, a white couple, John Ryle and Sarah Errington from England, visited our village to study our culture. I was probably seven years old. Despite their physical characteristics, what surprised me the most about the visiting strangers was them not knowing how to speak Thong Agaar. I was told the reason was because they came from a faraway country of white people. But the distance did not seem a legitimate reason for not speaking the language, so I thought the strangers were just *acëbëël* (dummies). Later, Mother explained to me that other people, such as white people and Arabs, misspeak (*guɛl*) in their languages and we, the Agaar, speak in our language.

However, despite being the only language that makes sense, the Jieng was a spoken language until the early1920s when missionaries came to spread Christianity in Sudan. One of the main obstacles the missionaries faced in converting the Jieng to Christianity was the language barrier. At first, nobody even paid attention to the strangers, who misspoke in a strange tongue, much less their peculiar religion. After acknowledging this obstacle, the missionaries' first objective was to learn the Jieng language first to understand their way of life. The missionaries overcame language difficulties by devoting their spare time to the study of Jieng language and by approaching Jieng in their own language to minimize cultural misunderstandings and distinctions between themselves and their potential converts. Daniel Comboni, one of the first missionaries who arrived in the Jiengland in 1856, was one of the first missionaries to learn Jieng language. Luckily, Comboni found an educated Jieng woman named Zeinab in Cairo, Egypt. Zeinab, from the Ciec section, and the missionaries then translated the first biblical texts from English into the Jieng language.[9]

The first 27 alphabet letters were developed, written in Latin script.

Uppercase letters:
A   E   I   O   U W Y B P
M   N   NH ŋ   NY R D DH T
TH L   K   G   Ɣ   C J Ɛ Ɔ

Lowercase letters:
a   e   i   o   u   w   y   b   p
m   n   nh ŋ   ny r   d   dh t
th l   k   g   ɣ   c   g   ɛ   ɔ

As shown above, there were seven vowels (*a, e, i, o, u, ɛ, and ɔ*) and 20 consonants (*w, y, b, p, m, n, nh, ŋ, ny, r, d, dh, t, th, l, k, g, Ɣ, c, and j*). If you compare the Jieng letters to English alphabet letters, you will notice a difference. For example, only 19 letters (*a, e, i, o, u, w, y, b, p, m, n, r, d, t, l, k, g, c, and j*) appear in the English alphabet and the other seven letters (*nh, ŋ, ny, dh, th, Ɣ, ɛ and ɔ*) are missing. Out of the seven letters, *nh, ny, dh,* and *th* are a combination of two letters. The letters Ɣ, ŋ, *dh, th, dh, ɛ, ɔ* do not exist in English. And letters f, q, v, and x do not exist in Jieng.

In Jieng tradition, men and women remove their six lower teeth to distinguish themselves as permanent members of their society. The absence of the lower teeth makes it difficult for Jieng to produce some letters (f, v, and x), which depend on the teeth for correct articulation. When creating the sounds of f and v, for example, you need your lower and upper teeth to bite down on your lip to cause the friction with the air source to make the sounds. To produce the sound x, you need to part your lips and use the upper and the lower teeth to restrict both the tongue and air to produce the sound. But since the Jieng remove their lower teeth, the pronunciation is often distorted. Even in English,

9   Werner R., Anderson W. & Wheeler A., *Day of Devastation, Day of Contentment*, Nairobi: Pauline's Publications, 2000, p. 131

most Jieng, especially those with missing lower teeth, find it harder to pronounce f and v. For example, they pronounce Francis, Prancith; very good, bery guud, and Victoria, Bictoria. Foreigners may not notice these differences in the pronunciation because of the heavy Jieng accent.

On the other hand, the missing set of teeth causes excessive movements of both the tongue and air from the mouth when speaking, and this produces an accent with long and irregular breathy sounds. So, after the establishment of the alphabet, it became clear that the original 27 letters were inadequate to express the complex series of Jieng sounds in the spoken language. The solution to the problem mentioned above was to modify the original vowels (excluding u) by adding two dots above each vowel to represent these breathy sounds. The six modified vowels became known as breathy vowels, and the seven origin vowels were clear or non-breathy vowels:

Original clear vowels: *a, e, i, o, u, ɛ, ɔ.*
Modified breathy vowels were: *ä, ë, ï, ö, ɛ̈, ɔ̈.*

After the modification, there were a total of 33 letters (20 consonants and 13 vowels) written in a Latin-based script and complemented with the signs of the International Phonetic Alphabet (IPA).

Even so, the 33 letters still could not produce other sounds in the spoken language. So, long vowels were created by doubling the vowel letters:

Short vowels: *a, e i, o u, ɛ, ɔ.*
Long vowels: *aa, ee, ii, oo, uu, ɛɛ, ɔɔ.*

Grammar

Jieng grammar takes a very predictable pattern; although some people may find it unpredictable. There are no Jieng dictionaries or encyclopedias, so the language keeps evolving. This evolution causes flexibility in grammar. What increase the volatility of the language are dialects. There are over 25 dialects, and each dialect has its rules and syntax, which are slightly different from others. Each dialect uses different words. For example, the word "see" based on different dialects can be *tïŋ, ɣoi, döt, daai,* ŋëm or ŋën. And "want" is *gör, guik, kɔr, wïc,* or *yuïc.* Because of these variations, a phrase used in Agaar dialect may sound grammatically incorrect in Bor or Rek dialect.

The Agaar dialect, called Thong Agaar, "the mouth of Agaar," has its own grammatical rules. To form sentences in the present, past or future tense, helping verbs (*acë, abë, a, aa, e, ee*) are used in conjunction with the main verbs.

Present continuous tense is formed by adding the letter (*a*) after the subject or before the verb. For example, *Dut a jam*, "Dut is talking." *Dut* is the subject, *jam* is the main verb, and the letter *a* is the helping verb. Sometimes, you can add the *a* to the main verb to make one verb—for example, *Dut ajam* can still be correct, though it is informal.

However, when you use double *aa*, as in *Dut aa jam*, it is grammatically incorrect. You use double *aa* when describing two subjects. For example, *Dut ku Yar aa jam*, meaning "Dut and Yar are talking."

Present simple tense is formed by adding single *e* after the subject or before the verb. For example, *Dut e jam*, "Dut talks" or "Dut can talk." Again, if you rewrite this sentence with double *ee*, the verdict will change from present tense to past continuous tense. For example, *Dut ee jam*, "Dut was talking." Or "Dut has been talking."

It is, therefore, crucial to know how and when to use the short vowels (*a, e, i, o u, ɛ, ɔ*) and the long vowels (*aa, ee, ii, oo, uu, ɛɛ, ɔɔ*).

Past simple tense is formed by adding *acë* between the subject and the verb. For example, *Dut acë jam*, "Dut talked." Or "Dut has (had) talked." In this sentence, *Dut acë*, you must keep the two dots above the letter ë in the word acë. Otherwise, the meaning can change. *Dut ace jam*, without the dot above *e* means, "Dut does not talk."

The future simple tense is formed by adding *abë* after the subject or before the verb. For example, *Dut abë jam*, "Dut will talk." Again, in the future tense, you need to keep the two dots in *abë* otherwise, "*Dut abe jam*, without the dots above *e*, can translate into "Dut is talking again."

It is, therefore, crucial to know the differences between clear vowels (*a, e, i, o, u, ɛ, ɔ*) and breathy vowels (*ä, ë, ï, ö, ɜ̈, ɔ̈*). The letter u is not modified.

Let's look at one example: *Yar akët*, "Yar is singing." This is in present continuous tense. Pay attention to the two dots in the verb *akët*. Now, to change this sentence from *Yar akët* (with dots) to *Yar aket* (without dots), it means: (i) "Yar is being carried on the shoulder." (ii) "Someone is singing a bad song composed against Yar" or (iii) "Yar is the song being sung." It is, therefore, vital to know when to use clear or breathy vowels.

Pronouns

The pronouns are simple and straightforward. Personal pronoun: I, me, ɣɛn; you, *yïïn*; he, she or it, *yen*. Plural form: us, ɣook; you, *week*; they, and them, *keek*.

Demonstrative pronouns: This, *kân*; that, *këtui*; these, *kakë*; those, *kakui*.

Interrogative pronouns include: who, ŋa; what, *kunu* or *kuŋu*; when, *nin*; where, *tëyo* or *tëno*; how, *kadi*.

A possessive pronoun is formed by adding prefixes *kë* (singular) or *ka* (plural). For example: *këdie*, mine; *këda*, ours; *këdu*, yours; *këdɛn*, theirs; and *këde*, his, hers or its. This is when the object being owned is singular. When owning two or more objects, you say, *kacë*, mine; *kaku*, yours; *kakuôn*, yours; *kakua*, ours; and *kakɛn*, theirs.

Nouns

Nouns have no grammatical gender; instead, distinct words are used to distinguish gender. For example: *moc*, man; tik, woman; *dhɔk*, boy; and *nya*, girl.

Animal sex is determined by *muor*, male or *ŋuôt*, female. In domesticated animals such as cows, goats, or sheep, the prefix *ma* is added to the name, which is the color, to make it a male. The absence of *ma* in the name signifies female. *For example*, majak, mading, and marial are names for bulls or oxen; ajak, ding, and rial are the opposite sex.

Singular and plural

There is no definite rule for the formation of the plural from the singular; some substantives have the same form in both singular and plural. In some instances, the vowel sound may be entirely changed, or one or two vowels may be omitted; and there are still other nouns of which the plural is altogether irregular. In most cases, both vowel and consonants may be changed entirely to form a plural or singular.

For example: *tik*, woman; *diâr*, women; moc, man; rôr, men; *nya*, girl; *nyiir*, girls; *dhɔk*, boy; *dhâk*, boys; meth, child; *mïth*, children. When talking about a group of people or crowd, the pronunciation and spelling change. For example: *muɔɔc* (large number of men), *dhâäk* (large number of boys), *nyääl* (large number of girls) or *diöör* (large number of women).

In most instances, singular or plural is formed by either shortening or lengthening the vowels. For example: *raap*, sorghum, *rap*, sorghums; *acuuk*, ant, *acuk*, ants; *alïïk*, bat, *alïk, bats*. This is shortening of the vowel to form the plural.

You can also lengthen the vowel to change from singular to plural. For example: *bith*, spear; *biith*, spears; *tim*, tree; *tiim*, trees; *abun*, priest; *abuun* priests; *sukul*, school, *sukuul*, schools; *alïp*, thousand, *alïïp*, thousands; *nyin*, eye, *nyïïn*, eyes; *atët*, designer, *atëët*, designers.

Comparative and Superlative

The comparative and superlative degrees are formed by placing *arët* (comparative) or *arëtdic* (superlative) after the adjective. For example: *arac*, bad, *arac arët*, worse (very bad); *arac arëtdic*, worst. Rek Jieng uses *apɛi* instead of *arët*. For example: *aciek*, short; *aciek apɛi*, shorter; *aciek apɛidït*, shortest.

Numbers

The Jieng are very poor in the language of numbers. Initially, the numbers only ranged from one (*tôk*) to a thousand (*tim*). *Sometimes, tim is called alïp*, which is an Arabic term for thousand. The numbers were designed for counting cattle, and no one owned a thousand animals, so there was no need to create names for a million or trillion. Hundreds of thousands were simply called *thiërcikuen* (infinite or countless).

The numbers are designated by distinct words from one to ten: *tök* (one), *rou* (two), *dïäk* (three), *ŋuan* (four), *dhïc* (five), *dhetem* (six), *dhorou* (seven), *bët* (eight), *dhoŋuan* (nine), and *thiär* (ten). However, eleven, twelve, thirteen, etc. are compounds of ten and one, ten and two, ten and three, and so on; as in *thiär ku tôk*, eleven; *thiär ku rou*, twelve; *thiär ku dïäk*, thirteen; and so on. The other tens are formed by placing the multiple units after the word ten, as in, *thiär*, ten, *rou*, two; *thiär-rou* (spelled *thiër-rou or thië-rou*), twenty; *thiëdiäk*, thirty; *thiërŋuan*, forty, and so on. The intervening numbers are formed by connecting the ten with the unit that follows it by the conjunctive particle *ku*, as in *thiërŋuan ku diäk*, forty three; *thiërbët ku dhorou*, eighty seven.

There are specific words designated a hundred or thousand, as in, *buɔɔt*, hundred; and *tim*, thousand. For example, one thousand nine hundred twenty five (1925) is *tiɛm tôk ku buɔt ka dhoŋuan ku thiërou ku dhïc (1925)*.

Even though Jieng is the dominant language in South Sudan, it's not the official language. After independence, English replaced Arabic as an official language taught in school. However, both English and Arabic are spoken in schools and government settings, but they are rarely used in conversation outside the offices or schools. Educated people often interject English or Arabic words when conversing in Jieng, and an increasing number of young people, particularly those who grow up outside the country, speak English, Arabic, or even Kiswahili. Among the uneducated people, on the other hand, speaking English or Arabic in public may be considered as showing off and is mocked.

The majority of people cannot write or read the language, but the grammar rules are followed correctly in the spoken word. People look with disgust at people who do not speak the language well, especially if they are Jieng. Anyone who does not talk in Jieng language is automatically considered *jur* ë *guɛl*—a foreigner who misspeaks.

The Agaar Calendar

In addition to grammar, the Agaar people knew their environment, their people, and their animals intimately. Their knowledge was based on the experience of a life; they noted the phases of the moon and watched the movement of the stars and planets.

The Agaar used (and still do) a lunar calendar to measure the times for planting, weeding, harvesting, fishing, hunting, or migrating every year. Month is called *pɛi*, meaning the moon. The month is determined by the appearance and disappearance of the moon. The disappearance of the moon is known as *muth*, and the appearance is *yuil*. From the first day the moon appears in the sky, to the last day it disappears, it is estimated to be between 13 and15 days. And from the previous day it fades to the first day it appears is between 13 and 15 days. Bear in mind that there are some factors which affect the observation such as weather conditions. If it's raining, for example, it's hard to tell whether the new moon has appears today or not. Thus, it makes an average of 28 days in a month, twelve equal months in a year, with a total of 336 days. The counting may differ based on geographical locations.

The following is the calendar with the names of the months: the names are the same, but the order may be also different because the Jieng ethnic groups are widely spread out in the settlement.

January, *Kol*; February, *Nyith*; March, *(Akɔ̈c) Akänydit*; April, *Akänythii*; May, *Aduôŋ* June, *Alɛthboor*; July, *Akoldït*; August, *Bildït*; September, *Biɛlthii*; October, *Lal*; November, *Hörbëklâi* and December, *Kônpïu*.

Generally, the Agaar used names of the month (*Kol, Nyith, Akɔ̈c*, etc.) when referring to seasonal activities such as farming, harvesting, fishing, migrating of cattle, etcetera. But in most cases, they use *Pen* ë Tök *(January), Pen ë Rou (February), Pen ë Diäk (March), Pen ë ŋuan* (April), *Pen ë Dhïc* (May), *Pen ë Dhetem* (June) *Pen ë Dhorou* (July), *Pen ë Bët* (August), *Pen ë Dhoŋuan* (September), *Pen ë Thiär* (October), *Pen ë Thiär ku Tök* (November), and *Pen ë Thiär ku Rou* (December).

Similarly, Monday, Tuesday, Wednesday, Thursday, Friday, Saturday, and Sunday are: *Aköl ë* tök*, Aköl ë Rou, Aköl ë Diäk, Aköl ë ŋuan, Aköl ë Dhïc, Aköl* ë *Dhetem, Aköl ë Dhorou*. You can omit the letter ë and still be correct, For example, *Aköl tök, Aköl Rou, Aköl Diäk,* etc. But the latter is informal.

You need to be thorough when talking about days, weeks, months and years. For example: Monday, January 6, 1983 reads: *Aköl ë Tök, pɛi nïn dhetem, pen ë diak, run ë tiɛm tök ku buɔt ka dhoŋuan ku thiërbɔ̈t ku diäk. Dates of births are expressed in similar manner.* For example, Yar was born on Thursday, June 21, 2012. *Yar ee dhiëth në Aköl ë ŋuan, ke pɛi ë nïn thiërou ku tök, Pen ë dhetem, run ë tim thiërou ku thiär ku rou.*

Seasons of the Year

There are five seasons of the year. *Kër* is the beginning of wet season. *Ruël* is the wettest season of the year. Then there are two springs: *Rut* Col (early spring) and Rut ɣer (late spring). *Mɛi* is dry season.

It is important to note that these seasons don't arrive at the same time throughout the Jiengland, as there is a progressive difference between northern and southern extremes of the Jiengland. For example, rain arrives early in Bor and late in Rumbek, as the Earth turns its top and backsides toward and away from the sun within the tropics, thus forming these seasons of the year.

Naming

(Note: the names which appear in this section or any other section of this book were stated without specific individuals in mind. So if you find your name in this book, it's just a coincident.)

The Agaar people have the most complex naming traditions, which help enrich their sense of identity. The naming takes on a predictable pattern. And because every name tells a story, every stage in life has its name. In their life stages, individuals can have four titles, including infant, adolescent, oxen, and Christian names. Each of these names represents a critical stage in life.

Infant Name

As soon as the child is born, he or she is given an infant name (*rin ë mεεth*). This descriptive name, usually provided by the mother, midwife, or female relative (men, including the father of the child, are not allowed in the delivery process), is derived from daily occurrences, such as weather conditions, time, event, or place of the birth. For example, a child born when it is raining is called *Deng* (male); *Adeng, Nyandeng,* or *Atuenydeng* (female). A child born when it is windy or dusty is called *Matur* (male) or *Nyitur* for females. A child born when the day is gloomy or cloudy is named *Maluet* (male) or *Aluet* (female).

In addition to the weather conditions, children are also named after the places they are born. For example, a child born on the road as the mother is traveling is called *Puoric, Dhel, Madhel,* or *Makuer* (male) and *Adhel* or *Nyankuer* (female). *Matoc* (male) and *Nyantoch* (female) are names given to children born in the savannah or swamp. *Madiria* (the Arabic word for the province) or *Matueny* (male) and *Nyanpen* (female) are names given to children born in cities or towns.

In addition to weather conditions or place of birth, infant names can also be derived from the time of the day the baby arrives. For example, a child born at dawn is *Bakgic*, early in the morning is *Nhiakdur*, midday is *Makol* (male) or *Nyanakol* (female), afternoon is *Magang*, dust or sunset is *Cholruel* (male) and midnight is *Amakou* (female). Similarly, *Muothich* is a child born in the darkness, and *Sawat* is a child born at one o'clock—a common name in urban areas where there are watches to track the time.

Urban dwellers also have a unique way of naming infants. Although they still use traditional naming, some people name their children after influential figures, even if the prominent persons are not Agaar, believing that the child could grow to become an important man/woman like the person he or she is named after. For example, there are children named Mandela after South Africa's first black president who fought against apartheid. Children born in the early 1980s were named Nimeri, after the president of Sudan. Children born in refugee camps in Ethiopia were named Mengistu after the Ethiopian president who helped the Southerners in the war against the Northerners.

The most common names among urban dwellers are the days of the week on which the children were born. For example, *Kamis, Jima (Juma), Sebit,* or *Lahat* are names given to male children born on Thursday, Friday, Saturday, and Sunday, respectively. The only name for a female is Yomjima (Friday). These are Arabic terms.

An educated person could name his daughter *Nyanëgalam* ("daughter of the pen"), implying he did not inherit his wealth from anyone, but used his hard-earned salary, a result of his education, to buy the cattle and marry the mother of the child.

A positive or negative circumstance the parents experience around the time a child is born also influences the choice of names. Therefore, such names are not only complete sentences, but they also carry stories or statements. For example, when a child is born and the mother dies after delivery, the child is named *Amukpiu* (male) or *Apiu* (female), meaning the child "survives on water." When both parents die, the child is automatically named *Akec*, a gender-neutral name, literally meaning, "the bitter one." The name Akec is derived from cricket (*akec* or *akeny diir*) that the Agaar believe to give birth and die, leaving its child behind. So a female child may be named *Nyëdiir*. The only surviving child after other children have died is known as *Derkeny*, implying the ultimate survivor. *Cingoth* (hopeless) is given to a child born after many children have died. In other words, the parents feel hopeless, thinking the child may die.

Parents who are hopeful or optimistic may name their children to express their mood. For example, *Cholhok* ("pay back the cows") is the name given to a girl they believe to be so beautiful that when she grows up, she could be married with many cows to "pay back the cows" the father paid as a bride-price when marrying the mother. On the other hand, *Wade* (male) or *Akolde* (female), which means "future," are names given to children with potentials. Other names for male children which illustrate optimism or resilience included Gum and Agum ("shoulder your burden bravely and silently"), *Muorater* ("man who never gives up"), *Muorwel* ("man of his words"), or *Rilpuou* ("strong-hearted" or "tenacious"), *Tokmac* ("kindle the fire of the family"), or *Konybaai* ("help the country").

While some names reflect the mood or circumstance of the family at the time of birth, others serve as warnings or rebukes. For example, when one parent is expecting a male child, and it turns out to be a female, the other parent may name the child *Kochkedhia*, meaning "they are all human beings," so it doesn't matter whether the child is a boy or girl. *Kochkedhia* is a gender-neutral name. Such a child might also be called *Puondak* ("doubtful"). Others will make a strong point or statement: *Lingudi* ("So what!"), *Pingke* ("listen" but pay no attention), *Tingke* ("just watch" but don't react), or *Welken* ("to hell with them") are other names individuals use to rebuke those who are against their decisions within the family or clan.

When parents have disputes during the pregnancy, and they go to court or the council of elders to solve their conflicts, the child is named *Maluk* (male) and *Aluk* (female), meaning "court."*Alam* ("conjure") or *Bith* ("sacred fishing spear") are names given to children who don't want to arrive until a spear-master conducts prayers. A child who is born in the modern hospital is named *Akim* or *Diktor* (male) or Nyanakim (female)—all mean "doctor."

The Agaar also have a unique way of naming twins. They refer to twins as *diet*, which means "birds." And when one or both of them dies, they are said to have "flown away," not died or deceased. Animals' twins are called *acueek*, not *diet*. The first twin is often named *Ngor* or *Mangor*, meaning "leading" for a male child. The second twin is usually named *Madit* or *Lual* (male) and *Adit* or *Nyandit* (female). Other Jieng groups use *Ngor*, *Chan*, or *Madit* for males; *Anger*, *Achan*, or *Adit* for females. A child born after a set of twins is automatically named *Bol* (male) and *Nyibol* (female).

There are also names for consolation. For instance, a child born after the mother has waited for a very long time without getting pregnant or after the first child or children have died is called *Dut* (male) or *Adut* (female), which means "consolation for the lost child or lost period without children". Similarly, a child born right after the first child has died may be named *Chol* (male) or *Achol* (female), which means God has repaid the grieving parents.

When there are complications or difficulties during the delivery, this is explained through the name of the children. A child who is born before the due date is called *Mapet* (male) or *Apet* (female). Similarly, a child born inverted during the delivery, feet first instead of head, is called *Maluong* (male) or *Aluong* (female), meaning "reversal."

Natural and human-made disasters are also included in the names. *Riak* or *Mariak* (male) and *Nyiriak* (female), all mean "spoil of the earth," are names for children born in civil wars. *Tong* and *Matong* for males and *Atong* for females are children born in a conflict or fight. On the other hand, a child born during the drought is named *Yak* (male) and *Ayak* (female). *Machok* (male) and Achok or *Nyikuân* (female) are the names given to children born during hunger or starvation.

You would think such names would be shameful. Far from it! Nobody is ashamed of his or her name, as long as the name is meaningful and historical. When children grow up, they will know the reason why they were given such names. For example, a parent may name her child depending on the accusation made against her. The idea here is to let the society know how badly and unfairly she has been treated. In the end, the insulter or accuser will be ashamed for the rest of his life, not the child or parent.

Some of these infant names are discarded after the child reaches adolescence, and others are kept. Names that tells meaningful stories of consolation, rebuke, or historical wars are kept permanently. But the names derived from daily occurrences such as weather conditions, time, events, or place of the birth are discarded as the child is given an adolescent name.

Adolescent Name

When a child reaches adolescence, he or she receives an adult name (*rin ë dït*). Usually provided by the father or male guidance, this is the permanent or legal name in the family tree. Remember, the Jieng don't have a surname or last name system. The name goes in order from child to father, to grandfather, great grandfather, and so on.

Unlike other Jieng groups, Agaar adult names exclusively come from the colors of their cows. For example, *Machar*, *Malual*, or *Mabor* come from the black, red, or white bull. The opposite sex of these names included *Achol, Aluel,* and *Yar.* Other common names include, *Makuei* (a black bull with white on the head), *Makuach* (a spotted bull or ox), or Manyang (a bridled bull or ox). The absence of *ma-* in the name or the presence of the suffix (a) signifies female sex. Therefore, the opposite sex of *Makuei, Makuach* and *Manyang* are *Kuei, Akuach,* or *Nyang.*

A father who names his children after cattle does so because they are the brideprice he has paid in marrying the mother of the children. For example, my name is Mayom, meaning a bull with a white body and a redhead. Mayom was one of the beasts my father paid as a dowry to marry my mother. I learned the story of my name when I returned home after more than thirty years away.

When I returned from Canada to Rumbek in 2017, I visited Mathiang village, where I met my maternal uncle, Majur Marial. Uncle Majur greeted me with my infant name, Makol (meaning I was born in the middle of the day). After the greeting, he delved deeper into the history of my name. "You are Mayom, aren't you?" Majur asked with a smile that said he knew a lot about me than I knew myself. "Do you know the bull Mayom you are named after?" Uncle Majur asked. It turned out the bull I was named after was given to Majur as his share when his nephew, my mother's father divided the brideprice paid by my father. The bull Mayom, according to Majur, was just a calf, and it was so weak he thought it would not survive the journey back to his cattle camp, so he ended up slaughtering the bull to eat at the gathering. I was named after such a weak bull because I was the last-born; my older brothers had taken the names of first-class bulls and oxen. How unfair to be the last born!

Oxen Names

The third name an individual receives is a nickname called *rin ë mör,* literally meaning "oxen name." Right after initiation, every Agaar young man (*apäräpuöl*) acquires his personnel ox, the *muorcien (song-ox),* which he cherishes as his beast. The young owner will eventually adopt a nickname for himself, usually given to him by his peers. Such a name is nothing but a work of art—a complete poetic paraphrase of the ox's color, physical characteristics, or behavior.

The size, shape, and color of the horn, as well as the color of the muzzle, are also considered. For example, a young man who owns a bull with a white and smooth horn may call himself *Matungböör* (white-horned), and *Matunglual* (red-horned) or *Matunglââk* (smooth-horned) are named given to young men who own beasts with such horns. If the ox has a red nose, which is the most desired, he could be called *Mawumlual* (red-nosed); or his name would be derived from the redness of his ox's nose in comparison to the redness in other things. Therefore, the young fellow named himself *Mawumcuur*, "the cuur fish with the red mouth," or *Dan-luat,* "the red seed." The redness can also be exaggerated and likened to the fire, moon or anything that gives lights. For example, Many-cin-amör ("fire that does not burn") is given to a person with red-nosed ox. Similarly, *Atit-hok-pɛi* ("lighting the cows until the moon arrives") is given to a man who owns a white bull, believing his beast is so bright that it gives light in the darkness when the moon is absent.

A young man with a malou ox (dark grey) may liken the color of his ox to the color of the elephant. Therefore, he will be known as *Adhong-tim*, ("breaker of the tree") because of the elephants like to break trees. Similarly, a young man with a mayen ox (light-cream) will liken its color to that of the lion. Therefore, he may call himself *Ayaplai* ("hunter of the animals") or *Adhɔmläi* ("stalker of the animals").

In addition to color-configuration, the name may be derived from the general character of the beast. For example, a young man from our village named himself *Saluk,* meaning "criminal" or "thief" because his ox stole the show from other oxen and bulls. So, the young man's boasting phrase included, "My name is Saluk. But I'm not a criminal who steals; it's just that my ox is doing the unthinkable deeds."

After the acquisition of the name, the young man would be addressed with it by everyone, especially his friends, as a sign of respect. A junior has to address a senior by his oxen name. Addressing him by his real name is disrespectful.

Christian Name

After infant, adult, and oxen names, Christian names are the fourth name an Agaar might get in their life circle. When Christianity first arrived, the convert received Christian or saint names when they were baptized. So when I became Christian, I was named William. More than 90 percent of the Agaar people are Christians, and they have Christian names in addition to their infant, adult, and oxen names. Educated individuals who live in cities and towns and don't have an oxen name often use a Christian name in the same way oxen names are used.

Greetings

Greetings and salutations are crucial among the Agaar people. When two or more people meet, the first thing they do is to get greetings and salutations out of the way. There are many phrases used in greeting, but the most common ones include *Kudual* ("greeting") and *ci baak?* ("Have you reached the dawn?") The response is usually *acin kërac* ("nothing bad; all is good"). Other greeting phrases include *ca pääc?* ("have you awakened?"), and *ca niin?* ("Have you slept?") The responses are "*acin kerac*" (nothing bad) or "ɣɛn *apuɔl* guɔ̂p" (my body is well or light"). Other Dinka groups use other greeting phrases including, *loidi?* ("How is it doing?"); *ci ruon?* ("Have you reached the dawn?") *Maadhu* ("greeting"), and *path-dhu* ("goodness").

A handshake often accompanies the verbal phrase. The handshake is crucial; without it, the greeting is incomplete. All people—men, women, and children—shake hands. No exception. Intentional refusal to shake hands is not only rude but also a sign of an existing feud or animosity. Even if your hand or palm is slightly wet, you must offer the tip of your fingers, or you can turn the back of your hand to be shaken. If your hand is dirty, because you are eating or cultivating, for example, you can just offer your wrist or even arm for grabbing while apologizing for the inconvenience. And if both parties have dirty hands, then they can only touch their wrists or arms instead of handshakes.

To shake hands, straightforwardly line up your right hands and clasp for one, two, three, or more seconds (depending on the duration apart or how well you know each other), and then release. It should not be too hard, soft, long, or short. For example, it is rude to withdraw your hand too soon or before a handgrip. Doing so will send a signal you are angry. It's not uncommon for someone greeted that way to ask, "Why do you spear my hand? What are we fighting for?" Similarly, squeezing someone's hand a little harder means that you are either flirting with them if they are of the opposite sex or you want to talk to them in private when they are in public. In other words, if you want to speak to one person in a crowd, you can squeeze his hand a little hard during the hand shake, and he will know you want to talk to him privately.

Hugs and embraces are frequent in urban areas, but they are usually reserved for friends and family members. You stand facing each other and use your right hand to tap your party's left shoulder or back before shaking hands. When you are happy to meet someone, or you are meeting someone famous, shake with your right hand and then use the left hand to either support your right arm or sandwich the dignitary's hand. This handshake is uncommon and foreign, and practiced by urban dwellers.

When entering a house full of people, you should greet everyone with a handshake first before sitting down. If the visitor is a grown-up or an important individual, he or she will be seated first, and then the hosts will come one by one to shake the visitor's hand. Children, even those who can't walk or talk yet, are trained to shake every visitor's hand. As a courtesy, "the woman of the house" usually holds a cup of water in her left hand, greeting the visitor with her right hand before giving them water to drink.

In urban areas, people often stand up to welcome or greet a visitor, especially when the visitor is a prominent figure or elder. But in rural areas, there is no need to rise; you greet while seated. Juniors must get up to offer their seats when a visitor arrives.

Addressing Individuals

In addition to the greeting and handshake, another component in greeting is addressing individuals correctly. Correctly addressing a person is crucial because the importance of one's place in society is reflected in the tendency to address people of seniority by title instead of name. *Beny* or *benydit* (master or big master) is used to address any leader, such as governor or chief.

Spouses don't call each other by their names. Instead, they refer to each other by their children's names. A couple with a child, who is named *Marial*, will use *Man–Marial* (Marial's mother) for the mother and *Wun–Marial* (Marial's father) for the father. A young couple who have no children may refer to each other as "Man of the House" and "Woman of the House". It is disrespectful for a spouse to call each other by name. Doing so sends a signal that they are quarreling.

Similarly, it is strange to call a woman by her name, especially if she has children. After 30 years away from home, I had forgotten the etiquette of names and learned the hard way when I returned in 2016. I stayed at my brother's house for two months and referred to my brother's wife as just Christine, her Christian name or Anguendek, her first name. The first time I called her that, she frowned, though she tried to hide the disappointment. At first, I didn't know why she acted that way until later when I heard other people calling her *Man-Sebit* (Sebit's mother), Sebit being her first son. After that, I called her *Man-Sebit* as well.

It is disrespectful for children to address adults by their names. Instead, they say uncle or aunt because the adult is your parents' age. Or they refer to adults by their oxen names. A junior addressing an elder they don't know by name may say *raandit* ("big person"). And it is okay to call seniors *monydit* ("old man") or *tiŋdit* ("old woman") provide they are old. A young person may refer to any woman or girl as mother-in-law or sister-in-law (*dhiɔp*). If you know the woman has children, you can just call her *Man-dhäk* (boys' mother), *Man-nyïr* (girls' mother), or *Man-mïth* (children's mother).

The same etiquette applies in urban areas. Instead of oxen names, they use the Christian name. But generally, people address each other based on their work titles. For example, honorable, teacher, headmaster, father, priest, professor, engineer, etc. Some people address each other as comrades, reflecting the communist roots of the SPLA.

In conclusion, greetings with handshakes and salutations are important rituals that must be observed by both the young and old. A handshake is a sign of respect, love, and civility. In addition to handshake, a person's mood and disposition are improved when they are asked about their general wellbeing: *Ci baak?* (Good morning); *ca niin?* (Have you slept?) *Ca pääc?* (Have you awakened?) *Ca but* or *cool* (good day), *ci yi thëi* (good evening).

Gestures

When talking, Jieng people frequently use elaborate hand gestures to help them express their thoughts more effectively. As devoted agro-pastoralists, culturally they depict or use hand gestures to imitate not only actions or movements but also to show the size and height of crops, animals, or objects. For example, to describe the age of a heifer, you press your fingers of one hand to resemble the tip of the horn, and then use your other hand to hold your wrist or arm, marking the length of the horn. For a mature cow, you throw your hands in the air to emulate the size, sharp, or direction of the horns. When dancing, both men and women curve their hand in the emulation of cows.

To show the various sizes of sheep and goat, you will straighten your hand, palm facing to the side, with the hand placed at multiple heights above the ground. When showing the height of objects, say a pumpkin, or a heap of manure, the palm faces down with your hand in a horizontal position. To describe the height of a human being, you extend your hand and bend your wrist so that the fingers point up.

Additionally, another gesture is pointing. Unlike Canada, where pointing an index finger at someone is rude, pointing at someone using the index finger is standard among the Agaar. However, it is extremely offensive to point at someone with the left hand in the horizontal position with the index finger extended, and the right hand raised over or behind your head. It means you want or wish them dead. Unlike in Western culture, where the middle finger is an insult, it's a sign of good luck among the Agaar. Before my father passed away, he showed me his middle finger saying, "You will be like this middle finger of mine," implying I would always have a higher status in the family and society. Can you imagine a dying American father gesturing his middle finger to one of his children? That child would have nightmares for the rest of his life.

When counting, you fold fingers one by one, starting with the thumb to the small finger. When you wrap a thumb and an index finger against your palm, it indicates two. The thumb, index, and middle finger folded against the palm mean three. A fist means five, and two fists are ten.

Fingers and hands are also used to call someone. When calling someone, the Agaar beckon by extending a hand with the palm facing forward or down, then opening and closing the fingers. You can also snap by touching your thumb and middle finger, then flicking repeatedly, producing a cracking sound to get someone's attention. For example, when visiting for courting purposes, a suitor often stands at the edge of the courtyard until he is welcomed. If he is not seen, especially at night, the suitor often snaps his fingers to get the girl's attention. If the snapping does not work, he will clear his throat or jingle his spears.

Sometimes a tongue is used to point at someone close by, especially when the pointer has ill feelings toward the person. Sometimes, people point with their faces by protruding their lips while looking toward the subject being talked about, or by looking in a different direction while protruding the tongue toward the intended subject. Pointing with your chin is allowed, primarily when your hands are occupied with things. Gossipers mostly apply the above techniques.

Shaking your head from side to side means "no," and nodding up and down is "yes." Also, to say "no," a person may also waggle an upright index finger from side to side. To say "yes," the person also makes a clicking sound in the mouth.

Eating Etiquette

Eating habits vary between urban and rural settings, but sharing is the common denominator. This communal eating is taken seriously. Eating alone is a sign of bad habits, greediness, and an unacceptable social norm. Family meals involve eating from the same bowls, plates, and gourds. Men, women, youth, and children eat separately. It is not uncommon to find one household grouped into five containers or shares: women, girls, men, boys, and the elderly.

The sharing expands to the entire village. Late in the evening, the *apäräpuööl* of the village would get together, going from homestead to another eating. Boys of the community also do the same thing. Girls do it differently: each girl takes her bowl of food to a designated home, usually a big house which can accommodate many people, where all the girls of the village can eat while gossiping about boys and everything.

When different age groups are sharing, if you are the oldest, you shouldn't finish the food with a junior. Instead, you should leave early, even if you are not satisfied, so the junior can finish it. When eating with elders, the oldest person should dig his spoon in the bowl first before the junior. The man of the house (father) always leaves a little food on his plate, even if he is not full, to indicate that the meal was filling. The man's wife or children usually eat the leftover food.

When eating, keep your eye on the plate or look away. It is rude to look at people's eyes or to watch their spoons as if you are trying to see how full or empty it is. When eating in a group, dig your spoon in the part of the bowl directly in front of you; don't cross over to over people's sides. Even if you have no meat on your side and there is plenty on the opposite side of the plate, you can't grab, unless it's offered. Usually, when you see all the meat is on your side, you can push some to the others. Not doing so is rude. Food is often shared, and in most cases, it's never enough. But putting food aside for your children or husband is very rude. *Aguän* (food set aside as a special treat for someone) is not allowed, though many mothers practice it.

Spirituality

Before the arrival of Christianity, the Agaar, like all other Jieng ethnic groups, worshipped *Nhialic Maayuäl* in their own way. Other Jieng call Him *Nhialic Madhol*. Maayuäl or Madhol was the Great ancestor, the ultimate Creator (the *Aciëk*), the Giver of life and behind everything that existed in the universe.

But there was no designated term for religion or *diin* (Arabic), and no designated days of the week where prayers were conducted. Nhialic was worshipped anywhere, anytime, as much as needed. There was no teaching or indoctrination because divinity came from within individuals and was born with people. *Nhialiny ë waa ku maa* or "God of my father and mother," believers used to say. To entice the divinity to live with individuals, who would pass the divinity to his descendants, they had to do the will of Nhialic regularly and strengthen their awareness and connection to the divine world through sacrifices and offerings.

Nhialic Maayuäl made it possible for people to live in this world. Even though Maayuäl lived in heaven, He kept a close watch on human beings and their activities on earth. When the human beings did not live according to His will, Nhialic intervened directly or indirectly in human affairs.

Maayuäl was not a hateful Divine who worked alone. He was a merciful God who worked with other groups of associates who assisted Him in running the universe. The first group of associates comprised of *jak* (singular *jɔk*) divinities. *Jak* acted as intermediaries between human beings and Nhialic. *Jak* were small deities that lived on earth with people, and they made themselves available for individuals or clans to own them, as long as they were appeased and adorned with sacrifice and righteousness. The most common small deities in our area included *Colwëc, Ring, Abiɛl, manthiang-guk, and Lirpuou.* The following song came from a clan who owned *Ring*, the flesh divinity, asking the divinity to help and protect when they were helpless:

Rïŋ oo, Rïŋ guöp!
Yin aba kuɔny akäl ee,
Të can nhom ciën raan e;
Raan ca maan, kë cɔk ë lɔ;
Raan nhiar ɣa, kë cɔk ë bɔ kek wëi ke.
Rïŋ ë waa aba kuɔny akäl ee,
Të can nhom ciën raan!

Translation:

Ring oo, Ring indeed
You will help me today,
If I have no one (to help me);
Anyone who hates me, let him go.
Anyone who loves me, let him come with his life.
Ring of my father will help me today,
If I have no one!

In addition to *jak* deities, ancestors (living dead) were the second group of divinities who acted as God's messengers or agents. The Agaar believed that ancestors died in the flesh but lived in the spirit. They were called *atiip* (singular, *atiëp*). These *atiip* formed another important spiritual segment of the society. As intermediaries, the *atiip* intimately linked their living descendants with Nhialic God. The primary function of the ancestors, therefore, was to promote the overall welfare of their descendants by providing protection and healing. Also, the *atiip* divinities were considered as moral and ethical judges, who guided and guarded the moral conduct of their descendants. The descendants obeyed the divinity, and from time to time conducted offerings and sacrifices. In exchange, the descendants had the right to demand all they needed from the divine world, such as applications for procreation, prosperity, general well-being, rain, or a good harvest. The relationship between humans and the divinity was a mutual relationship understood as the relationship between the creator (*Aciek*) and the created (*raan*). Between the creator and the created were the ancestors, the revered dead human progenitors of the clan or tribe, both remote and recent, who not only the custodians of this tradition but also linked descendants to the spiritual world.

Nhialic and His associates (*jak* and *atiip*) made their presence or absence known in many ways. They showed their presence to individuals in dreams or sensations. "It felt as though the divinity atmosphere has engulfed me and I became strong like a bull," said a spear master named Acien Malual, "and my body became light and warm with the blood running like water in the river." To show Himself to people, God also came through dreams, or caused minor illness or discomfort to the living descendants. If not diagnosed or attended to, the situation could escalate into a major illness or even death. Therefore, the Agaar believed that death, drought, and destruction were attributed to the overall unhappiness or absence of God and His associates; happiness, prosperity, procreation, good harvest, overall happiness, and wellbeing were signs of God's presence or happiness with the people on earth.

The spiritual leaders, the spearmasters whose sacred spears were a symbol of their holiness, diagnosed the happiness or unhappiness of the spiritual world. The spearmasters were hereditary specialists who had allegiance to Nhialic and clan divinities, and they acted as mediators or reconcilers between the people and Nhialic God. The spearmasters knew or predicted God's intention. By communicating with Nhialic through sacrifice, the spearmaster could determine the cause of a problem and ascertain its solution. Each Jieng section had its own spiritual leaders, but some could perform miracles and were well known such as Makuer Gol (from Agaar), Aguer Adëël (from Luäc), Ajiingdit (from Twic), and many others. These prophets and spear-masters had higher reputations and they were believed to be capable of killing those who offended them by just pointing the sacred spear at you. Therefore, they were feared and people paid the strictest attentions to their commands.

Also, every clan had its own holy man called *raan-kec* (the bitter person). *Raan-kec* acted precisely like the spear master, though he had no sacred spear and had less power. In the spear master's absence, *raan-kec* could conduct prayers and initiate offerings or sacrifices involving chicken, goat or sheep. If the event was big enough to require a cow, then a spear master was summoned to officiate the ceremony.

Tit diviners also played an essential role in the Agaar communities. *Tit (singular, tiët)* were diviners or healers who had occult knowledge and powers to diagnose and heal illness or misfortune. Unlike the spearmasters, *tit* usually offered their services for a fee. Some interceded to Nhialic, but most to clan divinities.

It is crucial to note that the power originated from *Maayuäl*, the Creator, though *jak* and ancestors possessed it to some degree. But only the above-mentioned groups, the spearmaster, the bitter person and the *tïet* diviner possessed this power and used it for good intentions, such as healing, rainmaking, or divination.

Some individuals in the society achieved divinity powers but used them for bad intentions or evil purposes, such as magic, witchcraft, and sorcery. *Apeth* and *röth* were in this category. *Apeth*, also known as *wuth*, were malign witches who possessed the evil eye and could inflict internal injury or organ damage. *Roth* was a malign witch who possessed an evil touch and could inflict physical injury, though it was not fatal. The act of inflicting internal injury was known as *lueng (lueŋ)*, and the act of inflicting external body harm was *rooth (rɔɔth)*. Such individuals who had the powers but did not conform to the rule of divinity were considered evil to be feared but not respected.

The existence of these people with spiritual powers had worked out a code of conduct for the Agaar people. Through divinities and intermediaries, the society knew what was evil or good, right or wrong, truthful or deceitful, and beautiful or ugly. They taught people of their obligations. Above all, they formulated the morals of the community, creating relationships among the people, and between people and Nhialic. Unlike Christianity or Islam where some believe and others don't, the entire society believed in Nhialic before the arrival of Christianity and Islam in Sudan.

The Creation Myth

Since Nhialic was considered the Creator, the sense of the sacred permeated various aspects of the universe and the spirituality mentality affected the way the Agaar viewed the universe. Like any other people who try to make sense of how their world came about, the following is the Agaar mythology of creation.

In the very beginning, there was the Great Master. His name was Maayuäl. Maayuäl lived in heaven where He sat on cushioned clouds and wore twinkly colored beards (stars). Because of this, He was called Nhialic Maayuäl (Heavenly Almighty).

Nhialic Maayuäl created heaven, earth, and all things. The two entities (heaven and earth) were close to one other and held together by a rope. Maayuäl used the rope as a ladder to climb up and down from heaven to check on the people, animals, plants, everything on earth. If people wanted to see Nhialic Maayuäl, they also used the rope to climb up to heaven. Everything was in perfect order.

After creating heaven and earth, Maayuäl took the remnant of the mud left after making the land and fashioned it into a man and a woman: Garang and Abuk, the first couple. He then blew the air inside them through their noses, and they became alive. As a result, the first couple with their descendants became black, beautiful, and majestic, just like Maayuäl Himself.

After creating the first couple and placing them on the land, Maayuäl used a wooden mallet called *puööt* to beat down the rocks and lumpy ground into fine soil, where Abuk and Garang could live and grow crops and rear cattle. Maayuäl then collected the debris and pushed them away from the Jieng land. The debris formed hills and mountains, which we see today. And this explains why there is no single hill or mountain in the Jiengland; Maayuäl pushed the trash away because He did not want Abuk and Garang to hurt their feet. After all, they were His children, and He loved them.

Maayuäl made it rain so that people and animals could have water. But the rainwater sank deep into the soil, leaving people and animals with nothing to drink. In other words, there were no rivers, lakes, seas, or oceans. Garang and Abuk climbed up the rope to heaven, and they complained to Maayuäl that they needed water.

So Maayuäl came down from heaven and walked towards the rising sun where He uprooted an *aguot* (papyrus). Water came out of the hole where the *aguots* were uprooted to form a big pool. Then, He walked towards the setting sun and uprooted an even bigger *aguot,* creating a bigger pond. The two pools formed Lake Victoria and the Mediterranean Sea, respectively. In the Agarland, Maayuäl uprooted two small *aguots* to form Lake Akeu and Lake Nyiböör, respectively. While he was walking from east to west, Maayuäl dragged his pronged walking-staff, called *kuarang*, creating lines, which turned into Ciir or Kiir River (Nile, the world's longest river) and its tributaries.

Garang and Abuk had two children, Deng and Benykook. While all other tribes were the descendants of Deng, the Agaar people were the progeny of Benykook. Maayuäl blessed Deng and Benykook, and they had many children and grandchildren. These children and grandchildren also had their children and grandchildren, and so on. It didn't take long before they grew into many clans and tribes.

As the population grew, the traffic to heaven increased, because the people climbed up and down regularly using the rope to see Maayuäl. But the cable was blocking a robin's pathway. With many people going up and down the line every day, robin and its family could not fly freely. The robin complained to Benykook to remove the rope. But Benykook could not remove it because it was the only way they could see Maayuäl.

After she complained and nothing was done, the robin became very angry. So she used her beak to cut the rope thread by thread until it finally snapped. Heaven floated up into the sky with Nhialic Maayuäl. That's how heaven and earth were separated. Garang and Abuk, with their children Deng and Benykook, and their grandchildren lost contact with Nhialic Maayuäl.

Benykook built a big *luak* (shrine) and initiated a sacrifice. People gathered around the altar to sacrifice a white bull. They prayed and sang:

Waa Maayuäl
Yin ee Bëny dan thɛɛr,
Yok aa ruai oyi ee;
Waa Maayuäl yin ee Bëny dan thɛɛr!
Waa Maayuäl,
Waa atɔ nhial!

Translation:

My father Maayuäl,
You are our Master forever,
We are related to you;
My father, Maayuäl,
You are our old Master!
My Father Maayuäl,
He is in heaven!

Since that day, Nhialiny Maayuäl has not come down from heaven in the flesh because the rope is no longer there. Instead, He comes in the spirit, and He has to communicate with people through intermediaries, such as the *jak*, the ancestors, and the spear masters, the bitter people and the *tit* diviners.

The Shrines and Sacrifices

There were many shrines in the Jiengland. The largest shrine (*luak*) in the entire Agarland was the great shrine of the divinity Maayuäl. Gol Meen first built the shrine in the early 1950s, the greatest master of the fishing spear in the region. In the early 1980s, Makuer Gol, who had inherited spiritual powers and influences from his father, Gol Meen, initiated the rebuilding of the shrine. The construction started in 1982 and was completed in 1983—the same year fighting erupted between the SPLA rebels and Khartoum government. The neighboring tribal sections, such as Aliamtoc, Rup, and Kuei, participated in the building of the shrine, which was dedicated to the Divinity Maayuäl. When I was five years old, I accompanied my uncle who took a pole called *kau* to the shrine during the construction.

The shrine was located in the seasonal cattle camp in the Amoth-nhom area, less than 15 miles northwest of Rumbek, the biggest town in the Agarland and the capital city of the Lakes State. The structure was a magnificently circular building with a conical grass-thatched roof and a wooden wall. Inside the byre was a sacred drum that no one touched, except once a year when the drum was played to summon the believers to attend the annual sacrifices, offerings, or dedications to Nhialic Maayuäl God.

Makuer Gol was not just a spiritual leader; he was also the president of Rumbek Town Court, the only leader who combined both institutions (law and spirituality). Known by his oxen name, Con-Aguot, Makuer Gol, the master of the fishing spear was over six feet tall. He had a medium build with an erect posture, and six scarification marks running on his forehead that marked him as a permanent member of the Agaar people. Full of divinity, Makuer Gol rarely spoke unless he was in the court or at a gathering where he initiated the sacrifices. Nevertheless, Makuer Gol was the only spearmaster who had an outstanding reputation amongst the Agaar. For example, when the rain did not come, clan elders gathered at the shrine asking Makuer Gol to pray for rain to rescue their withering crops. The spearmaster did not even pray. Instead, he said to the people, "Go to your homes quickly to seek shelter before the rain ruins your hairdos." It was not long before clouds gathered and the rain poured down.

Like any other master of the fishing spear, Makuer Gol owned a sacred fishing spear, which was the symbol of his divine powers. And like any other Agaar warrior, he owned several other fighting spears and barbed fishing spears. The sacred fishing spear was unbarbed (*binh ë lääk*) and much bigger than the other spears. The holy spear was kept inside the byre, next to the holy drum. Makuer carried the sacred spear only when traveling, for spiritual purposes.

The shrine of Maayuäl linked people to the spiritual world. Prayers, rituals, sacrifices, and thanksgivings songs addressed to the spirit world:

Oo, Maayuäl
God of my father and mother;
The Aciek (Creator) who shines on the earth with the sun, the moon and the stars;
He covers me with the cloud when I'm hot;
And He spits on my head, blessing me with the drizzles;
The wind blows to give me the breath I need;
This is the work of Maayuäl;
The divinity of my ancestors;
Oh, Maayuäl, you are our master!

Sacred places or shrines, like *Luaŋ Makuer Gol* (the shrine of Makuer Gol), were not only the abode of the divine but also served to entice the divine to reside at a given location or to take up residence at a new site. About five miles south of the shrine of Makuer Gol was another holy ground in Biling Daldiar, where Maayuäl had taken up home. The sacred place of Biling Daldiar was located one house away from where I was born and grew up, so I knew everything that took place their daily. Unlike the shrine of Makuer Gol, where there was a physical structure, there was no building at Biling Daldiar. Instead, the biling tree, after which the place was named, marked the holiness of the site.

The biling tree which still exists today is an ancient tree that has been there for ages. The place was first inhabited by the Jurbel tribe before they were defeated by the Agaar centuries ago, according to my uncle, Mathou Majok, whose great grandfather first settled in Billing Daldiar:

A long time ago, said Uncle Mathou, the Jurbel tribe inhabited the area. A war broke out between the Agaar and the Jurbel. The battle went on for days as each side tried to evict the other and claim the territory. The Jurbel used arrows and bows. But the Agaar used spears and shields. The shields easily stopped arrows. But the Jurbel had nothing to stop the spears from penetrating their bodies. Eventually, the Jurbel were defeated, and they ran southwest where they are located today. The Agaar women supplying food and water to the warriors stood under the biling tree, dancing, thrilling, and laughing for the victory. So, it was named Biling Daldiar, meaning "biling of laughing women."

The victory was dedicated to Maayuäl, and sacrificial pegs were lodged under the tree to mark the sacredness of the site. For several years, the biling tree grew vast and shadowy. It stood there in the center of a million green panes of grass, its branches fanned out wide, separating from each other. The tree stretched up, as if proud to stand there under the sun, hardly shedding its leaves in all weather conditions. Massive and ancient, the biling tree was a shrine where people believed Nhial Maayuäl God dwelled. Under the tree, a buffalo skull hung from a center sacrificial pole. Its sharpened horns were carefully aligned upright, ready to gore any evil spirits that might attempt to dwell there. Several small poles stood around the perimeter, symbolizing the ancestors and the *jak* divinities standing around Maayuäl. Carved sacrificial forked-pegs, adorned with *kuol-ë-jɔk* (sacred cucumber) and other spiritual amenities, were implanted on the other side of the tree. Like the shrine of Makuer Gol, Biling Daldiar was a holy site where Maayuäl was honored.

All the locals and travelers, who passed through Biling Daldiar, visited the shrine to pay their respects, offer gifts and seek blessings. You could offer whatever you had. If you had milk, you could pour some onto the shrine. If you had sorghum grains or groundnuts, you could grab a handful and throw them on the site. If you had nothing to bring, you could just uproot a single grass and place it on the shrine. Maayuäl was not a greedy God.

Worship came in many forms, such as sacrifices and offerings, prayers, invocations, blessing and salutations, and intercessions. Sacrifices and offerings were everyday acts of worship. Through worships and sacrifices, the Agaar woke up Maayuäl and His associates, including ancestor's divinities, tapped into their higher soul, their spiritual selves, and demanded from spiritual world what they desired such as overall health of the society. Offerings and sacrifices were given as gifts to appease Maayuäl, to have communion with Him, and thank Him. By sacrificing or offering, they were renewing their binding relationship with Maayuäl God.

I attended several ceremonies at both Biling Daldiar and Makuer Go shrines, but I don't remember them in detail because I was too young. The last traditional prayer, which I vividly remembered, was in 1985 at Biling Daldiar holy site, two years before my departure to Ethiopia to join the rebels who were fighting against the Khartoum Islamic regime. It was the most meaningful ceremony in the area, and several masters of the fishing spears, including Makuer Gol, were invited. The sacrificial bull was a white bull, called *mabor-thon*, and was a magnificent beast with a massive rump and drooping hump. With its horn sharpened, the beast bellowed thunderously like a lion. It was the perfect gift for Maayuäl. The sacrificial bull was brought early in the morning on the day of sacrifice and tethered on one of the sacrificial poles under the biling tree so the crowd could form a big circle around it. The first session of the ceremony begun, initiated by the youth and recently initiated masters of the fishing spears—the powerful spiritual masters would come late for the final service. Young warriors crouched in ready-to-attack positions with their shields, spears and a shield in the left hand raised in defense and one spear in the right hand in ready-to-throw positions. Elders were on the other side, standing erect, each holding a spear in a ready-to-throw position, too. Women thrilled and ululated. Chants rang through the village as the warriors sang war songs in deep, thunderous voices:

You better accept peace,
Anyone who rejects the peace will be selected with a spear.
I spear in the back,
And spear another in the back of the head,
My spear doesn't miss (…)

After the song, the bull was untied and let go. By now, the beast was riled up due to the dramatic scene it had been subjected to. As soon as it was let go, it ran off wildly. This was the moment the young warriors had been waiting for. They had to showcase their speed, agility, stamina, and endurance. While brandishing spears and shields, the warriors chased the bull, each chanting his boasting phrase. They had to run the beast to exhaustion. While playing war games and shouting poetic expressions, the warriors chased the bull the whole day, running from village to village. The purpose was to chase off evil spirits that may try to possess the beast.

The warriors returned the bull late in the afternoon and tied it back down to the sacrificial peg. The entire community of men, women, and children gathered, including the top spiritual leaders, led by Makuer Gol. People formed a big circle again around the bull; women, and children on one side, *apäräpuööl* on the other side, and elderly on the other side. More battle songs were sung, which talked of bravery and previous victories before the invocation began.

The first to lead the invocation was a master of the fishing spear named Mabordit. I didn't know which section or village Mabor was from; he came from another village. The symbol of his office was a two-pronged fishing spear. Holding the spear in his right hand, he thrusted it downward to emphasize and seal every word. As Mabordit invoked, the crowd repeated every phrase he uttered:

> *You, the Thing (divinity) of my father, listen to my voice;*
> *And you, Maayuäl, I'm calling you,*
> *Come down from heaven.*
> *Here is the white bull; we are giving you.*
> *We need a lot of rain,*
> *We need a good harvest.*
> *Let our women give birth to healthy children.*
> *Let our cows give birth (...)*

Mabordit concluded his invocation with the following song:

> *The earth is ruined,*
> *So everyone must call the Thing (divinity) of his father*
> *You, the Thing of my father, come out.*
> *The Thing in the ground, come out.*
> *The Thing in the sky, come out!*

Several spear masters recited their invocations, and each one chanted requests the bull must carry to Maayuäl before Makuer Gol took the stage. The women thrilled and ululated as Makuer held the sacred spear in his right hand with the tip of the spear facing downward.

'*Gamkë!*' he called, 'repeat.'

But before he could continue with the prayer, the sacrificial bull urinated, so he had to conclude his prayers. The urination of the beast meant two things. First, it was a sign the bull had heard all the words, accepted them, and was ready to die and take the messages to Maayuäl. Second, that Maayuäl had liked and received the gift. So there was no need for Makuer to continue with the prayer. He just concluded by saying, '*Nhialiny ë waa, wëtkan*, (God of my father, that is the word)!'

Finally, the *apäräpuööl* seized the bull by the legs, tail, and horns and threw it down on the ground, where Makuer Gol used his sacred fighting spear to cut its throat. Chants, ululations, and thrills went out after the bull was slain. Mabordit was using a sacred device called *yuɛl* made from the tail of a giraffe, which he dipped in holy water and sprayed it on the people to bless them. Others used sacred ash, the *arop*, which they smeared on the people for the same purpose. Several battle songs were sung before the sacrifice ended at dusk.

The Arrival and Spread of Christianity

Fierce resistance to foreign cultures has primarily defined the Jieng's identity. But their fierce resistance of one culture made them vulnerable to another. The Arabs, who came first, used brute force to convert the Jieng and other Nilotic groups to Islam, but the Jieng resisted Arab culture and religion. Europeans came and took a different approach. First missionaries came and acted as a shoulder on which Africans cried as the Arabs persecuted them. Then, the missionaries offered Christianity and English as a means of resisting Islam and Arabism. Their tactic worked. The 64 South Sudanese tribes, who had no common culture, language, and beliefs to unite them together, accepted Christianity and English as tools for resisting Arab culture and influence.

In 1858, Daniel Comboni, a young Italian priest, reached South Sudan on what he called the "Holy Cross mission," intending to spread Christianity. Comboni spent one year among the Jieng, but he was not able to even convert a single Jieng. Some missionaries died of malaria, and Daniel returned to Italy for treatment. Two years later, the tenacious Comboni returned from Italy with more missionaries known as Verona fathers, and they opened several stations in Bhar el Ghazal and Upper Nile regions of Sudan. By the early 1900s, there were several missionary posts throughout the country, but despite missionary efforts, Christianity was only found in towns and cities, mostly in Northern Sudan. The indigenous South Sudanese did not want Christianity. The frustrated missionaries could not even find Jieng workers to pay, let alone pray; they had to hire Arabs workers from the North. Comboni and his team were extremely frustrated, and they did not know what to do.

However, Comboni's first breakthrough came when he met an educated young woman named Zenab, from Ciec-Jieng, in Cairo, Egypt. Zenab was captured and sold into slavery in Egypt. Because she spoke English, Arabic, and Jieng, Comboni, who could not find a single Jieng to work for him, decided to use the vulnerable girl to his advantage. So he bought Zenab out of slavery and made her work as an interpreter for the missionaries. It was Zenab who eventually helped the missionaries translate the first Jieng alphabets, catechisms, and dictionaries.

Having seen how useful Zenab was to the mission, Comboni had finally discovered a way to approach these stubborn Jieng: exploit them when vulnerable. So, Comboni went on a shopping spree, buying all the Jieng slaves. But instead of letting the freed slaves back to their communities, Comboni kept them in churches and made them Christians. After Zenab, the second young man Comboni found was a run-away slave name Deng Surur, who was captured in Abyei. Comboni freed and baptized Deng by the name of Daniel Deng Surur, and he became the first Jieng Christian to be baptized.[10]

Zenab, Deng, and other freed slaves were enrolled in schools in Cairo, and some of them, including Zenab, were eventually sent to study in Italy before returning to Sudan as catechists, teachers, and technicians who worked for Holy Cross missions. Zenab and Daniel worked in Suakin, Gezira, Melut, and many other missions in Sudan. The Catholic Church movement got a new impulse and a sense of direction when Jieng Catechists were among the Western missionaries. The Catholic Church recovered in the first decades of the 19th century and revived the work of evangelization in Southern Sudan.

The usefulness of Zenab and Deng had changed the missionaries' perspective. Daniel Comboni came up with the idea to "train Africans to convert Africans." Comboni had to gain the trust of the indigenous Africans by demonstrating he was there to help them. So he not only

10   Ibid 142

bought and freed slaves, but campaigned against slavery in the country. Missionary run schools and clinics were opened. The Jieng were introduced to written literature through Christian teaching; the very first books in their dialects were produced to advance the Christian cause. Both Catholic and Protestant denominations disseminated education in their attempt to win converts and to train Jieng catechists. They called this, "Transforming Africa by the Africans." The function of the missionaries was to initiate Christianity, but the Africans themselves were to accomplish the lasting work once they became Christians and apostles. The smart move the missionaries did was sending medical doctors and teachers to set up clinics and schools in the Jiengland. After attracting people, they introduced religion.

The news of the new trick to convert the Jieng must have spread among the missionaries, as both Catholics and Protestants flocked south, flanking the Jieng from all directions. In 1906, Archibald Shaw led a team of missionaries to Malek, Bor, where they were stationed for years. At first, no one wanted Christianity in that part of the world either. The village the missionaries had chosen was run by an older man called Biordit, who was an influential spiritual leader of Lirpiou divinity, a divinity who provided rain, good harvests, or animals. After ten years, no one attended the school or church Shaw had built. Eventually, Shaw started gathering boys from impoverished families together and paying them a heifer each after every semester. This encouraged the boys to return every semester and also motivated other boys to attend school and church, hoping to receive cows. Shaw stayed in Bor for ten years, studying the Jieng language and way of life, earning him the nickname "Macuor." After over ten years in Malek, Shaw made his first baptism: a young man called Aruor and his family believed in Jesus. Shaw eventually put together a team who produced Jieng bibles (Old and New Testaments or *Lëk Thɛɛr ku Lëk Jöt*), besides hymns.[11]

In 1918, Dr. Trudinger and his wife Lynda went to Melut, where they studied Jieng and eventually translated the New Testament into Padang dialect. He was an excellent linguist and concentrated on the Jieng dialect spoken in the Upper Nile. After thirty-three years, he completed the translation of the New Testament into Jieng language.

In 1922, two missionaries, Father Arpe and Father Olivetti, opened a mission among the Rek Jieng in Kwajok. Like anywhere else, their

---

11 Ibid 193

first attempt to convert the Rek Jieng was a failure. So they (missionaries) invented a link between Jieng and Christianity. Fr. Arthur Nebel integrated Jieng spirituality with that of Christian traditions, so he looked for links between Christian and Jieng spirituality.[12] First, he likened the *jak* and totems to the guardian angels in the Bible. Second, he linked Garang and Abuk, the first couple, to Adam and Eve. Nebel even went further by including Garang and Abuk in the catechism and songs. Finally, Nebel said Deng, the son of Maayuäl, was Jesus. Because of these affinities created by the missionaries, Catholicism developed roots in Bhar el Ghazal.[13]

While Catholics dominated in Bhar el Ghazal and Protestants in Jonglei, the Agaar in the middle remained untouched by the modern religion. But things changed in 1929 when the government opened the main road connecting Rumbek and Yerul. In the same year, two medical doctors, Rev. Macdonald, and his wife Kathleen came to Akot in the Agarland and opened up a clinic, followed by a school, and a church. First, they had to dig a well because there was no single stream or river in that area. The Akot location was strategically placed there to serve the people of Lakes State, the Agaar, the Aliab, the Atuot, the Ciec, the Gok, and the Jurbel. Later, three missions were founded in Panëkaar (Yerol), Rumbek town, and Bhar Gel (Cueibet) with Akot being the headquarters.

In Akot, the modern clinic attracted people as Rev. Macdonald, and his wife Kathleen treated more than 100 patients a day. Modern medicine was appreciated, but the school and the church were questionable. Parents did not see the future in modern education. The teaching of Christianity and the rituals and values of the church were incompatible with Agaar culture. The missionaries eventually transferred students and teachers from Malek, Bor to come and help in Akot.[14]

Moreover, the missionaries collaborated with the British government officials who were running the country to pressure chiefs "to lead by example" and send their children to school. Fearing the consequences, the tribal chiefs and parents selected children they deemed to have no future and sent them to school. It was not uncommon for a parent to threaten his children, "Behave or I will take you to where bad children are taken: school."

---

12 Ibid 200
13 Bid 226
14 Ibid 229

Gradually, the importance of education was instilled in some parents and students by the missionaries. Every year when final results were given to the pupils, the missionaries invited parents and government officials to the graduation ceremony. Students who had done well in their classes were given gifts of clothes and even heifers. This encouraged many parents, especially the poor ones, to send their children to school. But they allowed their children to go to school under the condition they should not be baptized. But after a while, some parents thought Jesus was a fantasy figure used to make children behave, just like the Tooth Fairy or Santa. So the parents did not worry much about Christianity. Because of this, Christianity became widely known as *Nhialiny ë mith sukuul* ("God of the pupils").

But in schools, conversion and education went hand in hand. The primary goal of all missionaries in the Jiengland was the winning of converts, and therefore, a massive religious emphasis was common to all mission schools and clinics. They established schools and clinics because education and treatment were deemed indispensable to their aim, but they always placed religion at the forefront of the school curriculum and Jesus was the ultimate curer. Most missions provided only basic education and treatment to ensure the inculcation of proper Christian principles and enable Africans to attend the mission schools and clinics to become good Christians. Schools expanded because the denominational rivalry; each denomination found its school system to attract new converts. Africans were thus provided with several educational options. The missionary domination of the education system was characteristic of all colonized areas.

Missionaries, who were also teachers and medical doctors, carried with themselves their cultural values, which determined the form of education and treatment provided. Both the Catholic and Protestant missionaries hoped that in providing education and medical treatment, they would also be able to form Christian character. The schools they established, for example, were often boarding schools. To the missionaries, the reason for boarding was to make it easier for children not travel long distances. But to parents, the missionaries wanted to remove and segregate new converts from the traditional cultural influences of their homes for easy assimilation. Moreover, the school system promoted Western values and desires. Missionary schoolmasters provided a total culture pattern, including church attendance, Christian morality, manners, dress code, and so on. Educated men combed their hairs, creating a gap line on the side of their heads to look like the European missionaries. Educated women started to wear wigs to look like the European women. Later bleaching of skins ensued. All this led to the segregation and alienation of converts from their families and their societies.

But, as you can imagine, the social alienation involved was painful to both the students and parents. Because of the changes the pupils had gone through, parents often referred to the children they sent to school as *mïth sukuul* ("the children of schools") or *mïth abuun* ("the children of the priests"). They saw their children in total different cultural Lens; not their cultures but foreign ones. Also, students were looked down upon by their friends who did not go to school. They were thought to have abandoned their traditions and adapted to a different culture. To prevent social alienation, some students quit school and returned to cultural practices such as the removal of six lower teeth and receiving scarification marks.

In school, the emphasis on reading gave the impression that literacy was necessary to learn Scripture, and uneducated people were unintentionally alienated. When I went to school in Pachong in 1980, I thought the only reason people went to school was to learn to read the Bible. The following song was sung every morning at the parade before we entered our classrooms:

I want to learn to read the Bible (x2)
If I read it (Bible), it will help me.
The Bible is an excellent book to read.
Jesus Christ, open my eyes to read the Bible.
If I read it every day and night, it will help me in my life…

The missionary's tactic of transforming Africa by Africans succeeded. In the late 1930s, the first round of solid Jieng Christians emerged full of spirituality and hope. For the first time, the newly converted Jieng composed songs in their own way, always full of cultural references. It was at this time Daniel Ayup from Yerol emerged, composing many songs still sung today. One of Daniel Ayup's first songs was *Waragaŋ tɔ nhial ee Bibol* ("The book in the heaven is the Bible"). Many other composers emerged from Rumbek, Wau, Bor and Melut. For the first time, these songs, entirely in Jieng taste (the rhythm, idiom or tune), were printed into a booklet and called *Diɛt ke Duɔ̂ɔr* ("Songs of Praise").

It was during the first Civil War of Anyanya One (1955-1972) that Christianity took off in a way that was not seen before. All the Anyanya One leaders were the results of these Christian schools. All South Sudanese influential figures were baptized and acquired saint's names: William Deng, Gordon Muortat, Joseph Lagu, Samuel Aru, and so on. The Second Sudanese Civil War (1983-2005) leaders, including John Garang, Kharbino Kuanyin, and William Nyuon, Salva Kiir, and James Wani were trained and baptized in that missionary school system. These leaders were taught in these missionary schools and used the Christianity and the English language they had learned to unite together to resist Arabism and Islamism.

In addition to the north and south existing divide, the Islamic government in Khartoum was alarmed, not only by the unity among the Southerners but also the acceptance of Christian values over Islamic ones. The fact the Jieng opposed Islam and readily accepted Christianity was unfathomable. The government wanted to bring the situation under control, by all means, before it was too late.

As a result, all the missionaries were expelled from Sudan. The accusation was that the missionaries were intentionally dividing the country into two. The Arabs did not want the Southerners to be anything but Muslims. After the expulsion, the government resumed business as usual: Islamism and Arabism. Arabic was introduced in schools, and a prerequisite to getting jobs or higher education was the possession of an Islamic name. This completely slowed down the work that missionaries had done, though it did not extinguish it entirely as some early converts took on leadership roles in their churches after the expulsion of the missionaries. But this pocket of Christianity was a threat to the Arabs. The army openly started to assassinate Christians and intellectual Southerners.

In March 1964, the Government of General Abboud expelled all Western missionaries from Sudan. The missionaries fled to the country, leaving the church to very few local clergy men and catechists. The government sent troops to assault all towns, villages, buses, and churches throughout the region and repress resistance in the South. The entire population was considered supporters of the Anya-nya rebels. Villages, schools, churches, and cattle camps were burned to ash, and the Southerners were displaced; some ran to neighboring countries, and others hid in remote bushes and swamps where the tanks did not reach them.

By this time, murder and destruction occurred in every city and town in Southern Sudan. The army hunted down Southern intellectuals in Juba, Malakal, Wau, and Rumbek. Thousands of educated Southerners were killed in July 1965. In Wau, government soldiers came to Cier Rihan's house during a wedding ceremony, and they selected women out and killed all the men in the party. Vicar General Fr. Archangelo Ali was killed in July 1965 during a raid of Arab soldiers in Rumbek parish. After attacking the Rumbek parish, the troops headed to Akot two days later, where they killed people and destroyed the churches along the way. Reuben Maciir Makoi, an Agaar priest who ran the congregation after the missionaries were evicted, was the main target of the attack at Akot. But luckily, Reuben Maciir and his family narrowly escaped the attack.

The killing in Rumbek and Akot was a signal for many Agars living near towns and main roads to flee deeper into the savannah forests' swamplands or into exile in neighboring countries to join the rebels. All the churches and schools were closed down in the Agarland except schools in Rumbek where Arab children studied. My parents often talked about the ruin of the Anyanya war. There was nowhere safe in the country. Government soldiers patrolled villages and cattle camps in Southern Sudan; anyone with a sign of modernity, such as wearing clothes or having no scarification marks, was killed because they were assumed to be either rebels or missionary-educated individuals with Christian values. Apart from those who had gone to neighboring countries, Christianity declined in South Sudan during the First Civil War because the missionaries were gone and the new coverts were fighting in the bush, leaving no one to spread the gospel.

In 1972, after 17 years of war, the Addis Ababa Peace Agreement was signed in Ethiopia between the Sudan government and representatives of the Southern Sudan Liberation Movement (SSLM). Sponsored by the World Council of Churches, the agreement ended the First Sudanese Civil War (1955-1972), established the Southern Region, and brought a decade of relative peace. For the first time since the arrival of Arabs, the South Sudanese tasted freedom. Islamic rules and regulations were only practiced in the North. South Sudanese were allowed to worship as they wished. Maayuäl worshipping flourished in the countryside, and Christianity grew in cities and towns in the region. Missionaries returned to pick up from where they had left off. The students the missionaries taught in Akot, Maleng-gok, Panekar and other places had already started the work for them, and Christianity picked up once more.

Schools were reopened in the same system the missionaries had designed: conversion and education went hand in hand. Villagers who moved away during the war returned to live along the road or near towns where schools were. By now, many Agaar people realized the importance of education, after having seen how significant those students who were taught in missionaries schools. Powerful politicians, governors, commissioners, and generals in the Army or police forces were all those trained in missionaries schools. Many parents started to at least have one child in school, usually a boy, and the rest of the children at cattle camps. Despite the fact that all students were baptized as Christians, many parents understood the value of modern education.

My uncle, Mathou Majok, the younger brother of my father, looked after me after my father passed, had a perfect reason for sending my two brothers and me to school. Once he attended a meeting in Rumbek where politicians wanted hear from traditional elders. In Rumbek, Uncle Mathou met Samuel Aru Bol, one of the most powerful politicians in the region, elected to the parliament of Sudan in 1968. Uncle Mathou noticed that whenever Aru Bol passed, all people, including the Arabs, stood up to welcome him. This was very new and strange to Uncle Mathou because in Agaar culture, you would never stand up for anyone, not even traditional chiefs and spearmasters. To do so was a sign of weakness or submissiveness—a trait loathed by the Agaar. Uncle came home that evening puzzled by what he saw: "Aru Bol is so educated that when he passed the entire Agaar, as well the Arabs, stood up," Uncle Mathou said, as he kept shaking his head in disbelief. "I have never seen anything like before. There is power in education!" Subsequently, Uncle Mathou sent all of us to school—myself and my two elder brothers, Manyang and Makis. In 1980, we moved from our traditional village Biling Daldiar to Pachong, where a primary school was located.

Pachong was a small town built with no planning in mind and had no enthusiasm for architecture. Unlike Rumbek, every building in Pachong was the same as any other traditional house, emerging from the earth with conical grass-thatched roofs and muddy walls. The sound of the blacksmiths beating iron into spears, hoes, or axes was the consistent and dull pounding that let you know the town was alive. In addition to a network of footpaths, which sprung up in whichever direction, the town was split into two by a modern road running from Rumbek to Yerul. This was the road which let the missionaries into Agarland. The unpaved, winding road ran from east to west and mahogany trees flanked it on both sides. Several shops were located alongside the road. There was a palm tree where all sorts of birds lived, including bats. On the far side was a big ler tree, where Chief Chut Dhuol conducted court cases. And on the opposite side were shea trees, where black-smiths manufactured and sold a variety of ironwork, mostly spears, hoes, and axes. On the far side of the town was a tamarind tree where a police station was located. There was only one platoon of policemen, commanded by Corporal Machuei Thondok. On the right-hand side, was Pachong Primary school, built in an L-shape. The school building was composed of about seven classrooms, with several other classes conducted under trees. The well that supplied the entire population of Pachong was several yards away from the school.

Pachong was divided into two: Pachong-dit (big Pachong) and Pachong-thii (small Pachong). Chief Chut Dhuol of the Athoi section resided in Pachong-thii, where he conducted his court cases. And Rok Reec was in Pachong-dit; his grandson, Marial Dongrin Rok, was the chief of Panyar section. Chief Majak Malok led the Kok section, and he conducted court cases at Panawach. The three section of Agaar lived side by side for generations.

In 1984, however, warriors from Panyar section killed a giant, named Matheen Mabor Reech, from the Panyon section of Rup, but he lived with Athoi, his maternal clan. Knowing the Athoi would revenge-kill, the entire Panyar migrated to Yek area where they are living today.

I was probably seven or eight years old when I was introduced to school and Christianity at the same time. There was no physical structure or church in Pachong, but a small congregation prayed in a classroom on Sunday or late in the afternoon after classes. Every morning in the school parade, *Abuna* (Pastor) Joseph Maker Nyinde came to conduct prayers before classes. And once or twice a year, *Abundit* (prominent pastor) Benjamin Mangar Mamur would come from Rumbek to baptize people in Pachong, Akot, and Yerul.

Benjamin Mangar from the Ciec was one of the Panekar students when missionaries first arrived there, right after Akot and later Rumbek and Gel River. Benjamin Mangar studied in Kenya and Nairobi with the help of missionaries and came back with a lot of potential for teaching and evangelism. Like Daniel Ayup, who was also from Panekar, Benjamin Mangar Mamur was also a great song-maker. He composed many songs, which are still sung today in churches. He also invented many Christian chanting phrases which he first taught in Lakes State before expanding to other areas. He taught us the following chant in Pacong in 1980:

Rem de rem (yo)
Rem de Nhial (yo)
Alelu—
Aleluya!
Athiɛi Nhialiny piïr
Amin!

Youth of the youths (yes)
Youth of God, (yes)
Hallelujah!
Blessed be the living God;
Amen

Benjamin Mangar Mamur composed many touching and moving songs that inspired every Jieng Anglican in their worship. Mangar's songs were mostly choruses. His songs were inspiring, like the songs of Daniel Ayup. In the current Jieng hymnal—*Buŋ de Diɛt ke Duöör*— the late Daniel Ayup has seven songs (179, 203, 210, 376, 450, 643 & 654). And Benjamin Mangar Mamur also has seven songs (192, 208,311, 330,419, 616 & 626). With a fascinating ability and capacity to compose songs, Fr. Benjamin Mangar was a real evangelist and source of encouragement to the church. He composed many songs we used even in Agaar traditional dances.

The teachings of Benjamin Mangar Mamur went rapidly through the Lakes State and affected all villages, towns, and cities of Rumbek, Akot, Wau, and Yerul. Later in the Second War, he became the pioneer of the Christian revival in the Lakes State.

Fr. Benjamin Mangar was not alone: another son of Agaar, Bishop John Malou Ater, devoted his life to spreading the gospel throughout Jieng territories. He worked with the Sudan Council of Churches as secretary for evangelism in the 1980s before becoming bishop of Wau in 1984. He established four missions in different Jieng regions: Twic, Aweil, Malual, Abyei, Ngok Kuol Aloor, Parieng, Pan-ru people. Meanwhile, Bishop Nathaniel Garang Anyieth worked tirelessly in Jonglei areas, mainly Bor and Twii, spreading the gospel in a way that was never seen before. The free South Sudanese worshipped God whichever way they wanted.

But relative freedom was short-lived. In 1983, President Nimeri started with the formal re-division of the South into three regions, Bhar el Ghazal, Upper Nile, and Equatoria regions, which were excluded from economic development. Then Nimeri undertook several decisions that overturned the critical terms of the Addis Ababa Agreement, including imposing Shari'a Law across the country and abolishing the Southern Sudan Autonomous Region. This reopened up the wound in the heart of Anyanya One fighters. The Southerners responded in a way that the Islamic regime had not seen before. Led by Dr. John Garang, who was a junior officer in the Anyanya One movement, the rebels formed an army called the Sudan People's Liberation Army (SPLA) with its political wing, Sudan People's Liberation Movement (the SPLM).

In response, the government cracked down on Southerners, especially Christians, in cities and towns. Apart from Rumbek Secondary School, all schools and churches in Cueicok, Maleng-gok, Pachong, Akot, and Yerul were closed down indefinitely due to fear of being attack by government troops. The Christians evicted from the towns fled deep into the countryside, bringing along their Bibles, the Old Testament and New Testament (*Lëk Thɛɛr ku Lëk Jöt*). For the first time, Christianity reached the illiterate population of Agaar. I was one of the people who first brought the Bible and Christianity to Biling Daldiar when Pachong was attacked and burned down by the government soldiers.

Government soldiers attacked Pachong in 1984; three years after the rebellion had started. By then, the SPLA rebels had returned from Ethiopia fully trained and equipped with light machine guns, mostly AK47s, and they began to attack towns and ambush government troops. The government responded by attacking villages and destroying or looting cattle camps and crops.

Pachong was attacked during the Christmas of 1984. A considerable congregation of over 1,000 people had gathered under the pig tree to celebrate Christmas. Bishop Benjamin Mangar Mamur had snuck out of Rumbek, which government soldiers controlled, to baptize people and celebrate Christmas with us in Pachong. Abun Maker Nyinde had prepared for the arrival of the bishop. I was nine years old, but I already knew how to read the Bible in Jieng. Abun Maker had told me I would read the bible when the bishop arrived. I did not have a Bible, but Abun Maker lent me his to practice the verses.

Bishop Mangar came before noon, and he began the first service. There were to be several services from morning to evening before Bishop Mangar returned to Rumbek. It was late in the afternoon when I began to read before the Bishop preached. I was very nervous, but I had practiced a lot. Abuna Maker went to the podium with me and stood next to me, occasionally correcting words that I mispronounced. I read from Matthew 5:1:15:

> Now, when Jesus saw the crowds, he went up on a mountainside and sat down. His disciples came to him, and he began to teach them. Blessed are the poor in spirit, for theirs is the kingdom of heaven. Blessed are those who mourn, for they will be comforted. Blessed are the meek, for they will inherit the earth. Blessed are those who hunger and thirst for righteousness, for they will be filled. Blessed are the merciful, for they will be shown mercy. Blessed are the pure in heart, for they will see God. Blessed are the peacemakers, for they will be called children of God. Blessed are those who are persecuted because of righteousness, for theirs is the kingdom of heaven . . .

I became stuck on a word that I could not pronounce, so I looked at Abuna Maker, but he was not paying attention. His eyes were fixed northeast, towards Biling Daldiar. Something was happening. I looked at the bishop; he was also looking in the same direction, and so was the entire congregation. Something was happening. Some people ran away; others were closing their shops quickly and running. Suddenly, I heard strange noises followed by bursts of loud sounds, boom, boom, boom, which shook the ground beneath me.

Everyone was running in every direction. "The government soldiers are here," the bishop said as he got up and ran. "Run. Run. Run! *Athiɛi*

Nhialiny Piir!" There were many soldiers, hundreds of them, wearing green khaki uniforms, and shooting people with guns. I had never heard so much screaming and shooting in my life. I saw people being shot and fall down and they never got up. I ran.

I raced after the Bishop, but he was faster than me. Abuna Maker was nowhere in sight. My heart and other organs were trying to leave my body. I saw one of my teachers, Ustaz Majak and Uncle Achuoth, also running. I ran after Uncle Achuoth, crossing the street and passing between the school buildings. I followed him like a thread through the eye of a needle. But instead of running straight to the bushy grass, which was just a few meters away from the school compound, Uncle Achuoth entered a classroom. I went after him. I wanted to follow him inside the class and hide under the benches. But as I was about to enter the class, Ustaz Majak came running at a speed and forcefully pushed me out of his way. I staggered and fell, grazing my knees. (I still have two big visible scars on my knees.) I didn't feel a thing. But the impact had forced me from following Uncle Achuoth inside the class room. Instead, I got up and ran passing the shea tree that was behind the school into the tall grass leading to the bushes. I ran for about an hour with a group of men until we no longer heard gunshots before we hid in the bushes.

Late at night, I saw some people returning to the village. I heard them, saying, "The soldiers have returned to Rumbek." When we returned to Pachong, I could not recognize the place. Everything had been burned, and ashes were left behind. I had never seen a dead body before; Agaar children were not allowed to see the bodies of those who had died. Now I saw many dead bodies. Several people were killed, including Chief Maker Kanac. Uncle Achuoth had been burned to death inside the classroom I saw him enter. I did not want to think about what would have happened to me had I followed him inside the classroom. Only one thing came to mind: it was Jesus who sent that heavy man to push me out of the way when I was about to enter the classroom. For the first time in my life, I became a firm believer in Jesus Christ.

After Pachong was attacked, we returned to our traditional village, Biling Daldiar. But I was a changed boy: a devoted Christian, a soldier of Jesus Christ who had saved me from death. I avoided Biling Daldiar shrine, and the shrine of Makuer Gol. I no longer sang hymns of the *Abiel, Ring,* or *Lirpuou* divinities. I only sang Christian hymns and read the Bible. The New Testament, which Abuna Joseph Maker Nyinde lent to me in Pachong to read the verse, had stuck with me. It was the most precious possession I had ever had. It was the only book I had, so I read it every day. I also talked to my friends about Christianity.

Another man named Marial Ademal, who also fled from one of the small towns, was a Christian. We were the only people who knew about Jesus and how to read and write. We prayed with friends under the trees in Biling Daldiar. Later, a woman and her two daughters (I don't remember their names) from Rumbek joined us. She was a deacon in Rumbek, and she became our preacher. The five of us prayed every Sunday inside a house. Later, others from Rumbek joined us, including Majak Akech, who is currently the Inspector General of South Sudan police. Majak was Catholic, but he joined us, the Anglicans, anyway. It did not take long before our congregation grew to about fifty members; some of them came from towns, and others were new converts.

Bishop Benjamin Mangar, who was the target in the Pachong attack, did not return to Rumbek after he escaped the assassination attempt. Instead, he moved to the Yek area, where he preached and baptized people. While others were in government-controlled towns and cities, it was Benjamin Mangar Mamur who went to the countryside, traveling from village to village preaching and baptizing people. He was later consecrated to be the bishop of the Diocese of Yerol in 1988.

In late 1986, Bishop Benjamin Mangar made a highly effective evangelistic tour of the Agaar, Ciec, Atuot, and Jurbel territories. He had heard of our little under-the-tree church in Biling Daldiar, so he visited us. Fr. Mangar did not just recognize me, he remembered my name. He told the congregation how we were attacked when I was reading the scriptures, and that God protected us as no one in the congregation was killed that day. Benjamin Mangar had a great evangelistic gift. He punctuated his speech with *Athiɛi Nhialiny piir* to maximize the impact of his service.

After the prayers, the Bishop said I should go with him on the evangelical tour. This was 1986 or 85. He asked my mother for permission to go with him, saying, "God protected us in Pachong, and He will not forsake us now either." My mother was a devoted Maayual worshipper, but she let me go anyway. It was a two-month-long tour wandering from village to village preaching, baptizing, praying for the sick, and burning traditional *jak* shrines. There were about 20 boys and girls, young men, and a few women, let by Benjamin Mangar Mamur.

On our tour, the Bishop challenged the local spiritual powers. One day in Makuaar village, we went to the house of a man called Madol. Several elders were sitting under a tree in the courtyard. Without hesitation, Fr. Mangar approached the elders and said, "I greeted you in the name of God. We are the people of God, and we have come to your village to tell you about God. Our God does not need offerings or sacrifices of a cow, goat, or chicken. God has already sacrificed his son, Jesus Christ, to redeem our lives. I will not force you, but anyone who the word of God touches will be baptized in the church." None of the elders said anything. We left.

Half an hour later, Madol showed up in the church to be baptized. Surprisingly, Madol was the keeper of Abiel divinity, and several sacrificial pegs were in his house. He was afraid to touch the sacrificial pegs, but asked the Bishop to remove them. We went to his house, and we broke down all the pegs and burned them. People thought we would die, but nothing happened to us. The next day, the church was jammed with people asking to be baptized. We also burned several sacrificial pegs in Makuaar.

Bishop Benjamin preached about repentance. "Without repentance," he said, "no one will enter the kingdom of God. You must repent and reject the devil. Then pick up the cross and follow Jesus Christ that you will see heaven. Madol is an example of repentance; he has left the life of the deceiving devil and chosen the true God."

Everywhere we went, the sick people were brought to Fr. Mangar to be healed. In the Makembele village of Jurbel, a woman approached us with a one-week-old baby. The baby had refused to suckle since she was born. The frantic mother did not know what to do. She said she dreamed about the people of God coming to rescue her baby the previous night.

"If you genuinely believe in God, "Bishop said, "then your child will be alright, and he will suckle."

We gathered around the woman with her sleeping baby, and we placed our hands on her head. Bishop put his hand on the baby. He began by his favored phrase, "*Athiei Nhialiny piir*," and we all responded, "*Amin*." Then Fr. Mangar asked me to start the song, "*Nhialic Wada*." He'd composed the song a couple of days ago, specifically for praying for sick people, and he taught us to sing it. I had a lovely voice, which is one reason he brought me along. I began the song, and they all joined in:

God our father
There is no reason why we believe in you, but our lives.
Like you said, 'sing if you are happy;
And pray if you are suffering'.
Now sickness has come,
We are placing our hands (on the sick person);
You put your blessing on the head of your loved one;
To heal, so that people know you are the most powerful God.

After he prayed, Benjamin said to the mother, "When your child wakes up, he will breastfeed if you truly believe in God." Two days later, the father of the child tracked us down and gave us the testimony that the child had breastfed for the first time. He was baptized on the spot.

There were many stories of this kind on our tour. We, the Soldiers of God, marched, processed, and burned down sacrificial *jak*-pegs of those who had just renounced them and become Christians. There was also fellowship and the sharing of food and eating together after prayers. We did not carry any food, but we were welcomed with food and milk everywhere we went.

Bishop Benjamin Mangar was (and still is) a blessing to the people throughout the history of the Anglican Church in the Lakes State. His teachings spread rapidly through the Lakes State and shook the grounds of every village. We did not record the number of people who were baptized in that two-month tour, but it was estimated to be tens of thousands. New churches and preaching centers were established throughout the Lakes State in villages, cattle camps, and even fishing grounds.

The Agaar became very receptive to the new faith of Christianity. The civil war and all war-related causes such as hunger, disease, and displacement shattered traditional cultures, so the new religion (Christianity) seemed attractive. People had seen their traditional spear masters helpless in the face of mass death and displacement. So they came to embrace Christianity, and the real and true God, as Bishop Benjamin put it. They beat their drums for prayer in the morning and evening, and people came in significant numbers in villages to church. Also, in the Toc Swamp, in the fish camps, they gathered in groups to pray on Sundays and every evening and morning, asking God for protection for their children on the front lines. So they lamented and sought God's victory over the enemy unjustly persecuting them. The Jieng saw Christianity as a form of spiritual liberation, whereas Islam was deemed to despise Christianity and takes Black Africans as valueless souls and people that deserve only enslavement and exploitation. The following song says it all:

> *Lord, you created the earth and put us in it.*
> *Our father, the mud that you took (molded) and breathed air in it*
> *Is the reason why we are fighting now;*
> *The enemy wants to take our land,*
> *The land which is as black as our skins;*
> *Will the black soil be taken with our skins, or will our skins remain?*

This change was not only happening in the Lakes State, but throughout South Sudan. The South Sudanese sought encouragement and words of comfort and hope from the scriptures. Gathering together at times of prayer and listening to elderly Christian leaders was very important. The same change was happening in refugee and the SPLA training camps in Ethiopia, such as Bongo, Bilpam, Dimma, Panyudu, and Itang. It also continued in Kenya and Uganda and in other neighboring countries where South Sudanese had taken refuge.

I joined the movement as a devoted Christian. Then when attended guerrilla warfare training on top of mountains, and at the same time, the radio SPLA went on air opening with a trumpet, I knew we were the God chosen people. What was next, the Bible openly talked people of Kush (kuc). Prophesy against Kush, Isaiah 18:1:7:

> Woe to the land of whirring wings, along the rivers of Cush, which sends envoys by sea in papyrus boats over the water. Go, swift messengers, to a people tall and smooth-skinned, to a people feared far and wide, an aggressive nation of strange speech, whose land is divided by rivers.
>
> All you people of the world, you who live on the earth, when a banner is raised on the mountains, you will see it, and when a

trumpet sounds, you will hear it. This is what the Lord says to me: 'I will remain quiet and will look on from my dwelling place, like shimmering heat in the sunshine, like a cloud of dew in the heat of harvest.' For, before the harvest, when the blossom is gone and the flower becomes a ripening grape, he will cut off the shoots with pruning knives, and cut down and take away the spreading branches. They will all be left to the mountain birds of prey and to the wild animals; the birds will feed on them all summer, the wild animals all winter. At that time gifts will be brought to the Lord Almighty from a people tall and smooth-skinned, from a people feared far and wide, an aggressive nation of strange speech, whose land is divided by rivers—the gifts will be brought to Mount Zion, the place of the Name of the Lord Almighty.

After over 120 years, the South Sudanese finally liberated themselves in 2011, forming their own state. But the freedom came at a cost. After the first civil war, less than ten percent of the Jieng were Christian, and Christianity existed in cities and towns. Over 90 percent were worshipped *Nhialic Maayual* or *Madhol*. Currently, over 95 percent of South Sudanese are Christians and only less than five percent has traditional spiritual practices. On top of that, English is the official language in the country. Their fierce resistance to Islam and Arabic had forced the indigenous South Sudanese into Christianity and English.

Subsistence Strategies

Cattle Keeping

In 2017, I met an Equatorial man named Kenyi in Shalom Hotel in Juba. After talking with Kenyi for a while, he said, "This is the first time for me to talk to a Dinka without discussing cows. Dinka talk about cows all the times, in office, on the street, everywhere. I don't know why the Dinka are so obsessed with cows? Even President Kiir, who has all the money, still talks about cows. In fact, President Kiir has cattle herds here in Equatoria."

Kenyi's remarks reminded me of the same observation made by John Ryle, a British man who studied the Agaar way of life in the early 1980s. In his book, *Warriors of the White Nile*, John Ryle wrote:

> Almost everything in their life revolves around cattle, and every conversation returns eventually to this topic, if indeed it ever leaves it . . . No one who spends even a single day among the Dinka could fail to be impressed by their preoccupation with cattle, and the time and labour they devote to looking after the beasts.[15]

---

15   John Ryle, *Warriors of the White Nile*, Amsterdam: Time-Life Books, 1982, 84

John and Kenyi were right. The Jieng are obsessed with their cows. Apart from the Nuer, who are also devoted cattle lovers, all other non-Jieng groups, including Arabs, look in disgust upon Jieng because of the obsession with their cows. But anything which connects Jieng to their herds is not considered an insult; it's praise. The Jieng are inextricably linked with their cows. The love for cows is one of the main characteristics connecting the Agaar to the other Jieng groups. Much of the Agaar's culture and history is derived from the importance of cows. Therefore, cows are the embodiment of culture, tradition, and livelihood.

Cows have indefinite practical uses. Without an animal to offer or sacrifice (as explained in religion section), then the prayers or invocations are not completed. Without the exchange of cows or promise to provide them in the future, the marriage is not legally binding. Without milk or meat in the diet, the food is not complete. Most of the terms for colors are derived from cattle, so without cattle the Jieng would have very limited terms to describe colors.

Both people and herds follow the same social groupings, and the terms used to describe these social groupings are of course derived from cattle. A tribe or section is called *wut* (the plural form is *wuot*), which means cattle camp. A sub-section is *gol* (*gͻl*), which means byre. Similarly, much vocabulary describing people is also derived from cows. A gentleman or handsome individual is called *awuot*, "one who stays in cattle camp", or *ajööt*, "mover of the cows." A warrior is called *apälräk* or *apäräpuöl* (plural*, apäräpuööl*), meaning "one who has stopped milking," and a recently initiated individual is *acööt*, meaning "hornless cow."

Apart from deriving social groupings terms from them, young men and women also learn their social cues, such as masculinity and femininity, from their cattle. A young man identifies himself with oxen or bulls accordingly. The beasts define his maleness. He must be physically strong, yet gentle, like his ox. Sometimes he identifies with his bull; he must be the embodiment of power, aggressiveness, and fearlessness. The protective and territorial instincts enable him to defend his territory or community and be ready to die. An Agaar warrior would lay down his life in protection of both the people and cattle.

To better understand the behavior I'm trying to explain here, it is best to see how every young person treats their bulls and oxen. The ox, called *buoc (buɔc)*, is subdued through castration and the cutting of the horns so they grow asymmetrically. The horns are then adorned with objects of beautification such as tassels. The songs dedicated to display-oxen are called *kёp* songs. Such songs are often slow-paced and gentle in tone. A young man, called Mabor Dak, who owned a marial ox, sang:

> *My ox marial,*
> *You were not brought by theft;*
> *You are the beast of my father.*
> *The designer carved your horns,*
> *Then I pierced your horns and adorned them with the tassels*
>   *of buffalo.*
> *Marial, you are my other half;*
> *That is why I'm attributing these songs to you.*
> *I moved you to Alou, Awai, and Buktiam [cattle camps].*
> *My ox is like Agum Mading,*
> *A tall girl with white teeth and dark gum;*
> *My ox marial will get such a beautiful girl.*

On the other hand, the bull (*thɔn*) represents aggressiveness or violence. The horns of the bull are sharpened so it defends itself. It is not uncommon for bulls to gore each other to death. The owner of the killer bull is delighted with his bull's aggressiveness, though he may end up paying for the damage done by it. The songs attributed to bulls are known as *tuar* songs. Such songs are not only vigorous, but they are also full of aggression, violence, and the sexual potency of bulls. A young man sang:

> *My bull Manyang is fearless.*
> *He rumbles like thunder.*
> *He mounts every cow in this cattle camp.*
> *Other bulls don't stand a chance when Manyang is around.*
> *I have sharpened its horns;*
> *Manyang gored the bull to death.*
> *That is how we are, Manyang.*
> *I have never turned my back on the enemy.*
> *I'm brave like a buffalo bull,*
> *That dies with its eyes open.*

These *tuar* and *këp* songs are permanently his, even after the bulls or oxen no longer exist. The songs will define his mood for the rest of his life. At night when a man can't sleep because he is very angry about something, say if someone insults him, he sings his *tuar* songs, attributed to his bull. When happy, he sings *këp* songs. In the Agaar village or cattle camps, it's easy to know who is happy or angry by listening to what they sing.

An Agaar young girl, on the other hand, identifies herself with the cows. The cow reminds her of femininity. She is loving, caring, and the embodiment of nurture, patience, and fertility, and the mother of earth. Girls show their gender through conventional feminine characteristics of cows. Learning these feminine cues is crucial for portraying gender successfully. For her, a young man must show his love by paying up to a hundred cows as a brideprice.

Besides their social importance, cattle have other practical uses. Cows are the chief currency of the traditional court system of the Agaar. For example, when a young man injures another young man, and the matter is taken to court, cows are given in compensation. For adultery, the man pays seven cows to the husband, even if it is the woman who initiates the act. If you impregnate a woman and you don't marry her, later on you may pay seven cows to take custody of your child. For murder, a total of 31 cows are paid by the killer; 30 cows go the deceased's family and one belongs to the court. The cattle are generally used for payments of debts, loans, or fines.

No modern pharmacy is needed at a cattle camp because the cows provide all the necessary medicines for curing and disinfecting. Cow urine contains properties which kill bacteria, funguses or insects. All milk containers are disinfected with their urine. When water is not available, individuals wash their hands with cow urine before milking. Also, a repetitive application of urine in the hair kills lice and also thickens and dyes the hair yellowish; a style loved by people of all ages and sexes.

Similarly, the dung also contains antiseptic properties which cure wounds. When I was a little boy, a rusty bicycle wheel cut my left leg, and it became infected. I was in a village where there were no cattle. My mom tried several herbs, but the wound kept getting worse. I was sent to a cattle camp so my wound could be cured there. After applying ash to the wound, it healed instantly, and I returned home in less than one month. I still have a big scar on my leg.

The dung has other practical functions. Besides providing manure, it is used as fuel for cooking and warming, and repelling insects. The routine collection and drying of dung is exclusively done by boys and girls. I was the expert in this job. First thing in the morning, I would collect the dung from our byre using my bare hands. Watery dung went to a separate heap as it does not dry quickly. The thick dung goes into a well-prepared ground where it's spread in the sun to dry. Now and then I used a pronged-stick, called *kuarang*, to break up the dung into sizeable pieces and spread the pieces to dry all day.

The burning of the dried dung is another work of art that every boy or girl masters. First, you light a fire using grass, leaves, or twigs. Then, you add the dried dung to the fire to form a conical shape. If you want smoke to flow horizontally, you open the base of the mound. If you want the smoke to flow straight up, you open up the top of the heap. The smoke is used for repelling mosquitoes, flies, and other insects.

The ashes from the dung are important elements with many practical uses. People who live in a cattle camp, young and old, are coated with ashes from head to toe. The ash is used to protect their skin from heat and insect bites. But the main reason people wear ashes is to show they are *awuot* or cattle camp dwellers, as it is honorable. For decoration purposes, water is added to ashes, and the paste is applied to the body in desired patterns and left to dry, forming living art on the body. Additionally, in the swamp where there are no twigs to use as toothbrushes, you grab a handful of ashes and use your index finger to clean your teeth and gums with it, and then rinse your mouth with water. Your teeth and gums will be clean and germ-free.

Furthermore, ashes are also used for spiritual purposes. Not any ashes, but cow dung ashes called *arop*. Ashes are carefully processed and mixed with special clay, forming a red or white powdery mixture which is stored in sacred gourds (*gut*) specifically used for this purpose. It is stored to be used by spiritual leaders for blessing, healing, and other spiritual purposes. In fact there was a free divinity called *Arop, meaning ash.*

Because of their importance, cows are highly prized and cherished, so they are rarely killed. No one kills a cow just because he is craving meat. This is because every Agaar's self-esteem extends to his cattle. Besides, it's not economically feasible to kill a cow for meat. A cow provides meat once in its lifetime, but it provides milk, urine, and dung for over twenty years. Most importantly, a cow produces over 20 calves in its lifetime. So you have to be really foolish to kill a cow for meat.

The daily diet of people living in a cattle camp is milk and they drink it twice a day. The remaining milk is churned into butter by swirling it in a container and then boiling to turn it into butter oil, which is used for both cooking and moisturizing skin for decoration.

When killed or if they die naturally, there's nothing wasted. Meat is eaten fresh or dried for future consumption. Their skins become sleeping mats, ropes, halters, belts, or drums. In the old days, married women wore the skins of sheep and goats as loin garments. Currently, sheep and goat skins are used for carrying babies. Horns are used for musical instruments and spoons. Their bones are manufactured into labor-saving devices such as beaters, pounders, and scrapers.

Herding

Livestock herding is a hell of a job! If you haven't done it before, you have seen anything yet. Boys and girls learn hard work, endurance, and stamina from cattle-herding. Before herding cows, a small boy starts with goats and sheep. Livestock herding is performed every day from sunrise to sunset and is a physically demanding job. First thing in the morning, the boy takes the sheep and goats to the wilderness for grazing. At around midday, when the sun is hot, he returns them home to rest. While the animals are resting, the boy grabs a sickle to cut grass to feed the lambs and kids (baby goats), which are too young to graze in the field. Then the boy cleans the dung from the animal shed. Before he knows it, it's afternoon, and the boy takes the animals back to the forest for grazing.

At the end of each grazing session, the boy provides water to the animals to drink. But finding a water source is a hell of a job by itself; sometimes, the boy walks for hours to the river, stream, or pool where the animals can drink. If he lives in an area where there are no surface water sources, he goes to a nearby well and draws water for hours for the animals to drink. A good shepherd makes sure his animals are adequately fed and watered every day so they appear fat and healthy.

If the animals are inadequately watered or grazed, the boy is beaten. If the animals destroy other people's farms, the boy is whipped. If an animal is lost or eaten by wild animals, the boy is whipped. When an adult sees a boy goofing around, he whips the boy even if they are not related. Sometime when a boy is being whipped, another man will call the crying boy saying, "Come here, I will help you," but will beat the boy even more. That's how cruel they are. Whipping, whipping, and more whipping are part of being a boy or girl.

However, the cattle-keepers say the purpose of the punishment is not to abuse the boy or girl. Hell no! It's to discourage laziness and bad manners, and encourage hard work and good manners. Prominently, the pain and suffering the boy endures from the whippings will prepare him to endure other great pains in life. When he is about seven or eight years old, he sits still as his six lower teeth are pried out with a spear, marking him as a permanent member of the society. When he's about 15, he endures the knife when scarification marks are cut bone deep into his head, as he transitions from boyhood to *apäräpuölhood*. When he becomes an *apäräpuöl*, he endures the heavy blows to the head with a fighting stick from an opponent in battle. Or when speared in the battle with a barbed spear, he sits still as the spear is pried or spun out of his body. Enduring pain is part of being a warrior and boys are trained at a very young age how to endure it.

Boys are also trained to cope with hunger. Sometimes, the herd-boy is intentionally starved. While he is away tending the animals, people will cook food and eat it all, leaving nothing for the boy. When he returns from the wilderness with the animals, there's nothing to eat. Some boys stick his hand into the ashes where food is cooked; when it's hot, he knows food has been cooked and eaten in his absence. You would think the boy is being mistreated. No! He is being trained to cope with the hunger so that when he becomes an *apäräpuöl*, he will be capable of fasting for days. When there is a war, warriors spend days fighting in the wilderness without food or water. When the food is scarce, an *apäräpuöl* always fasts, letting the women, children, and elderly eat the little food available. When unexpected visitors come, *apäräpuôöl* usually leave their food to the visitors. Complaining about hunger is a weakness—a trait that is completely unacceptable. This stamina is instilled in boys at a very young age.

Herding is a job done from sun rise to sun set every day. While herding the animals, the boy cheerfully chants *alangdol,* no matter how hungry he is. *Alangdol* (only Agaar may know this term) is a sing-song chant usually performed by herd-boys. While chanting at the top of your voice, you stimulate your throat with your hand to produce robust and melodious rhythms. The purpose of the *alangdol* is to mark your grazing territory and alert other herders of your whereabouts so that friends may join and the enemy may stay away. The *alangdol* is so important that a man who has never done it when he was a boy will be insulted even when he is old: "Are you a man? (*Ee moc?*)" the incompetent one is asked. "Where have you ever performed an *alangdol?*" The implication is that if you have never performed an *alongdol* as a boy, it means you have never herded cattle; and if you have never herded animals, it means that you are weak. Herd-boys are strong, sturdy, and tenacious. They work hard while enduring pain and hunger. There is a saying, "He is as tenacious-hearted or strong-hearted as a herd-boy *(aril puou cë dhöŋ ë thök)."*

City boys are weak. They eat three times a day and do nothing, yet they complain about everything. They are nothing but *athumaa* (city dwellers) who don't know the importance of the cattle. An *athuma* (singular) lacks decent manners and the term can be used for a street-boy, criminal, or thief. *Athumaa* are considered weak compared to the herd-boys.

There in the wilderness, the boys test their strengths and weaknesses through wrestling, boxing, and even clubbing or stick fighting. Unlike the *athumaa* who box with fists, herders box with open hands. If you are weak and you have no brother to come to your rescue, you will have to take care of other boys' herds while they sit and play. You have to be strong to earn respect among your peers.

There are herd-girls, too. Parents who have no male children allow their little girls to herd their goats and sheep. Herd-girls are just as strong as the herd-boys. Trust me; you don't want to mess with a herd-girl, for she'll show you your position. I remember this one particular girl in our area, who herded with us. She was very strong, mind you! In fact, she challenged every boy to wrestling and defeated them. She became confident enough to say, "Whoever defeats me in the wrestling, will sleep with me." Let me tell you, she had knocked me down several times before to the point I had given up on challenging her, but when she said this statement, I was the first one in line. I had to try my luck, right? I mean, who wouldn't? Deep down in my heart, though, I knew I stood no chance against her, but I was determined. I guess I was being misled by my testicles. But before I knew it, my skinny behind was wallowing on the grass, as the lady in question moved on to challenge another determined immature herd-boy being misled by his testicles too. She beat every boy.

The cattle-keeping teaches every boy or girl all the facts of life. The difficulties they face prepare them for real life experience.

Song Oxen

I was walking through an intersection in New Westminster, BC, when the car appeared. It was just a few months after I had immigrated to Canada. The car was a thing of beauty and precision engineering. The silver, gray Mercedes S600, 389 horsepower, and six-liter engine cruised down the freeway. All details of the car (the rims, the leather seats, the chrome, etc) were designed to fill the owner with nothing but prestige, beauty, pride, and social status. Holding the steering wheel in one hand, the young owner leaned back in the leather seat as the beast zoomed on, weaving in and out of the traffic before stopping at the intersection. Three young Canadian girls were walking ahead of me as we crossed the intersection. The girls looked at the car and the young owner with admiration and honor. To entice the girls, the young owner cranked the stereo to the maximum, and he was bopping and singing along. The rap song playing on the stereo was explicitly produced for glorifying such fancy cars:

> *We roll tight whips every day*
> *Bentley, Lex, Mercedes, and Escalades*
> *But they like my rims when I stop; they keep running away*
> *What [girl] in her right mind is going to turn it down . . .*
> *They call me Richie Rich; I got my name in the seats*
> *X-Box in the front and the back DVDs*
> *Got TVs in the headrest with the big widescreen*
> *Got the navigation system with the phone in between*
> *Driveway like a dealership, don't walk anymore*
> *Because this is my life...*

It became apparent to me that cars are the most precious possessions of young Western men. As I watched the young man impressing the girls with his beautiful car, my memory flashed back to the other part of the world where such showmanship is taken to the next level. But instead of cars, bulls and oxen are the most precious possession every Agaar young man can have.

Every man must own a song ox or bull. This beast can be his most precious possession he cherishes for the rest of his life. Through this beautiful animal, he will acquire a nickname for himself. This nickname, often given by friends, is purely a poetic paraphrase of his ox's color name or its behavior. For example, "fire that does not burn" (*many cin amôr*), is the nickname for the owner of an ox with a red nose. Or "mixture of color" (*aguelbuk*), is for the owner of an ox with *maker* or *marial*. "Criminal" (*thaluk*), is for the owner with an ox which steals the show. The young man will care for his beast and compose songs and boasting phrases, which identify him with his animal. To grunt, moan, or express shock, you must call the name of your ox or utter a boasting phrase. Expressing or grunting without calling the name of your beast implies you have none. For example, when I visited home from Canada, and I met one of my uncles whom I had not seen in 30 years, he chanted his boasting phrase, "I have rushed my marial bull to the swamp. Is that you, Mayom, the son of my brother?" In a battle when a young man successfully dodges the spear or his spear hits the target, he chants his boasting phrase or calls the name his beast.

There are many ways a young man acquires a bull or ox. The most common way a young man gets a bull or ox is from his father's herds. When a father has more than one son, the oxen are given according to seniority; the first son gets the first ox, and so on. If his father does not have cows, the young man may trade in cows to buy an ox. Oxen are very expensive. One ox can cost up to five cows. If the young man does not have cows to trade in, another way is to cultivate crops or fish and sell the product to buy an ox. Lucky are those who have sisters because they bring in brideprice. If an ox is among the brideprice, the brother of the sister often takes the beast. The bottom line is every young man must have a song ox (*muɔr-ë-ciën*).

Song oxen or bulls come in a variety of colors. Solid black, white, or red are called *macar*, *mabor*, and *malual*, respectively. A combination of both black and white forms a variety of different colors: *majok, marial, mangar, maker, makur, makuei,* and *mabil.* A combination of white and red form *mayom, majak,* and *malek,* and so on. The colors of the Agaar cows are limitless.

Even though every color is desirable, a highly valued color pattern is a combination of black and white, forming *marial, maker, majok, makur, mangar,* or *makuei.* To make it exceptionally desirable, an ox must have additional attributes. For example, its horns must be long and white, and its muzzle must be reddish or pinkish.

When a bull calf with such beauty is born, the young owner would be so thrilled that he would kill (*gut*) a relative's cow in celebration. Even though he will eventually compensate the owner of the cow he killed with up to five cows, the killing is worth it, because he's not only marking the occasion but also welcoming and blessing his newly acquired song ox.

The *gutgut* killing was crucial for a young person back then. When we were small boys, my friends and I decided to practice *gutgut killing* because our sheep had produced colorful lambs. But since we were not eligible to kill animals, we decided to kill pumpkins. We walked in a group going from farm to farm, each choosing several pumpkins which we speared and cut up while uttering boasting phrases. Even though some parents considered our act as creative and hilarious, some of us, including me, were thoroughly punished for ruining farm produce. The punishment made the whole episode real because there were always consequences when one killed an animal for pride.

The first step in raising the bull calf is castration. Castration is done to reduce aggression and increase the physical growth of the ox. A knife is used to cut through the scrotum and open the sac to expose the two testicles. Then each testicle is pulled out with a long cord attached. The wound is checked regularly to make sure it is not infected.

When the horns grow to specified lengths, a special horn designer is asked to carve them. The carving is a delicate task which requires attention to detail. Using a spearhead, the designer cuts a smaller amount of the inner core of the living bone than the outer cover of the horn. Cutting too much of the inner core of the living bone may cause excessive bleeding, which may lead to infection or even death. Cutting too much or too little of the outer cover may also lead to the wrong design. The cutting must be perfect, which is why it's crucial to find a renowned designer with proven skills. After cutting, the horns are allowed to grow in the intended fashion: asymmetrically.

The final stage is the piercing of the horns. The tips of the horns are pierced with a hot fishing spear. The hairy tassels made from buffalo tail are suspended on the tip of the jutting horns for decoration purposes. The ox also uses the tassels to swat flies away from its eyes. Additional beautification accessories, including neck collars, bells, and jingles, are also added.

Remember, every step from castration to carving and piercing of the horns deserves poetic boasting phrases of their own: "I have carved the ox's horns!" Or, "I have pieced the horns of my ox and adorned them with buffalo tassels!" These phrases are later coined into songs.

When not being used, the accessories that the beast wore are given to a girl to care for them. The tassels (*dhuɔr*) must be kept cleaned and neat. They are oiled and combed regularly. They are entrusted in the care of girls who don't often take vacations. So a young man gave *dhuɔr* to a girl who was always at the cattle camp and sang:

> *My tassels are being cared for by Ayen Ater Gol;*
> *She is a girl, who does not visit and stay away,*
> *So that buffalos tassels becomes messy like a cob eaten by a bird.*

Everything that has to do with both the master and the beast is nothing but an exquisite work of art. For example, when quoting or describing his ox, the owner emulates the shape of the horn with his arms. The ox is trained such that as the owner sings the beast bellows thunderously, punctuating its master's rhythm. As far as they are concerned, both the owner and the animal are one. Just as a Western young man takes his prestigious car for a ride to entice girls, a young Agaar parades his ox from hearth to hearth. With his body meticulously painted with ashes, he walks slowly and majestically, while holding a fighting stick upright in his right hand and a collection of thoroughly polished spears in his left hand. A young boy or girl is leading the beast as the master proudly sings a *kêp* song:

> *My ox, Mangar*
> *His horns were meticulously curved by a specialist (atêt),*
> *Until the gossipers (who disproved my ox's beauty) swallowed*
> * their gossips;*
> *Then I pierced Mangar's horns.*

The smoke filled the earth,
The beauty filled my heart.
That's why I decorated his horns with the buffalo tassels;
The black bull with red lips has many colors,
That's why I'm called Ajuec-buk (numerous colors);
I'm also known as Buk-thiar (ten colors).
I'm a bull whose horns are sharpened,
I don't turn my back to the enemy.
My ox Mangar will bring me a good wife,
A well brought up girl, like Ayen Ater;
The girl with the teeth as white as an elephant tusk!

Of course, the owner of the ox, the *ajööt* or *awuöt*, is not exempted from the beautification, either. He is adorned from head to toe. His hair is groomed into a mushroom-like shape, which is then dyed yellowish or reddish with cow urine. An elegant plume of ostrich feathers, called *nok* (*nɔk*) is then planted in the hair and set off with a scarf, which keeps both the hair and *nok* in place. Gleaming on his wrists are several brass rings, called *madhiɛk*; several bigger brass rings, called *pajakrial*, are also shining on his legs. Two large ivory armlets are on his upper arms and two other smaller armlets are on his lower elbows. A tassel (*cöt*) is tied on the armlet, as a replica of the ox's tassel.

A young fellow named Makuen-Gok, adorned with *madhiɛk* and *pajakrial*, used to sing:

Makuen-Gok has madhiek on his wrists.
What gentleman!
Don't you see pajakrial on his legs?
What a gentleman!

I also remember a young man who wore four armlets in our village. When he danced *kobulo* (a robust hopping dance), he spread his elbows far and wide, intentionally keeping other dancers away with his massive ivory bangles. When asked why he danced like that, his response was, "The big guys, elephants (referring to the ivory bangles on his arms) always need plenty of room." In contrast, there was a story about a woman who was married to a poor man who couldn't afford to buy an ivory armlet. At night, the woman grabbed her husband's hand and shoved it into the fire. "Why would you do that?" the husband cried. "Sorry," the woman replied. "I thought it was a block of wood because your arm is so dark and naked" (implying that there was no ivory bangle on the arm to distinguish it from the wood).

I still remember young fellows from our area in the early 1980s, who were very famous because of their oxen, bulls, and songs. One of the young warriors was Mapiu Magäk Ater. He owned an ox, *Makuei*, with a stiff neck and a prominent dewlap. Its horns were massive and extraordinary white—the *matung-boor* or white-horned. As a finishing touch, the velvety ox muzzle was exceptionally reddish—the *mawum-lual*. Mapiu had composed many songs, which I still remember up to now, but I can't add them here because they are too long.

And who didn't admire Majok Agook with his ox marial? The ox had a striking color pattern: black with a bright white patch running on each side. The ox was patched on both sides with black colors from rump to neck. Because of such a unique pattern, the owner seized the opportunity and oxen-named himself *Muor-ci-mang*—literally meaning the ox is slapped or patched with exotic colors.

Then, there were young fellows from Panyar sections, including Panyakum Mapuor (who passed on in 2020 when I was writing this book) and Amerga Makueng, who were very famous too. It was before Panyar migrated from Pachong areas to Yek. Pinyakum was a troublemaker, who, when things didn't go his way, would always say, "We must test our muscles!" And with that, the cracking of the fighting sticks ensued. Pinyakum owned an ox maker, and one of his friends, who owned an ox marial, oxen-named himself Saluk, meaning criminal. To distinguish himself, his boasting phrase was, "Yes, my name is Saluk, but I'm not a criminal who steals; it is just that my ox is doing the unthinkable deeds at the cattle camps."

At one point, Pinyakum Mapuor and five of his friends, including Amerga Makueng, all had oxen with the similar colors: *muokëër* (plural maker), almost blue-black with a white line down their backs. The roan coloring on their sides varied from nearly black to nearly white, with either red or black noses. All the variants were stunning, especially against a background of green grass of the Aramweer or Majak-ajok cattle camps, where they often kept their cattle. Pinyakum and his crew sang the following song:

I moved my Majok and Mangar. We are the soldiers of Makuen-thiang who never get tired of war chants. My ox has left the salty soil of Majak Rual and Adet; the bull rushed to Akam [Cattle Camp].

Maker Ater Dier is rushing the cows to the river . . . These are cattle camps of makers: my Maker, Kuet-Toong Makueng Rok's maker, Meen Modok's maker, and Magual's maker. Then, there is an ox of Pinyakum called maker of Pinyakum. The ox rushes to Akam; Maker Ater Dier is rushing the cows to the marshland. My Majok has been inside the Nuer's savannah . . .

Then, there was a young fellow from the Bar Aguoc area named Majak Benyther, famously known by his oxen name, Maleng-toong (-tɔɔŋ). He owned an ox which was *malek* in color—a magnificent beast with a deep chest and high, curving hump. He claimed to have acquired the ox from the Nuer, using spears, earning him the named Maleng-toong (Malek of spears) implying the ox was acquired by force. The ox was unique because of its color patterns, size, and even behavior. With long and large horns, the ox was massive in size and elegant in appearance: dark red spots dominated the white skin.

When performing a mock fight (*gör*), the Maleng-toong's style was unique. While holding a shield and spears in the left hand and one spear in a throwing position in the right hand, he leaped up high in the air and then launched the spear in midair before landing. He did this in one swift move, mind you. He was the only one who had mastered that style, which he claimed to have learned from the Nuer.

The only reason a young man may give up his bull or ox is when he gives it away as a dowry for his wife. Even so, the beast remains part of his life. The nickname which he acquired is permanent. And when his wife gives birth to a boy, he will name the child after the bull or ox. The songs, chants, and boasting phases attributed to his beasts are his for life.

Crop Farming

In addition to cattle-keeping, the second subsistence strategy is crop farming. The Agaar followed a similar pattern of seasonal activity throughout the year. Divided into economic units in their families, the Agaar move in regular patterns between permanent villages, cattle camps, and fishing stations. These activities are predictable and give structure to the seasonal activities. In summer, many families congregate at fishing stations located along the Naam River and Lake Akeu. They fish using line hooks, nets, or fishing spears.

Like other African people, the Agaar people depend on subsistence farming, where an individual or family plant small-scale agriculture for direct consumption by individuals, families, or small communities. They grow a wide variety of crops such as sorghum, maize, millet, groundnut, sesame, yam, cassava, and many other crops. The majority of people still use traditional hoes for cultivation. More recently, some people have used plows pulled by two oxen trained for that purpose. A few individuals even have tractors for commercial farming.

The preparation for the land begins in mid-summer, usually February or March, where individuals clear the farms by cutting trees, uprooting the stumps from the previous year. The rain usually starts in April or May. When the first rain is heavy, people cultivate in the second rain. If not, people plant after the third rain. Groundnuts are first planted one by one in holes. Then, the sorghum, millet, and sesame are mixed and scattered on the plot. Then, the farmer uses a hoe attached to a bamboo pole to plow the land, producing four crops in the same land. The groundnut is harvested by the end of August, and the sesame is ready by September. Millet and sorghum are the last crops to be harvested in December.

In separate farms, beans and Agaar lentils, called *aguoth (aguɔth)*, are grown separately. *Rap* are mixed with them so that when the beans and *aguoth* are harvested, the *dura* will remain until December. In addition to the main crops, other cereals, tubers, and vegetable are also grown. Pumpkins, yams, cassava, okra, *amokbek*, and other vegetables and tubers are grown. Most of these vegetables and tubers are perishable goods, which are consumed as soon as they are harvested.

July is the worst month of the year. At this time, all of the last year's produce has been depleted. The planted crops will not ripen in two months. In this period, people survive on vegetable and leaves. Some people die of hunger in this period. But soon, the groundnuts will ripen, followed by all other crops. In September, all the crops will ripen including sorghum, pumpkin, yams, cassava, maize, beans, you name it. *Diët ee yuil ku ye Bil.* "I wish every month is September."

Farming Practices

The Agaar use two farming practices that have helped shape sustainable farming systems and practices: crop rotation and mix or intercropping.

Crop Rotations: Crop rotation is the practice of growing different crops on the same piece of land. For example, sorghum is grown on one piece of land this year and groundnut will be grown the following year. The advantages of the crop rotation farming method include prevention of soil depletion, an increase in soil fertility, and reduction of soil erosion. All of the above help to maximize yield.

Mix/Inter-cropping: This is when a farmer sows more than two crops at the same time on the same piece of land. Each crop must have enough space to maximize cooperation and minimize competition between the crops. This practice is very common throughout the Jieng land. For example, on one piece of land the farmer mixes sorghum, millet, sesame, and groundnut. After four or five months, the groundnut will be harvested, and this allows the remaining crops to get enough space, water, nutrients, and sunlight. After that, the sesame will be harvested. And finally, the sorghum and millet will be harvested at the same time. Inter-cropping practice helps prevent pests and diseases from spreading and increases soil fertility. Most importantly, it is efficient and effective because it reduces the labor needed for weeding.

Being a drought resistant grain, sorghum is the most important cereal crop grown by the Jieng followed by millet and maize. And it is planted at the beginning of the rains, usually in April or May. Grain sorghum has leafy green stalks and distinctive grain heads with many colors when ripened. The grain head can take on many shapes and sizes ranging from a tight-headed round panicle to an open, droopy panicle that can be short or long. It has a wide variety of colors such as red, orange, bronze, or dark brown.

Planting

There are two ways to plant sorghum. One is raw planning where a farmer digs holes in rows and throws between three to five seeds in each hole and then closes it with soil. Another method is when a farmer marks a piece of land and randomly throws the seeds and plows the land to bury the seed. You have to be quick in plowing the land and burying the seeds; otherwise, the birds and ants will take the seeds.

In less than one week after planting, young sorghum plants will emerge from the soil. As the plants grow and mature, the stalks grow taller and taller, producing up to 20 leaves. Each leaf measures the phase in the growing stages. Depending on the soil, mature sorghum can reach up to 10 feet tall in six to eight and a half months.

Weeding: Weeding takes place in the first four to eight weeks after planting. It is crucial to weed right away because weeds take away water, sunlight, and nutrients from the soil, leaving the grain to die. A hand hoe, attached to an L-shaped wood, called *kembee*, which maneuvers easily without damaging the crops, is used for weeding. Also, some weeds look like dura, so you really have to know the different types of weeds. Some farms require constant weeding. The trick is to remove weeds without soil attached to their roots or they will keep growing.

Guarding the Farms

After weeding, the farms are protected from animals and birds. Boys do this job. Cranes always know when groundnuts are ready, and they know to dig the groundnuts from the ground. Monkeys and even cattle eat dura and other crops, so the farm must be constantly guarded from morning to dawn. This was my job when I was a small boy. A rickety platform, called pöm, which was over 10 feet tall was built in the middle of the farm. Armed with a traditional catapult and hard mud balls, I would keep away animals and birds.

Harvesting

The sorghum (raap) and millet (awuöu) are finally harvested in December. This task is done by both men and women. First, a farmer would harvest grain sorghum by cutting off the seed clusters with a few inches of stalk attached and then spread them on the ground under the sun to dry for a week or so. She has to be constantly on the watch and ready to bring the cereal inside the house in case sudden showers cause spoilage. If you let the rain flood your grain, that's it; they are wasted and your family will be hungry until the next season. So keeping the cereal from the rain is an important task. It's also important to protect the cereal from birds and animals while drying; a job for both women and boys.

When dried, she places the cereal on a well-plastered floor to avoid the soil from mixing with the grains, and then uses a piece of wood (usually a pestle) to thresh the pile to separate the kernel from the stalk. When thoroughly beaten, she winnows out the debris.

The threshing and winnowing processes are exhausting. It's not uncommon to find women with blisters on their hands as a result of threshing the cereal all day. Additionally, the dust (*ayiel*) of the grains, especially millet, causes extreme itching and irritation. In fact, the dust is called *ayiel (ayiɛl)*, meaning "itching" or "irritating". This can sometimes lead to skin diseases or even scabies. But women have to do it; it's their job.

Winnowing

Another step is the separation of chaff from the grain, the winnowing. The most important element needed in this step is patience. Nature is in control here, not the women. You need wind to complete the winnowing process. But not just any wind: too much wind can blow away the grain with the debris, and too little wind will not separate the debris from the pure grain. You need a moderate wind to do the job. When she feels the wind is right, an experienced woman scoops the threshed content with a big gourd, stands up straight, holds the gourd up high above her head, and slowly dumps it on the ground; the lighter chaff and straw are blown away and the heavy grain falls on the ground. This process is repeated several times until all the debris is gone, leaving only pure grain.

Finally, a winnowing tray called *lɛth* is used to complete the final winnowing process. Also, stones, twigs, and other materials are removed by hand. Then the grain will be stored in granaries, where only the daily portion will be scooped out and pounded for meals for the day.

Fishing

Fish have always been and continue to be an essential aspect of life in rural Agaar societies. But they are seasonal occupations, usually done in the dry season. Fishing or hunting all year round implies that you have no cattle, and this plunges you into the bottom of the social hierarchy. Individuals who do hunting or fishing as a fulltime occupation are often frowned upon by those who have cows.

Floods usually come between June and August, when the Nile River and its tributaries including Bhar Naam River overflow their banks, and the entire Toc Swamp becomes sodden. All cattle camps along the river bank are deserted as they move to higher ground near the permanent settlements. Keeping cattle on wet ground can cause hoof disease.

At this time of the year, many people come to permanent villages to help in the cultivation of crops, leaving only a few members to take care of the cattle. The cattle are moved to temporary cattle camps near the villages. The grass and fish in the marshland flourish in the absence of men and animals.

At this time of the year, a small group of people who have no cattle can live and fish in the swamp all year round. They are called *atooc*, meaning "swampers". They use small boats made of palm trunks to sail along the river as they set up their lines of hooks, which they periodically check for fish.

In November or early December, the crops are harvested, and rivers recede. Gradually, wells in permanent villages dry up, and the grass on the open plains wither and brown. The cattle are moved to camps located along the river banks where grass and water are plentiful. Soon they will be followed by seasonal fishermen who will also set up temporary fishing camps along the River Naam, which gradually shrinks to muddy pools.

I attended several fishing seasons in 1985 and 1986. In November, everyone heads to Pachong or Rumbek to buy fishing equipment from the blacksmiths. At this time of the year, the blacksmith market booms as people buy fishing spears, hooks, and nets. Each fishing man buys his equipment according to his favorite fishing techniques, nets, hooks, or spears.

The two different nets include casting and scooping fishing nets. Casting nets have a mesh with an opening on the upper side. Fishermen throw these nets into a school of fish swimming in shallow waters. Scooping nets are strung on round wooden frames, which are then submerged and suddenly lifted out of the water to catch fish.

My favorite fishing method was rod angling. I attached a simple pole to a fishing line and hook. Historically, the hook was usually fitted with bait. Then I would lower the line into the water, usually from an elevated position like a riverbank. When a fish swallowed the bait and pulled the line, I swung it to pull the fish out of the water.

From January to April, all Agaar youth gather along the River Naam and Lake Akeu for the annual fishing festival. Before the fishing festival begins, elders gather to conduct the ceremonial sacrifice of a rooster or even ram to cast off evil spirits, and dangerous animals such as crocodile, snakes, or hippopotamuses from the river. Another function of the sacrifice is to ensure abundance of fish.

As the fishing begins, each young man is armed with a slender fishing spear, which he repeatedly and forcefully thrusts into the turbid waters. Thousands of people fish in close quarters so accuracy is vital or you could stab your neighbor. Spearing your neighbor's foot often results in a fight as the relative of a speared individual tries to beat the culprit. The relatives of the culprit defend their relatives.

In April, the biggest annual fishing festival takes place at Lake Akeu. It takes three day's fishing before the annual fishing ends. Most of the fish are cooked for daily consumption, and the leftovers are filleted and hung to dry in the sun to be taken home.

Tobacco Planting

During the dry season, the cattle camps near the permanent villages are deserted as the cattle are taken deep into Toc Swamp, where grass and water are plentiful. The deserted cattle camps become vocal points for youth who don't want to fish. Instead, they grow tobacco in these deserted cattle camps. So between January and April, every deserted cattle camp (wun ë ɣɔk) turns into a tobacco camp (wun ë macer). The tobacco is used for sale.

In 1986, I grew tobacco at Adiid Cattle Camp, located about seven miles away from our village. We left at dawn and returned at dusk every day for four months to work on our tobacco farms. This is where I learned tobacco planting is a very delicate job.

There are a few things that every tobacco farmer should know. First, tobacco needs a dry and warm climate to get the best quality of tobacco. It takes up to four months between transplant and harvest, so the tobacco should be ripened without heavy rainfall, as excess water causes tobacco plants to become thin and flaky.

The planting begins by preparing seedling beds where you sow seeds. Tobacco seeds are tiny, so be sure not to plant them too thickly; allow adequate spacing between seeds to avoid overcrowding. You have to water the tobacco thoroughly every day, three times a day or so until the tobacco plants settle. Once they become better established, you should water less frequently, like twice a day, to avoid over-watering. Keep the plants well-watered, but be careful not to make the soil soggy.

While the seedlings are growing, prepare other garden plots for transplantation. Make sure the area you plant the tobacco is continuously exposed to sun, well-drained, and thoroughly tilled. Lack of sun often results in spindly plants, poor growth, and thin leaves. When your seedlings are healthy and large enough, you transplant them into larger plots.

When the plant mature enough and begin to flower, you must top them. Topping means the removing of the primary bud to encourage more axiliary buds or suckers to grow, increasing the yield and quality.

To weed the plants, hoe gently around your tobacco plants to remove the weeds and loosen the soil. Also, you can pull up soil around the base of the plant to help strengthen it. Tobacco roots increase, and the root structure is quite complex, with some roots grow deep in the soil and many other small roots grow close to the soil surface. Pay attention when tilling or hoeing, as penetrating the soil too deep can damage the roots.

When the plants are ripened, the leaves on the bottom are harvested, leaving the soft upper leaves to mature. The final harvesting is accomplished by either removing leaves from the stalk in the field or by cutting the stem off at ground level. The leaves are then removed from the stalk after they have dried. The second method is that tobacco leaves and soft stalks are chopped, pounded, and formed into a conical heap called *thon macer* (tobacco bull). The tobacco is sold in the market.

Hunting

Game hunting was part of the Agaar's survival, but it was more a leisure activity than an occupation. But the Agaar's survival as a hunter, fisher, and gatherer depended on each individual having extensive knowledge of the land and its resources. Material technology was less important than the understanding of how to construct and use this technology efficiently. The experience consisted of a detailed knowledge of animal habits, population cycles, climate, and topography. Knowledge was built up during an individual's lifetime in several ways. First, it was acquired through practical experience. As a child grew to adulthood, he learned through observation and trial and error, the techniques of hunting, fishing, trapping, and the unique features of the animal population, vegetation, and geography in his particular territory.

I remember as a child when we used to play the game of *anyook (anyɔɔk)*. A giant sausage fruit, the anyook, was tied on a long rope, and one boy would volunteer to swing the *anyook* wildly as we gathered around with stick spears and took turns spearing the imagined buffalo or elephant. The swinger charged the anyook at you swinging wildly. If you were not quick enough to get out of the way, the giant sausage could hit you. You also had to be careful not to spear others and be ready to dodge any spear deflected by the anyook. Some boys were injured during the play, but it was just part of the game; when you grew up, a buffalo could hurt or even kill you if you were not careful in your hunting knowledge and skills.

While survival depends on practical knowledge, it is also crucial for people to live according to specific standards of conduct. They believe that animals and inanimate objects in the world had a spirit, and their survival depends on their ability to maintain balanced relationships with the spirit of the land.

You also want to move silently, or as quietly as possible when hunting. You want to practice moving precisely, probing for breakable twigs and sticks with your non-dominant leg. Stalkers should walk heel to toe, keeping their feet in a straight line. As they move in a heel to toe method, their weight should be placed on their rear foot, with the front foot a probe for these noisy breakables. Hunters need to be aware of how their entire body affects the world around them, which includes how your chest and shoulder touch limbs and brush, and how your knees and shins shake the base of these same bushes. The Agaar warriors mastered these tactical moves before the arrival of guns.

The guns have ruined our culture. The traditional armed warriors often resort to firearms now, even for a slight provocation. Who would blame them? They are called *Gelwong* ("protector of the cow"), a name with an economic (not cultural) connotation. It is no surprise that the *Gelwong* are morally corrupted, just like their politicians who arm and equip them. Killing, cattle-rustling, looting, raping, drinking, and all other culturally unacceptable practices are standard in society today, and a result of this toxic culture of firearms.

The previous warriors carried spears, not guns. Guns are for cowards, and they encourage cowardice or barbaric acts. You hide in a trench or behind a tree, and then you squeeze the trigger, killing everything that moves. That's just cowardice and barbaric.

The combination of spears and a shield was the display of art. The speed and agility, the leaping up in the air and landing, and the launching or dodging of a spear; each move was artistically calculated and accompanied by personal boasting phrases or poetic expressions. The fitness and stamina involved was art at its purest.

Everywhere an *apärapuöl* went, he carried a bundle of thoroughly polished and light, flat-bladed spears balanced over one shoulder. He bravely faced an enemy or a beast, say a lion, with these weapons."I have stabbed the lion until the beast broke the shaft," boasted a young warrior. "The cowards ran away."

A young lad named Maker Meen Ajuong from our village Biling Daldiar, had taken the art of spear fighting to the next level. He was famously known as Maker-Gok because he was initially from Gok Arol Kachuol. According to the story I heard, Meen Ajuong impregnated a girl given to a man from the Gok section. So Maker was born in Cueibet area, where he grew up and received the Gok's scarification marks. When he became an adult, he traced his biological father back to our village, Biling Daldiar/Loiyic area, in the early 1980s. His arrival was marked by a big celebration, where bulls were killed to welcome him into the family.

Maker-Gok turned out to be the bravest warrior. He met his brother, Marial Meen Ajuong, who was also a renowned warrior. They were joined by their cousin, Beny Cuar, over 7-feet tall warrior. The triples, from the Pan-Ajuong sub-section of Athoi, were killers in the art of spear fighting.

Maker-Gok invented the style of intercepting spears in midair. When speared in a battle, Maker-Gok avoided the tip of the spear, and then caught it in midair and launched it back at you. He speared you with your own spear, and he rarely missed.

Once, I challenged a friend of mine, a boy named Matoc Makuach, to spear me with a sharpened stick (*wai*). He obliged and hauled the shaft at me. I dodged and tried to catch the shaft in midair, Maker-Gok's style. Bad idea! The shaft speared my hand, and its tip broke inside the flesh. I still have the scar on my right hand. I had never tried Maker-Gok's move again.

Maniong Akot, from the Amoth-nhom section, was another renowned warrior. I neither met Maniong nor saw him. But I heard a lot about him. Everyone talked about Maniong Akot. He was the bravest in the land, and his spear-throw was the most accurate and deadly. I heard Maniong killed an elephant with a single strike which made him very famous among his peers.

Remember, hunting with a spear was more dangerous than hunting with a gun. If you missed with a spear, you only scared the game away. If you struck a beast, such as an elephant, buffalo or rhino, then you had to face the wildest wounded animal, which was extremely dangerous. Maniong always hit the vital spot, the heart or lungs, on the chosen game, killing it instantly.

The big games were hunted not just for meat but for material needs. Buffaloes were hunted because of their skins, which were used as shields. Rhinos and elephants provided horns or tusks, which were produced into beautification accessories. Whoever speared the beast first got the trophy. For example, if you speared an elephant first, then the right tusk of the elephants (*tung cuëëc*) was automatically yours. The second hitter got the left tusk (*tung ciɛɛm*). The rest (all the losers) would get a piece of meat each. Maniong always received the right tusk or both.

In 1985 or 1986, I watched young men in action at Gän Ayuol cattle camp. A rogue male elephant had arrived at the camp late in the afternoon. Women and children, myself included, climbed on the platform, called *kät nhom*, for safety, as the *apäräpuööl* grabbed their spears and encircled the beast on the outskirts of the camp. I watched the whole episode while standing on the *kät* platform.

A recently initiated young lad, named Maper, charged and launched a spear at it first. The weapon found its mark on the back of the beast. The young lad was ecstatic. "*Tung cuëëc dië*," he shouted, letting people know that he had struck the beast first and that the right tusk was his. The young lad then did the unthinkable: he left the action before the beast was even killed, and he went to find a tall anthill; the only vantage point in the plain's flatness, where he climbed on top so everyone could see and hear him. Then, he chanted at the top of his voice, uttering his boasting phrases.

The elephant was killed, skinned, divided, and cooked; meanwhile, the young man was still standing on the top of the anthill, singing and boasting. The young lad chanted all night. The following morning, every girl in the camp was singing his song.

Agoi Marol

There was a young fellow from our area who did the same thing. His name was Agoi Marol. Agoi liked to be the center of attention. He did things that were incredibly stupid and obnoxious.

One day, a bull elephant invaded Gän Ayuol Cattle Camp. While all the young men grabbed their bundles of spears to drive off the elephant, Agoi grabbed a fighting stick only (without a spear) and ran after the beast. As the elephant was walking away, Agoi approached from behind and hit it with the fighting stick and fled before the elephant turned around. This stupid act stunned the crowd. Later on, the *apäräpuööl* taunted Agoi for his stupidity of messing with the deadliest beast that could have killed him instantly. But Agoi mocked them back, "You picked up spears just because of one elephant? How cowardly!" From that incident, Agoi coined one of his famous boasting phrases: "My name is Agoi, the son of Marol. I'm a fearless man who faces the beast with a fighting-stick. A big man like Agoi Marol doesn't need spears to drive off small animals like elephants!"

Even though he called himself a big man, Agoi was the opposite. He exaggerated everything about himself. He was only about five-feet tall and slimly built. Perhaps it was his physical condition that drove him to such extreme attention-seeking quests. During a dance at Biling Daldiar, Agoi pulled off another scene. While people were dancing, Agoi arrived with girls who were carrying containers full of milk. Before he invaded the dance floor, he instructed the girls to pour the milk into a bathing gourd (*atiël*) and placed it right on the edge of the dance ground. As the entire crowd watched in awe, Agoi took off his clothes and started bathing with the milk. The crowd watched in amusement, some laughing and others jeering, but he didn't care. He continued scooping the milk with his cupped hands and dumping it all over his body, as he bathed thoroughly from head to toe.

The message he was conveying was that he was the wealthiest and most prestigious man who bathed with milk. But in reality, Agoi didn't even have that many cows. He was the poorest compared to his peers. But he just pulled off that stunt to wow the crowd. Talk about extreme publicity or fame-seeking behavior? Well, you got it!

As he bathed with the milk, Agoi intentionally turned his back, side, and front to the people, demonstrating that he was a well-built gentleman without physical deformities or disabilities. By this, he was mocking one of his rivals, a young man named Majak (last name withheld) who was also in the crowd. Agoi and Majak were courting the same girl. Their fierce competition over the girl turned into insults. They indirectly exchanged insults. Majak said Agoi was short, skinny, and ugly. Agoi countered by calling Majak *"Muony-Rek"* because Majak's private parts didn't have enough skin that covered it all. He wasn't circumcised though; it had just happened naturally. But Agoi was far from being sympathetic.

"God can be very unfavorable toward other people," Agoi remarked. "He created Majak with enough skin that covered his entire body, but didn't give him enough skin to cover his private parts? And if that was not cruel enough, God put him here in the Agarland (to be mocked) instead of taking him to the Rek-land where people with such disabilities live? What a curse!"

This was when wearing clothes was optional and those who had physical disabilities like Majak were mocked and bullied to death. The worst disability to have in the Agarland was the absence of skin from your manly thing. Now that wearing clothes is the norm, that disability doesn't matter that much anymore. In fact, circumcision is becoming popular among the Agaar, the Atuot, the Aliab, the Bor, etc., especially those who live in town and cities. The city dwellers are divided into two groups: circumcised and non-circumcised (don't ask me which group I belong to; I'm not telling you!).

Anyway, let's stop guessing the group I belong to and go back to the main story; shall we?

After Agoi finished bathing with the milk, he stood in the sun for a few minutes to dry his body. Then he invaded the dance floor. As he danced in that typical Agaar high-leaping dance, Agoi chanted over and over again, "*Lɔc ê kin oo* (here is the prestigious man *oo!*)" Remember, his dance wasn't even that exuberant or stylish, but he covered it all up with the persisting chant,"*Lɔc ê kin oo! Lɔc ê kin eei! Lɔc ê kin wei!*" The chant resonated, especially with the girls, because he was the most prestigious man (*lɔc*) who bathed with milk. Even though there was no social media at that time, Agoi Marol's behavior had provided people with a source of entertainment and a medium to laugh. He died in the late 1970s.

Gathering/ Shea-tree

Alongside hunting and fishing, gathering food in the wild remains crucial to the Agaar's eating habits. The gathering of food, also known as foraging, is still widely practiced by the population to enable them to meet their food needs. The most common fruits include mangoes, shea, palm, tamarind, lang, cum, and so on.

Shea is the most important fruit in the Agarland. Its flesh is eaten fresh, processed for drinking, or made into pastries to be eaten later. Its kernel is processed into butter used for cooking, lotion, and other uses.

The gathering of wild Shea fruit is exclusively done by boys, girls, and women. The fruit becomes ripe from April or May to August and falls on the ground before it is collected. When it is windy, children will race to the tree to collect the fruits shaken off by the wind. Green or light yellow, the Shea fruit is oval or round. It is divided into four layers: the soft cover of the pulp, edible pulp surrounding the seed, the hard cover of the inner seed, and the inner seed. Both the soft cover and the pulp are edible.

After the collection, the sweet flesh is separated from the seed. The flesh is eaten fresh or made into pastry for later consumption. The seeds or kernels are dried in the sun for days until they are thoroughly dried. This is to loosen the kernel from the shell for easy shelling.

When dried, a stone, wooden hammer, and a mortar are used for shelling. Winnowing is achieved by holding a basket filled with nuts at arm's length and gradually pouring them down. If there is a strong wind, the piece of shell will be blown away. If not, the operation is repeated. *Lɛth* is also used to separate the hardcover from the kernel. Then this inner seed is broken into pieces and put into a roasting pan to be roasted in a fire to increase the oil extraction. When roasted, it is black and greasy.

The next step is to put the roasted seed into a mortar and pound it with a pestle. After pounding, it is also ground into a smooth paste which looks like chocolate. Sometimes water is added, and then whisked for hours to remove some of the shaft. The solution is then cooked for several hours until the oil separates from the black residue; oil on top and the residue on the bottom. The oil is gently scooped away from the residue. You continue cooking, stirring, and scooping until you can no longer see the oil. When scooping, you make sure the black residue doesn't mix with the oil, for it will ruin the taste because this black residue tastes awfully bitter.

Finally, the processed oil is put in a container and left to cool and solidify. In addition to cooking, shea butter is a great product for smoothing, soothing, and the conditioning of the skin.

Alcohol Beverages

The artisanal fermentation of cereals into beer and wines is an ancient Agaar tradition. These beers have socio-cultural, economic, and nutritional value. Cereals, mainly sorghum, millet, and maize, are the most important crops used for fermented beverages. These ancestral beverages are widely used in various festivals and Agaar ceremonies such as marriage, praying for rain, communication with ancestors, the handing-over of a brideprice, and farming festivals (*kutkut*), and the popular annual festivals.

Back then, it was culturally unacceptable for young men and women to drink alcohol. You started drinking socially when your children had grown. But you didn't want to get drunk regularly; or else your reputation would ruin, and it would be hard for your children to get married. No one would be interested in the children of a drunkard.

Two types of drinks are made from cereals (sorghum, millet, or maize): *muon-col* (black beer) and *muon-ɣer* (white beer). Made by a quick process for immediate consumption, *muon-her* is mostly used for rituals and festivities and *muon-col* is produced for commercial purposes.

To produce the artisanal beverages, multiple steps of malting are required. The first step is malt production. After selecting the grain such as sorghum, millet, or maize, the grains are cleaned, washed thoroughly before being soaked and left overnight at room temperature. In the morning, the grains are drained and placed on a lay-out sack, covered with another sack, and kept at room temperature. The soft grains are covered and placed in a dark area for two to three days for germination. Water is sprayed sometimes when the ambient air is dry or when the temperature is hot. Alternatively, the grains are left on the ground and sprayed until the germination process starts and rootlets appear. The high temperature facilitates the beginning of germination. In this case, the germination time can last for four days. The germination of the grains determines the quality of the alcohol. Both over-germination and under-germination can ruin the quality and texture of the beverage. Moderate germination is needed to produce the good quality drink.

The germinated grains called *luwou (luwɔu)* are placed on a well-plastered ground and left to dry in the sun for days. When thoroughly dried, the *luwou* is ground by hand using grinding stones to produce a rough powder. Out of this malted grains, two types of *mou (mɔu)* are produced: *muön-col* (black beer) and *muön-ɣer* (white beer). Both products are processed differently.

To produce white beer, the powder is then mixed with warm water and left overnight to ferment and bubble; two characteristics of the sour odor of the beer. The mixture is cooked again, cooled, vigorously mixed, and placed in a large pot. The container is well covered and placed in a warm place, usually inside the house to encourage further fermentation for several days. In towns, yeast is added in this final process. But in rural areas, no yeast is required; only yeast present in the grains and *luwou* are responsible for the alcohol production.

After the fermentation, the product is filtered through a suitable fabric mesh called *dhïm* to retain some of the solid particles, while the liquid goes through the sieving device. The whitish-brown local beer with an alcohol content between one to seven percent is sold on the local market, served to visitors, or used in special celebrations and ceremonies.

The preparation and production of the black beer is lengthy and more complicated. In fact, this is where real traditional science and ingenuity are required. When cooking and distilling, two factors determine the quality and quantity of alcohol: (1) how severe the heat is when applied in the cooking process, and (2) the pot's surface area. The bigger the pan or pot, the more surface area, and the more alcohol that evaporates during cooking.

Water is boiled in a pot and the fermented and dried *luwou* is added and stirred vigorously for about an hour until it turns into a thick porridge-like paste. Then the paste is spread out on the well-plastered floor and left to dry in the sun. After it's thoroughly dried, it turns into pastry-like, chunky, crunchy balls. Using her hands, the woman preparing it will break the pastry into smaller pieces and fine powder.

Now, here comes the real stuff. Water is boiled in a big pot and the dried, bally pastry is added and stirred vigorously while cooking at a maximum heat temperature. Placed next to the big boiling pot is another pot with cold water. The two containers are connected by a tube called *aruor*. The boiling pot is sealed so the generated vapor escapes through the *aruor* into the coldwater pot, where the vapor condenses into liquid. Placed inside the coldwater pot is a container where the liquid alcohol is collected. While maintaining the maximum heat under the boiling pot to generate the vapor, the cook keeps drawing out the hot water and adding in cold water for the maximum condensation. The same procedures are repeated several times while the alcohol is collected and put in bottles for sale.

To advertise the availability of the beer, a long pole with the *dhïïm* or a piece of cloth is erected in the middle of the courtyard to alert the neighbors and passersby that there is a sale going on in that homestead. And when the beer is completed, the flag is removed.

Staple Food

The main food of the Jieng is *cuïn* (other Jieng call it *kuïn*). *Cuïn* is a cooked, thick, porridge-like starch made from sorghum, millet, or maize flour, served with vegetable stew mixed with fish or meat. It is the main food eaten every day, twice, or three times a day. Without *cuïn* in the dish, it's not a complete meal; it's just a snack.

Even though cuïn is plain in taste, it is heavy, so it is used to carry richer sources of meat, fish, vegetable, or milk. Because of its weight, limey vegetables such as okra or *malokia*, mixed with meat or fish and thickened with peanut-butter (*makuaŋa*) are preferred. A condiment called *awai* (a processed liquid or powder made from ashes of a special tree) is added to enrich the flavor and to help in the digestion.

The *cuïn* seems simple, but it takes a great deal of power and time to prepare it. It starts with planting of the dura, millet, or maize, then weeding, protecting it from animals and birds, harvesting, threshing, winnowing, pounding, and finally cooking. From the planting to harvest is both men's and women's job, and from threshing to cooking is women's job. Men don't cook.

Being the lastborn, I was always closer to my mother, and I watched how she prepared *cuïn* every day. Jieng boys were not allowed to be close to women in the kitchen, but when you were the lastborn, like me, you could get away with it now and then, especially when your friends were not there to laugh at you.

The first stage is pounding the grain into flour. The first step in producing the flour is dehulling—the removal of the husk or the outer coat of the grain: you put the grain in a traditional bowl called *aduok* or *atiël*, made from gourd. You add water to soak the grain in order to make it easier to remove the husk. Then you use a wooden mortar (*dooŋ*) and a pestle (*lek*). Put the soaked grain in the mortar and pound it lightly, so that you only remove the cover or husk. The husk can cause stomachache, which is why it is removed. Additionally, the husk of the millet is better, which is why it should be removed to improve the taste.

After that, the contents are spread on a plastered floor to dry. Then a winnower is used to winnow the husk from the clean bran. The removed husk is stored to be processed into alcohol beverage.

The remaining pure bran is moist with water and pounded with the mortar and the pestle. Remember, I'm not talking about the small mortar and pestle in urban kitchens; the Agaar mortar is hollowed out of a tree trunk and the pestle can be over five feet tall and thicker than a man's leg. You raise the pestle with both hands and thrash it down with force to crush the bran into the flour. Throughout the day, you hear the thumping of mortar and pestle as women pound the grains, a task every woman must learn at a very young age.

After it is thoroughly pounded, the contents are removed from the mortar and winnow with a winnowing tray (*ßth*) to separate the flour from the bran. Pounding and winnowing are repeated several times before a good quality and quantity of flour is obtained. The remaining bran is stored for emergencies. For example, when an expected visitor comes, the bran is easily pounded into the flour and cooked for the visitors. Manually pounding the grains is painful, time-consuming, tedious, and labor intensive. Inexperienced, weak, or sick women find it difficult to produce a daily meal for their family.

The final stage is the preparation of the *cuin* or *asida*. This is a very crucial stage for any woman, especially young and inexperienced women who have not mastered the art of cooking the *cuin*. Many things could go wrong in the cooking and no one will value her cooking, which means all her hard work, threshing, dehulling, pounding, and winnowing have been in vain. Even her marriage is at stake, because Agaar men may divorce women who don't know how to cook, which is also an insult to incompetent mothers who didn't teach their daughters properly. The *cuin* has to be perfectly cooked. Improperly cooked *cuin* may be described as watery (*lau*), solid (*köi*), lumpy (*nguäl*), uncooked (*bony*), or overcooked (*cuël*). No woman wants to hear any of these terms about her cooking.

To cook *cuin*, first you boil water in a traditional pot. Aluminum pots can make the food smell like it has burned (*cuël*). Only city women who have mastered the art of cooking with steel and aluminum pots can use them. When water is boiled, fine bran is added and stirred constantly as it cooks. When the bran turns into porridge, fine flour is added slowly while mixing rapidly. After the right texture, smell, and color is obtained, the *asida* is ready to be served.

There are two ways to eat *asida*: either by hand or with a spoon. To eat with your hand, you cut a sizeable piece using your right hand, mold it between the fingers, use your thumb to create a hole in the middle, scoop the stew with it, and place the contents into the mouth. Mostly city dwellers eat with their hands. Their counterparts, rural-dwellers, especially men, use a spoon. When using a spoon, you cut the *asida* with the spoon and make sure there is enough space on the spoon in order to accommodate the stew, and then you scoop the stew and stuff it into the mouth. Sometimes, the stew is not enough so you have to be conservative when scooping, otherwise you will complete the stew, leaving *asida* only, which is not enjoyable to be eaten alone because of its plain taste.

Even though *asida* is also popular in town and cities, the urban dwellers' staple food is *kisira*. Just like *asida*, *kisira* is a type of bread made from sorghum, maize, or millet flour and served with stew, soup, or broth of beef, chicken, or fish and mixed with vegetables, thickened with peanut butter, and seasoned with *kombo*—a powder or liquid condiment extracted from ashes.

In both urban and rural areas, the most important meal of the day is dinner. Even though the majority of people can't afford three meals a day in towns and cities, rich people eat three meals a day. Breakfast, which is served in the morning between 6:00 am and 9:00 am, consists of tea with bread (*alagemat*), cakes, biscuits, or roasted groundnuts. Lunch is served between 1:00 pm and 2:00 pm, and *asida* may be served. Other food such as rice, lentils, beans, and macaroni are also common in towns and cities. Dinner, the heaviest meal of the day, is served between 8:00 pm to 9:00 pm or later, especially when a member of the group is missing. Three stews may accompany one tray of *asida* or *kisira*.

Tea is served anytime, before and after the meals. Everywhere you go, you will be welcomed with a cup of tea. The tea is sometime flavored with traditional herbs (*nana* and *grumpul*) which can enrich the taste and smell.

In rural areas, food is usually plentiful during harvest season, but it may be scarce at other times of the year. Even if the food is plentiful, there is no way a woman can pound enough flour for three meals every day. Most people eat one main meal in the evening and various small snacks throughout the day. Popular snacks include roasted groundnuts (the Agaar don't eat raw groundnut), cassava, yams, sorghum-canes, mangoes, Shea-tree, palm fruits, and other fruits. Other fruits such as tamarind, kunyuk, cum, akoncit, lang, muona, alangkol, and coloc are often eaten by children because they are beneath an adult's dignity. They are considered snacks for children; grownups don't eat snacks.

Traditional Dances and Games

Traditional Dances

Traditional dances are an integral part of the Agaar culture. These dances serve recreational, religious, and all other social functions. Dancing is a means of marking life experiences, celebrating weddings, marking rites of passage, and welcoming or honoring of guests. Dancing provide the Agaar with adequate ways of verbal, physical, social, and emotional expression. Full of singing, clapping, and drumming, the Agaar traditional dances consist of a range of movements; some fast-faced and athletic and others graceful and slow. All consist of arm, feet, and body moments—every move and gesture is executed to tell a story or two.

There are five major dances of the Jieng and each tribal group has its dance. These included Bul, Magong, Ngok, Malual, and Guak dances. Out of these five major dances, the Agaar performed three major dances: Bul, Magong, and Guak dances.

Bul Dance

Bul, also known as *kobulo*, is a robust hopping dance both men and women perform. Although it is the major dance of Aliab, Bor, and Twii tribes, the Agaar perform it as a preliminary dance before their main dance, *Guak*. *Bul* dance, therefore, serves many purposes. It warms up the muscles before the main dancing and accommodates those with physical disabilities who can't perform *Guak* dance which requires extreme physical fitness.

Bul is a flirtation dance. To understand this, picture how alpha males attract females. In the natural world, females typically choose the best males by selecting those that produce the loudest, brightest, or strongest signals, and every beast tries to demonstrate these qualities in front of the herd to increase the chance of finding a mate. The same concept is incorporated in the *Bul* dance. Every male dancer's body is meticulously painted, his dance moves are unique and catchy, and he sings loud so his voice is above everyone else's. The females watch and listen attentively as the men sing and utter boasting phrases before choosing their dance partners.

Before the dance, the dancers run in a single line, and the procession of the *apäräpuööl* dancers snakes among the huts and pegs, as they jog from hearth to hearth to gain maximum exposure. Each dancer chants his poetic expressions or boasting phrases. This disorganization can sound chaotic to untrained ears. But trained ears distinguish every boasting phrase uttered.

Of course, every dancer wants to look his best. He is adorned from head to toe. His hair is trimmed and groomed into a mushroom-like shape, which is then dyed reddish or yellowish with cow urine based on an individual's taste. An elegant plume of ostrich feathers (the *nɔk*) is planted in the hair and set off with a brightly colored scarf. The warrior has two large ivory bangles on his upper arms and one or two smaller bracelets on his elbows or wrists. With the body meticulously painted with dung ash, he holds a collection of a thoroughly polished bundle of spears and a heavy fighting stick carved from ebony or rhino horn. Most distinguishing of all are the six scarification marks running from ear to ear, cut bone-deep, with no anesthetic, of course, when he transitioned from boyhood to manhood. His six lower teeth are removed, and this gives him volume and rhythm in his speeches and songs.

The dancers jog from village to village to gain maximum exposure. Now and then, the dancers get together and sing a song in a robust voice before they continue jogging in a line. Women don't jog; they watch silently. Soon, they choose dancing mates from these males.

Upon reaching the dancing ground, the group invades the staging ground and step on the drum itself or stop the drummer from playing the drum, completely interrupting the rhythm of those who are already singing and dancing. You must be a well-known warrior or a group of warriors to interrupt the dance and get away with it. Sometimes fights break out when a person with lower status steps on the drum. An immature bull can't disturb the alpha male in the herd and get away with it. The new group starts their song, which all the dancers sing as they perform a slow, marching dance as they move clockwise or anticlockwise. A man known for his clarity and beauty of his voice starts the song.

The following was the most popular *bul* song in our area in the 1980s:

The son of a gentleman migrated his bull in the afternoon,
The children of a mother were watching (in amusement)
   all things we, the owners of the beasts, were doing.
My name is Matung-boor [white-horned] because makuei's
   horns are white;
The bull of Mathei's son; its horns are like gourd flowers.
I move my big beast marial with nephews…
Our bulls with the son of Dhal Malith; we have mangar oxen;
These are the bull we migrate between December and April,
   heading to the swamp.
We moved our beasts to the land of Jul Machok . . .
My majok eats the grass in that area until he becomes sick
   with malaria.
But the red-nosed bull does not need modern medicine,
The only medicine he needs is awai (salty ground).

By now, the girls have joined in the dance. Each girl chooses her dancing partner or a group. When chosen, the young men engaged by getting closer to the girls, dancing, twisting, singing or shouting their bulls or oxen names with hands curved to emulate their beasts. The

other male dancers do the same thing to other girls, as scores of atten-
dants dance around the dancing ground. Foot jingles made from iron
or locally made from woven palm leaves filled with pebbles are worn
on the ankles, creating a sound that reverberates until the entire village
seems to be alive with the music. Then over 100 people form a giant
circle and dance. The men's voices sound like a wave, singing. Plumes
of dust hug their feet. The Bul dancing goes on for an hour before the
dancers switch to the main dance: Guak.

Guak *Dance*

After bul dance, the dancers start the main dance. The leading dance
of the Agaar *is Guak*, affectionately referred to as the high-jumping
dance. The old generation called it *Guak*, meaning "high jump." And
the new generation called it *Dhëëng-nhial. Dhëëng* means beautifulness,
handsomeness, or gentlemanliness. And *nhial* means up or sky. *Dhëëng-
nhial*, therefore, means displaying beauty in the sky.

Guak is an impressive dance of energy, power, and agility, often
fueled by rhythm provided by a combination of meticulous drumming,
clapping, and singing. Though the dance may appear rudimentary or
not exuberant, it carries a much more profound meaning and reason.
Unlike *Bul* dance, *Guak* is a dominance dance—a way a young warrior
demonstrates his strength, agility, and dominance to attract and retain
females. In other words, the *Guak* theme was based upon a dominant
male in the herd.

Dancers form a circle with the women inside the ring. Then one
male enters the loop to dance with the women. Women dance in a
pack, but two men can't dance at the same time. Two alpha males can't
control the same herd, can they?

The dancer inside the circle dances, the back of his heels touching
his buttocks as he jumps up as high as he can, with hands curved to
emulate the horns of a bull. He repeatedly makes high jump attacks,
charging left and right, trying to keep the women in a pack, just as
alpha males do with the herd. Sometimes, the dancer intentionally
kicks the straying female to keep her in the pack or to flirt with her.
Once a dancer achieves his maximum height and tires, usually after a
dozen or more jumps, he exits, and another man takes the center.

As men take turns executing high jumps with their hands curved, the women perform shuffling and scuffling moves as they dance with hands curved to emulate cows (to show feminism), getting closer to the men, and retreating flirtatiously. When her hands get tired, she dances with her hands down—she is a hornless cow (*acööt*).

All the while, the male dancers forming the circle are singing and clapping, matching the pitch and volume of their voices and hands to the heights of the jumps. The clapping is deafening (a single clapper cracks like a gunshot). The drumming is meticulous. The voices are loud, often punctuated by a grunt, chants of the men, and thrills of the women. The crescendo of the pressure encourages the warriors to jump even high higher. A lead singer, known for the clarity and attractiveness of his voice, sometimes calls out the name of each dancer praising them:

> *Ater, son of Machiek,*
> *He goes up as if he is related to birds.*
> *Marial, son of Majak,*
> *He goes up high in the sky.*
> *Majok, son of Maker,*
> *He loiters up there.*
> *I clap very loud,*
> *We are men who clap with cracks;*
> *Yes, I clap very loud when Machol dances!*

The dancers take turns leaping as high as they can to the music, to showcase their stamina and strength. A dancer is assessed primarily on his ability to jump up high while matching the percussive musical rhythm. The higher, the better. That is why the Agaar speak of "loitering up there in the sky" when they talk about a good dancer. The movement of his body or how well his hands are curved in the positions also matters.

Some dancers like to kick the women in his last jump. "The beast has gone wild," seems to be the message. A confused woman (*abuotbai*) who has never been to the cattle camp is always the victim of such brutality. She lacks milk in her diet, so she is weak and not quick enough to get out of the way in time. But the sturdy women of the cattle camp know how to dodge the kicks from the male dancers. With intricate movements of their feet, each woman dances while paying close attention to the man's progress. As soon as she anticipates a kick coming her way, she jumps out of the way, leaving the man to kick nothing but the air. Fearless women even catch a man's foot in mid-air, knocking the man down.

The intensification of *Dhëëng-nhial* is not static; it repeats from one level to another until ecstasy, euphoria, possession, saturation, and satisfaction have been reached. *Dheeng nhial* is powerful, eloquent, and productive; it is a complete and self-sufficient language of its own. It defines the Agaar.

Magong Dance

When the dancers are tired of the high-jumping dance, they start the *Magong* dance. *Magong* is a sharp and vigorous stamping of the feet with the hands curved in the emulation of bulls and oxen. While punishing the ground with his feet, the man chants or calls out his bull's name at the top of his voice. The female dancer twists her hands behind her back, tiptoes, one foot slightly ahead of the other, the chest extended forward to expose the breasts, and the buttocks extending backward to expose the buttocks, as she shakes her body in motions and waves, dancing to the beat of the drum.

It is mostly small boys that dance *Magong* because they are too weak to perform the high-jumping dance. Usually, small boys and girls participate in the *Bul* dance with the warriors. When *Guak* dance starts, the boys and small girls also start the *Magong* dance.

Just like Bul, *Magong* also originated from the Agaar before being adopted by the Rek Jieng (Tonj, Twic, Apuk, Aguok, etc.) as their major dance. The Rek still called it *loor Agaar* (Agaar dance).

Nyomluel Dance

At the end of all dances, *Dheeng-nhial*, *Bul*, and *Magong*, dancers relax with the *Nyomluɛl* dance. *Nyomluɛl* is the dance of selecting and rejecting. Dancers often form one big circle or line with men on one side and women on the other. As they sing and clap, two or more girls dance toward the men and they choose one or more men by stepping on their feet or pointing at them. The wanted man or men will be delighted, for they are the most handsome ones in the dance. Then the chosen man picks another man to challenge him. Both of them dance toward the girls, and they choose one girl by placing their sticks on her shoulder. The woman must to push one stick off her shoulder, leaving the chosen man's stick on her shoulder.

Dany Dance

Another dance is *Dany*. Women exclusively dance the *Dany*. They form a circle and clapping and singing; no drum is needed. While most girls clap and sing, a few girls haul themselves in the air dancing, some inside and others outside the circle. Unlike *Dhëeng Nhial*, where men jump up high and fold their legs backward until the heels touch the buttocks, women jump up with their legs straight.

Endurance and jumping high are the aim of the dance. As they dance, the women challenge each other as to who can jump higher or last longer during the dance. The dance theme is based on an elegant series of leaps, because in the tall elephant grass, survival depends on high leaping and endurance. Therefore, the dance is a symbolic of outrunning and outmaneuvering a predator.

Even though it is performed in every gathering, *Dany* is often performed in the evening right after the supper meal. Girls who arrive at the dancing ground early can sing a song mocking those who don't attend, encouraging them to attend quickly:

Girls, what is it now?
Why are you ruining the dance?
Why are you not attending?
Is it because the food is not ready yet?
Is it because your cows are not milked yet?

Dany songs are long, repetitive, and full of cultural references and metaphors. Because it's for women, *Dany* is where women practice their freedom of speech. Sometimes, they sing song against the men. The following is a song composed by a woman who was married to an abusive man:

My private part has climbed up the anthill.
I tell her to look out for me (find me a good man),
But she brings the garbage.
That's why I say to my paternal relative:
'I have found one thing about my private part;
I tell her to look out for me;
But she keeps bringing the garbage'.
When there is a little in the bed,
The man exasperates.
And he runs to a city, a place of two bosses;
The young man hits me like a dog
The old man hits me in the back of my head
I'm f**ked up, girl!
'You deserve to be in prison;
You are like a gossiper;
You are worse than a witch.'

Ruäi Dance

Another Agaar dance is ruai. Performed by females only, ruai is a type of dance performs in marriage ceremonies. The name ruai means marriage or relationship. Ruai is an elaborate stepping dance with the emphasis placed on the dominant foot. So the act of dancing is called stepping of the dance (*ruai käj*).

Ruäi, like all other Agaar dances, is tonal. The most common instrument used with the dance is a bell, accompanied by the human voice and body. The dance is performed by two or more dancers moving in exact unison with the tune. One of the most striking parts of the dany dance is the polyrhythmic nature of the movements, complemented by stamping of the feet, swaying of the body, and swinging of the arms. As she sings, the dancer can synchronize different parts of her body and moves them to the same rhythm and beat. For example, the dancer swings her left hand in motion to keep the balance while matching the rhythm, flicks her right hand to ring the bell to the desired melody, stamp both feet with the empathy on the dominant foot, and at the same time, she moves her entire body to the rhythms and beats.

The most significant movement in the dany dance is the ending. The dancers don't stop dancing until they are engaged in a process known as *nguang*. As the dancers dance and sing, a woman of the house would fetch an old pot, gourd or tin. With the device in hand, she joins the dancers, trying to match their tune and rhythm. When the time is appropriate, she suddenly bangs the device on the floor until it breaks into pieces, the louder, the better, and at the same time, she thrills at the top of her voice: Ayii-yii-yiiii! This completely interrupts the dancers who now stop dancing and singing to allow the welcoming dancer to utter her boasting phrases. If she does not have one, she chants her husband's phrases or songs. Or she shouts out the poetic expression of her clan or totem. Each clan has its poetic expression connecting them to their totem. "*Lou maguäät*," is the chant used by the Palou clan (people who are related to bamboo), capitalizing on the shape of the bamboo, long and curve (*maguäät*). "*Maayöl dhuur*," is a chant used by Pation (people who are related to the fox), capitalizing on the fox's bushy tail. "*Maager ruaal*" or "*luɛc-luɛc diïtdë*," is used by those who are related to the sausage tree, capitalizing on the shape of the branches (*maager*) or the size of the "hanging" (*luɛc-luɛc*) sausage fruit. The dance usually ends after this ritual.

Wak Dance

The final dance of Agaar is the wak dance. Wak is a seasonal dance performed once a year by warriors. It begins when young men (and occasionally young women) go through a process called "sleeping" (*tëc*). All warriors selects their finest cows, including lactating ones, and go to a secluded camp where they will do nothing other than drinking milk and sleeping in order to get fat. The fatter, the better because it means you are wealthy. Because the idea is to get fat and sleek, the participants are called *acëliib*, meaning fat and sleek.

The fatting session usually occurs in the rainy season between June and December, when there is plenty of grass for cattle to produce milk. While at the fatting camp, the *acëliib* compose wak songs and practice their dance moves. Each warrior has two or three songs in which the entire group of up to fifty or more warriors can learn the songs. In December, when food is plentiful at the villages, the *acëliib* return to their villages and towns to showcase their songs, dance moves and fatness.

Remember, it is prestigious to attend these fatting camps annually. It means you are rich. But not every young person can afford to participate in the sleeping camp every year. If you have no cows, you stay home to "eat disgusting food and pick your ass with the index finger," said a young man from our area, named Majok Agok, who attends fatting camp every year. Majok sang the following Wak song with his crew:

> *We don't stay home to gossip.*
> *Every year we sleep in the fatting camp;*
> *I don't spend autumn at home,*
> *To pick my ass with the index finger,*
> *I don't do that!*

During the harvest time, when food was plentiful at home, the *aciliib* return to the villages and towns to showcase their fatness and sleekness by performing their wak dancing and singing. These songs are often long and repetitive, and they could be confusing or even meaningless to untrained ears or listeners.

As a small boy, I had a very sharp memory, so I was very good at cramming wak songs. Whenever I heard a song one time, I would know the whole song from beginning to end. So, when *aciliib* arrived to dance in Pachong, big girls like to employ me. My job was to cram the songs of their chosen man. Later on, the girl would learn the songs from me. I liked the job. I mean, who wouldn't? It allowed me to hang out with big girls. You have to be insane to hate a job like that! I crammed many songs by famous singers and repeatedly sang them to the big girls who gave me the assignment. This explains why I still remember all the songs, more than 30 years later.

One of the young men that the girls asked me to cram his songs was Majok Agok, famously known by his oxen name *Muor-ci-mang* ("the ox that's slapped with exotic coloring"). Majok Agook, from Patiop Clan, one of the greatest entertainers in the Pacong area, was known as *alueeth* (liar). You see, in Jieng, the term *'alueeth'* has both positive and negative senses. In a negative connotation, alueeth means "liar." But in a positive sense, it means someone who is exceptionally creative and entertaining.

So, Majok Agook was an *alueeth* in a positive sense, because he was very creative and entertaining in dancing, singing, or talking. Remember, members of Patiop (people relating to the fox— the shrewdest animal), can also act just like the fox. Majok was such an example.

Majok Agook was one of the greatest composers. He was particularly famous for composing songs against his paternal uncles, insulting and criticizing them for not giving cattle for his bride-price. An uncle, who refused to help Majok, would die in shame. Every time Majok Agook went to the fattening camp, his uncles in question would be worried about the guilt they would endure again this year due to the shameful songs.

Most of his songs are inappropriate to be repeated here, but the following are short abstracts of the mild ones:

> *But my father has died; He's in the ground.*
> *And the Patiop clan of my father left me hanging in the middle.*
> *What a mystery that has found me.*
> *It's a big-headed-dick-thing (kë ŋuäŋ ŋuel) that has found me!*

His uncles didn't help Majok marry a wife that year, so he threatened to compose even more derogatory songs. He was not joking. The following year, he sang:

> *Everything I say is accepted by all clans:*
> *Kook, Panyar, Thiyith, and two Athoi: Gony and Dhiei.*
> *But it's not accepted by these dogs:*
> *the Patiop clan, where I belong!*

No one exempted from Majok's insults, including relatives who lived in towns.

> *When I visited my uncle in the city (Rumbek);*
> *He welcomed me with a big cup (nur) of a very sweet juice.*
> *I told my uncle, you sweeten my mouth with the juice,*
> *but you haven't given me the cattle*
> *for my bride-price to marry a wife*
> *so that my crotch can be sweet, too.*
> *You haven't done a damn thing to me.*

When Majok Agook finally got married, his uncles were off the hook. But he turned his attention to corrupted tax collectors in Pachong. He composed many songs against corruption in the tax collection. The songs' main target was Maker Waar, who was the meanest tax collector in Pacong areas. If you didn't pay your taxes on time, Maker Waar would shoot his gun up, then demanded you to pay extra cows for the "wasted government's bullets." If you refused, Maker Waar would confiscate your cows and take you to jail, as well. One-eyed, Maker Waar was a former Anyanya One fighter, so no one messed with him. Majok Agook composed the following song against him and fellow tax collectors:

> *One tax collector is sent to Pan Awac,*
> *Another one in Pan Agong Machol Noi, then Majak Ajok*
> *   and Cueicok*
> *The tax collector leaves early in the morning to collect taxes*
> *   on the other side of the road.*
> *When he returns, he spends some of the tax money on the tea*
> *   and alcohol.*
> *When the big boss asks him, 'where are the taxes?'*
> *The tax collector fucks his ass saying, 'There are no taxes'*
> *No taxes? You spent them on tea and alcohol.*
> *Then, they say taxes are overdue.*
> *Overdue where? It is within the tax center.*
> *I wish the cow can poke out the only one eye of Maker Waar.*
> *The one eye must go, gone forever!*

Like dany dance where women practice their freedom of speech, Wak is where young men practice their freedom of speech through song, as shown by Majok Agok. But the majority of the dancers don't insult their relatives like Majok Agook. Instead, they dedicate their wak song to their parents, relatives, and clans, as well as their oxen, bulls, and their girlfriends.

The Agaar traditional dances are slowly but surely disappearing. During conflict and war, efforts to secure the well-being and safety of one's family replaced all these traditional dances and recreational activities. The youth devoted their time to protecting their cattle, people, and property. Others were displaced from their traditional fields and homes and ended up in cities, towns or refugee camps where they spent many idle hours. To keep themselves preoccupied, the youth spent their time playing board games, cards, or watching soccer. In towns and cities, modern dances such as African disco dance, rap, and reggae are replacing traditional dances.

Games

Adiir

Adiir is an outdoor game played by two opposing teams; each player uses a stick curved at the striking end to hit a small, hard ball into their opponent's goal. The number of people available determines the number of players on each team. If there are 20 players, then each side would have ten players.

The ball, called *dök*, is made from locally available materials. Sap from the *dök* tree is collected and fashioned into a ball, or plastics are collected, melted, and fashioned into a ball. Sometimes a piece of wood is cut and chiseled into a ball. Because there are no protective devices, *dök* made from sap is encouraged because it is too soft to hurt someone; wooden and melted plastic balls are discouraged because they hurt people.

The objective of the game is to hit a ball with a stick to a goal. There are no goal posts, though. Lines are drawn at each end; the ball should cross it to count as a goal. Every time the ball goes into the goal, a point is awarded to that team. The team with the most goals at the end of the game is the winner. In the event of both sides scoring the same amount of goals, a draw is called.

The play starts in the center of the field. In a face-off, two players, one from each team, face each other with the ball in the shallow hole between them. After alternately tapping the ground and then his opponent's stick several times, each player tries to strike the ball, thus putting it into play. There are various provisions for placing the ball into play in case it goes off the field—the game restarts by a pass-back in the center of the field after a goal is scored.

The outfield players consist of defenders, midfielders, and attackers. The amount of each position varies depending on the formation that the team adopts. There are no designated goalkeepers.

A goal is scored when a player hits the ball over the line. The ball has to be struck with the player's stick, and any use of the body was an infringement. You could catch the ball and place it in the right spot for a better hit, provides the opponent is far away.

For boys to make the game exciting, each team counts their scores at the end of the game. Each score represented a girl or woman. If your team scored ten goals, for example, and there were five players, each player had two scores, which equates two women. When a team has fewer scores, some members of the team would have no wives and would die unmarried which is very shameful. If that is the case, the next day you have to play harder to score more goals.

Wet

The most popular game played by the Agaar is *Wet*—a board game commonly performed by the Jieng and all other African tribes. Played by two or many people divided into two teams, *wet* is a game where players take turns distributing the counters around the board, and each player tries to capture the opponent's counters.

Though wooden or clay boards are used, the easiest and most common way is to scrape small hollows in the leveled ground consisting of four rows, with each row having ten to fifteen holes. Each player or team has two rows of thirty hollows. Whether they carve a piece of board or scrap on the ground, the hollow must be round and large enough to hold fifteen or more counters which are accumulated during the distribution of the play. The counters are usually seeds or stones that change hands several times in the game.

To begin the game, each hollow contains two counters, making 120 counters in sixty hollows. Each player has thirty holes in two rows: an interior and exterior. Before the play begins, each player must "mix" his counters in his two rows. The player chooses one hollow and picks up all the counters in it. Then he distributes them by dropping a single counter into the next hollow in an anticlockwise direction, a single counter into the hole after, and so on. When the last counter lands in a hollow, he picks up the counter in that hollow and continues the distribution. This is known as "sowing." The mixing ends when a player's last seed falls in an empty hollow. This is known as "sleeping."

There are many ways players decide who plays first. Both players can start mixing at the same time, and whoever drops his last counter in an empty hollow or "sleeps first" will start the play. Or one player will hide a stone or seed in one of his fists and the opponent chooses between the two fists. If the opponent correctly guesses which fist holds the counter, the opponent starts the game. Sometimes, the winner lets loser start the game.

The purpose of *Wet* is to capture all the opponent's counters so they can't make further moves. The act of capturing the counters is called *cam* ("eating"). The act of playing *Wet* is known as *cam* or "eating" *wet*. The most common tactic used in the game is to capture the counter on the right side of the opponent where the counters loop, forcing the opponent to empty most of the hollows on the other side of the board to cover the empty holes where the counters were captured. This is known as *tök nhom* or "the cutting of the head." Or you can destroy the left side of the opponent. This is "cutting the tail." Or you can destroy the middle; "the cutting of the back in half."

After mixing the counters, the real play begins. The aim of the game is to capture the opponent's counters; each player calculates his moves that will loop many times and catch the opponent's counters while defending his seeds from being captured. Then the player chooses a non-empty hollow from one of his rows, picks up all the counters contained in it, and drops a single counter into the next hollow in an anticlockwise direction, and a single seed into the following hollows. When the last counter falls in one hole in the interior row, the opponent's row directly adjacent to the hollow where the last counter lands are captured, provides that those two rows contain counters. If one or both rows are empty, nothing will happen, and the player continues to distribute the counters. When the last counter falls into an empty hole or sleeps, the move ends, and the opponent starts his move to recapture what was captured from him.

Riddles

One of the most enigmatic games the Agaar play is the game of riddles (*meek* or guessing), where a player comes up with a term or phrase others have to guess. Riddles are simple and elegant ways to communicate a lot of meaning in a few words.

Riddles play an important role in the traditions of Jieng speech, conversation, and creativity. Played by children, the riddles are presented in a series of organized sessions, and the search for a solution to each riddle implies competition, as everyone wants to see who emerges victorious: the player who proposes the riddle, or the opponent who guesses the correct answer.

Played by young boys and girls, riddles are normally played in the evening after supper and before going to bed. Adults don't take part, but may be part of the audience who laughs or arbitrates if confusion arises among the players. Adults secretly learn which children are eloquent and show ingenuity during the play.

Like all other activities, riddles are based on observations of nature. However, with riddles, the player is expected to come up with legitimate statements or questions and the listener is expected to provide quick, witty answers. For example, "Guess which two people compete forever?" The answer is hands or legs, when walking. "Guess which two bulls face each other, but don't meet to fight." The answer is heaven and earth. "Guess the guests who eat with you even if you don't invite them." The answer is flies.

Riddles can also be just a sentence that makes you have a sudden realization. For example, "Guess three people who arrive at the same time: one goes with air, one sinks into the ground, and other one coils up on the ground." The answer is urine, farts, and feces.

The purpose of the riddles, besides being fun, is to help sharpen children's minds and open up new thought processes and improve their memory retention.

Tongue Twisters

In addition to riddles, another important game children play is tongue twisters. This is when a child attempts to recite tricky terms and phrases as fast as possibly without tripping over or jumbling the words or phrases. While riddles improve cognitive capabilities, tongue twisters are designed to enhance pronunciation skills and improve a child's oral and speak functions.

The tongue twisting game requires a player (speaker) to utter, without faltering, a sequence of phrases that are difficult in articulation, specifically designed for this function. With each word or phrase has its own basic meaning and pronunciation, the intention of the game is that the speaker (player) will likely mispronounce the word or even confuse the meaning, thus generating laughers among the players (judges) who are listening to the speaker. For example:

Ee Nhial en acë Nhial luɔp nhial bë ya lɔ nuaai nhian nhial, go Nhial löny go nhial duɔɔny. ("It's Nhial who followed Nhial upstairs to tickle his testicles, so Nhial fell and broke his knee.")

The main function of the game is not only to demonstrate oral literature, but also test and improve children fluency in the language. It also teaches children to avoid the embarrassment of misspeaking. So sexual matters are incorporated in the play and children (both boys and girls) recite these phrases without shame. For example: *Bït awec meei në ŋaap thar* ("the womanly thing is digging a root beneath the n*gaap*-tree"). In this phrase, it's easy for a child to say, *bït awec meëi në maa thar* ("the womanly thing is digging a root beneath my mother"), which will generate laughter. To avoid such embarrassment, the player will practice many times to get it right. Without even knowing he or she is not only mastering the articulation but also increasing her vocabularies.

Puzzles

In addition to riddles and tongue twisters, children also play oral puzzles. The puzzles are told in form of stories called *akökööl or alaŋkööl.* This game tests a child's ingenuity and knowledge. In this game, a player provides a puzzle, and the solver is expected to put pieces together logically to arrive at the correct or fun solution. For example, you could have a sheep, a lion, and sorghum grain. You want to cross a river with them. There is one boat that only takes two things at a time. What do you do? In this mystery, the player must think logically. If he takes the lion across, leaving the sheep and the grain behind, the sheep will eat the grain. If he takes the grain, the lion with eat the sheep.

To solve the problem, first you must take the sheep and cross the river with it, leaving the grain and the lion on the other side. The lion will not eat the grain. Then you leave the sheep on the other side and you come back to get the lion. You leave the lion on the other side and bring back the sheep to the first location. Leave the sheep and then take the grain to the other side. Leave the grain with the lion and then come back to get the sheep.

Oral puzzles are mystery riddles intended to improve a child's thinking and problem-solving skills.

Tricksters

Tricksters also reflect the Agaar's environment, daily life, and worldview. Stories about heroes, tricksters, and monsters provide an allegorical form of explanation for how the world works. A trickster can be a character in folktales that usually appears as an animal with human traits—like being able to talk. Trickster tales are used not only to entertain, but to teach lessons about how to behave and treat other people. The Agaar people have used trickster stories to teach their children for many years. Tricksters are smart and they use their knowledge to play tricks, bend the rules, or solve problems.

The fox is considered the most elusive trickster of all the animals. Nicknamed Muorkueu or Kueudit, he is mischievous, cheeky, or a rascal. Kueudit, with some exaggerated human-like characteristics, can be reckless with a humorous side and create havoc for no reason. The trickster dupes other animals. The following is the story of how Kueudit solved dispute between two beasts: lion and hyena.

Once upon a time, a lion and a hyena visited a distance relative. The hyena was given a pregnant heifer, and the lion had a bull. On their way back, the beasts spent their night near a pool. It was getting dark, and both beasts were exhausted, so they decided to spend the night. At night, the hyena's pregnant cow gave birth. While the hyena was still sleeping, the lion took the calf and put it beside his bull.

In the morning, the hyena woke and noticed the calf in front of the lion's bull. When he asked, the lion said that his bull gave birth.

"My bull gave birth last night," the lion said.

"How is that possible?" asked the hyena. "The calf is mine because my cow was pregnant."

"I don't know about that," said the lion.

The case was taken to court, presided over by all the animals. All the other animals spoke, but to no avail as the lion kept saying his bull gave birth.

Kueudit was not in the court, and other animals wanted his opinion. When they summoned him, Kueudit arrived, carrying a pot of water.

"My father gave birth last night, so I'm taking this water to him to take a bath."

"Stop it," the lion roared. "How can your father, a man, give birth? That's impossible!"

"Exactly!" Kueudit said. "My father did not give birth, and neither did your bull."

Case closed. Kueudit's wisdom had solved the problem.

The actions of a trickster can even change the course of a tribe's history. For example, Patiop, who are related to the fox, are considered very shrewd.

Folktales

Through tales, morals and values are taught to children. The following story about a young man with a talking skull teaches a lesson.

Once upon a time, there was a very arrogant young man. He always thought he was the wisest. He liked to argue, but he did not listen to anyone. His father kept warning him, "Son, stop being arrogant. I'm worried about you."

"Don't worry, Dad," the young man said. "Nothing is going to happen to me. You know how smart I am."

"Remember, son," Father said, "sometimes, an individual can die because of his own mind."

The young man did not listen to the old man's advice.

One day, the young man went to play in a nearby forest, and he found a skull in the forest. "Oh, my God," he said. "How can anyone die in this peaceful forest?" He suddenly remembered what his father told him, 'anyone can die because of his thinking,' so he started laughing and kicking the skull, saying, "You died because of your thinking."

The next day, he returned to the forest and started kicking the skull again, "You died because of your own thinking." On the third day, he returned to the forest and did the same thing. As he was about to leave, the skull spoke: "Yes, young man, I died because of my thinking."

The young man was shocked. "You can speak? Well, tell me then, how did you die?"

"I already told you," said the skull, "I died because of my thinking. But what I did or how I died is irrelevant now, because I'm already dead. But let me tell you something, young man," the skull continued. "You will die because of your thinking too."

"No, I won't," said the young man.

"Yes, you will," said the skull.

The next day, the young man returned and kicked the skull again: "You died because of your own thinking."

"You will die because of your thinking too," said the skull.

"No, I won't.

"Yes, you will."

After doing the same thing for a week, the young man finally ran home one day and told the story to people."There is a talking skull in the forest," he said. But no one believed him. Everyone was tired of his arrogance, so no one even paid attention to him anymore. The young men insisted that they should come and see the talking skull. Eventually, the young man swore that if the skull would not talk, they could kill him.

The young man's dad tried to convince him not to make such foolish promise, but he was stubborn. "Come on, Dad, you know how smart I am. I would not bet my life on it if it weren't true."

Finally, the warriors, who were tired of his cockiness, took their spears and followed him. He led them to the skull and said, "This is the skull. Do you think I'm lying? Watch, it will talk. He kicked the skull like he always did, saying, "You've died because of your thinking." But the skull did not reply. Knowing people would kill him, he kept kicking and talking to the skull, but the skull did not respond.

Knowing he had lied, the warriors killed the young man. As they were about to leave, the skull finally spoke. "I told you, young man, you will die because of your own thinking!"

The warriors returned home, and people inquired whether or the young man was lying. Their response was, "Lying or not, he died because of his thinking."

The narrator often concluded by providing the moral of the story: "Cocky or arrogant people talk a lot, but don't listen. It is always wise to listen more and talk less. There is a reason God gave you two ears and one mouth."

Material Cultures

Dress

IN THE OLD DAYS, the Agaar, like any other African tribes, did not consider clothes necessary for warmth and protection. This was because the weather was consistently warm. Instead of clothing, people developed body ash-coating, piercing, and scarification. For this reason, the Agaar wore few clothes.

The original clothes were made from animal skin. The clothes were called *buoong* (*buɔɔŋ*). There are no examples of early Agaar's *buoong* have survived because the clothing was perishable. Leather clothing could be as simple as small aprons. The Agaar's traditional apron for women consisted of two pieces; a back apron, called *buong ciën,* and front piece, called *buong tueng*, both tied around the waist. Some garments were left unadorned, while others were decorated with shells, beads, or metal ornaments.

Skin clothing was processed the same way as the sleeping mats. You laid the sheep, goat, or deer hide on the leveled ground, hair side down, and used the long-bladed knife to remove all the flesh from the skin. Then the leather was left to dry all day. When dried, you removed the hair using the back of a knife blade or spearhead, and then rinsed the skin in clean water. Then the hide was designed and cut into two oval pieces that covered back and front of a woman. The parts were then tanned soft with oil, fat, or animal brains. And then it was handcrafted into aprons and richly decorated with traditional geometric designs. The wearer also wore copper rings, bungles, and beads around their necks, ankles, and arms.

Only married women had reasons to wear *buong* clothing at all times: (1) pregnancies and births had altered their bodies, and (2) they were off the market so no need to show their bodies. Unmarried girls had no reason to wear clothes because pregnancies and births did not alter their bodies. Men proudly went nude. In the dance, they wore wildcat, leopard, or Columbus monkey hide, which they tied around their buttocks. A mature man of higher status wore leopard skin, which he slung over one shoulder.

A headdress called *jööng* was an immense, intricately crafted piece of headgear, like a fancy hat a designated warrior wore in society. The traditional headdresses, which were made from extraordinary fabric or cloth, were typically decorated with feathers, beads, or cowry shells. Along with these headdresses, the mighty warrior would wear leopard or wildcat skin, the *dhök*, which was tied around the waist and secured in front. In the battle, such a warrior was the target of the enemy; they wanted to kill him and get the trophy, which was why *jööng* was given to a warrior that could never be killed easily.

Gradually, the skin garments were replaced with traded clothes between the 17th and the 18th centuries. Women wore dresses and skirts and men wore robes called *jalabia*, a loose gown of Arab origin. Older men wore, and still wear, a long robe which covered the legs. Unlike Arab robes, which were only white, the Agaar robes came in different colors like red, blue, green, and black, just like the color of their cows.

The *apäräpuööl* used a short robe which ended on the thighs or knees, made for someone always willing to spring in action. It was called *cobwong* (*cobwoŋ*) because the cloth was so beautiful and pricy that a young person would "chase the cow" (*cobwong*) to the market to sell it and buy the piece of cloth. *Cobwong* robes were worn with *totin* shorts.

Now Western clothes are prevalent. In Rumbek, people dress nicely. It's a must to dress up when visiting someone or going to the market. Everyone keeps their most beautiful clothes for visiting or going to parties—young men wear skinny leg jeans with shirts. Men wear suits and ties.

When dressing up for an Agaar ceremony, one should not disregard the use of accessories as part of the ensemble: beads, earrings, necklaces, and other accessories all play an essential role in completing the clothing. No matter how poor one is, he or she always keeps clean clothes for special occasions.

Beads and Jewelry

Even though the Jieng groups share common traits, each group has its own distinct artistic traditions. Traditional arts, including basketry, pottery, beadwork, wood and ivory carving generally serve practical purposes. The Agaar produce a wide variety of tools, utensils, and ornaments on wood, bark, bone, and many other natural materials.

Like any other Nilotic groups, the Agaar engage in elaborate bodily beautification arts, making beads that they wear around their necks and waists. Worn by both men and women of all ages, these beads vary in size, length, color, texture, and shape. Because of their beauty and craftsmanship, beads transfer their essence to the wearer. Young women, for example, wear strings of beads around their waist for a sexy appearance and to entice a suitor.

In addition to beauty, beadwork is also used for communicating cultural and social messages, like the wearer's age or marital status. *Biiny,* the smallest beads with elaborate colors, are worn by young men and women. Old men wear bigger beads called *döök.* Infant beads are often mixed with cowry shells to protect them from harm, such as witchcraft. Brides or grooms-to-be always wear *guën Jäng* "Jieng bead")—a rare and expensive green and white beads.

Before modern beads arrived, the Jieng made beads of bone, claw, paw, stone, seed, and ostrich eggshell. Ostrich shells were very valuable. In fact, the first traders who visited traded ostrich shells and feathers. Porcupine quills and bird claws were also used as beads, and men and women wore them.

Currently, some beads come in the form of rosary and arm bracelets with either person's name engraved on it, or the flag. Town boys wear chains which they adopt from rappers and hip-hop artists. Urban dwellers wear gold and diamond necklaces. But traditional beads, including Jang, are still important in rural areas.

Basketry

Jieng men and women make a variety of baskets and mats out of plant materials such as reeds, grasses, and leaves which can be used for sleeping, storing, or carrying goods. Some items are plaited and others are sewn. A common basket known as *ahoth (aɣöth)* is made from strands of plant fiber and twigs which are soaked and then twined or woven to make a basket. In some community, baskets are used for carrying not only good but also babies. Such baskets are called *diaany*. Bee hives are also woven.

Most of the woven goods can be multifunctional. For example, winnowing trays for flour can also be used for serving food such as groundnut, sugarcane, or fruit. They can also be used for lids covering pots, bowls, or trays.

Most woven items are used as containers for serving food, storing items, or carrying goods. Some baskets function as tools such as traps for fish or rodents, and strainers or sieves for flour or homemade beer. On top of that, basket techniques are applied to other tasks, including curtains and framework for thatched roofs.

Animal Hide

The most important bedding items are mats made from either plant material or hides. Mats made from hides are smooth, durable, and expensive. They come in different colors and shapes.

To make a cowhide sleeping rug, first stretch a freshly skinned hide on level ground, and peg it down at the edges to keep it in place. Lay it out with the fur side down, and scrape off all the fat, tissue, and flesh still attached to the skin. It is crucial not to leave any of this behind, as it will render the hide useless. Also, you have to be more careful when scraping off the fur with a sharp blade; otherwise you will make unnecessary holes on the hide. When dried you use a knife, small hoe, or blade to scrape off the fur and then you cut the edges to make it either oval shaped or rectangular. If you need extra cushioning, leave the fur or hair on.

Shields are produced from buffalo hide because it is thick.

Weaving Mats

In addition to cowhide rugs, mats are also crucial. They are made from plant materials such as palm leaves and papyrus. The papyrus mats are mostly used in villages where palm trees grow and papyrus is used in cattle camps in Sudd, the largest swamp in the world, where papyrus plants grow. The papyrus mat is called *ayiɛk* and palm leaves mats are *birïc*. Both are woven differently.

The papyrus (*ayiɛk*) mat is easy to make. You cut the papyrus and leave them to dry in the sun. Make sure the pieces are same size and shape. When dried, use rope and needle to join them together.

Making palm-leaf mats is more challenging. First, you pull away the fronds from the branch and trim the edges of the fronds and strip the palm leaves into thinner sections. You can either remove the stick running at the middle of the fronds, or leave them on. Mats with fronds left on are durable. Place the required leaflets side by side on the leveled floor. Take another leaflet or a couple of leaflets and weave through the leaflets on the floor in an above and below pattern. Creative individuals insert different colors to create intricate patterns. Continue adding the leaflets until both sides are equal or larger. Make sure you push each row snugly against the preceding row and make points at the row ends. Continue weaving until you reach the right size, shape, and length. Finally, tuck the last remaining warp fronds into the weave from points on the last side, to finish the edges. Trim the edges and other protruding pieces.

Weaving can only be done when the palm rushes are slightly dampened to avoid breakage. Weavers usually work early in the morning or late in the evening when the condition or atmosphere is cool to moisten the rushes. He must wet his rushes constantly because when they are dry, they are brittle and can break easily.

The mat is ready for use or sale. A brand new mat can be rough at first, but smoothens when used. Sleeping mats are also multifunctional. In addition to sleeping, they can be used for wrapping and carrying goods, and for cover in cold or wet weather.

Blacksmith

A blacksmith, called *ajuong (ajuɔŋ)*, creates and repairs objects made from iron. Even though blacksmiths do not have a high status in the community, they are admired for their work. They use scrap irons to make tools and weapons such as spears, axes, bells, bangles, saucepans, hooks, hoes, and many other objects used by the Agaar for various functions.

In the early 1980s, there were several blacksmiths in Pacong and I spent my entire time watching and even helping them. Several things were needed. The first thing was to build a forge by digging a big hole in the ground. The size of the hole depended on what type of tools had to be produced, as bigger tools needed bigger forges. Sometimes, a wall was built around the forge, especially when it was windy. Two circular walls were built a few feet away from the hole. Two tunnels were burrowed, connecting the walls and the hole. Two pieces of soft leather, especially produced for this purpose, were attached on top of the wall. The two fluffy pieces of leather generated air which passed through the tunnel into the hole which was filled with charcoal. Using both hands, I sat on a stool and pumped the forge all day. I did this for fun.

Anvil is another tool the *ajuong* needs. The anvil is the tool used beneath the work the smithy is hitting. They are made of either forged or cast steel so it withholds the brutality of the blacksmith's force. The anvil helps the blacksmith by rebounding the smith's hammer with the same amount of power, which helps make the job less strenuous.

The blacksmiths also need hammers. Blacksmithing hammers come in various shapes, weights, and head styles that perform the different techniques of manipulating metal. Each is used to strike the metal to control the metal's movement. In addition to the hammer, many other tools are used to hold the metal in place while the blacksmith hits and manipulates the metal. Blacksmith's tongs and flyers are used to pick up and hold hot pieces of metal. They are generally made of wrought iron or steel and have large, flat, smooth jaw surfaces that do not scratch the work.

Heating the metal is the first step in blacksmithing to manipulate the metal. It has to be heated to the perfect temperature. When iron is heated in a charcoal fire to white-hot temperatures, skilled blacksmiths move the metal with the same ease as clay. Using hammers as an extension of their hands, they could model any shape they desired upon their anvils.

In blacksmithing, hitting the metal accurately is more crucial than merely hitting the metal with great force. There are specific tools used in the process of hitting that helped the blacksmith achieve higher accuracy and precision.

Blacksmiths make and repair hoes, axes, bells, spears, hooks, spoons, saucepans, bowls, earrings, bangles, and many other items throughout the Agarland.

A renowned singer of kêp songs, Dit Mariik Dit, praises a blacksmith who made beautification accessories (*ajaac*) for his ox. Dit who owns a hornless, white ox, the *mabor-acööt*, composes a song, a very famous one. The song is long and repetitive, but the following is an abstract:

We have a manufacturer (of accessories).
If you describe a designer, I say Maltih Abong is the one.
I didn't know Adol, where Malith Abong and Mabor Mawat,
*   was where prestigious people live.*
If God knows, anyone who has helped me will be healthy
*   until I pay him back.*
Blacksmith has many mysterious tools: anvil, many other
*   devices, and a flyer.*
I wish the son of Abong will never get sick.
I brought my ox's accessories from Malith Abong, who promised
*   to produce them.*
The son of Abong produced the accessories by jamming it on
*   the anvil and giving it to*
Mabor to cut it...
I say this to God with my whole heart: If another sinister
*   comes, Malith Abong will remain*
like Noah... To show [carry on] his father's name.

Traditional Arts of Molding Clay

One of the ancient arts and crafts of the Agaar is pottery. From cooking pots to storage containers to tobacco pipes, pottery remains a useful artwork to this day. In rural areas, villagers prepare cooking in clay pots rather than aluminum cookware because they believe food cooked with modern cookware does not have flavor. Additionally, clay pots are used as water storage containers. Unlike tins and other metal storage which contaminate water with rust, clay containers keep water cool and safe from contamination. Even urban dwellers have adopted clay water storage because it saves energy compared to fridges.

Pots look simple, but they are difficult to make. To be a potter, you need patience and determination, then you need a clay source, a fire, and of course the skill.

In our village Biling Daldiar, our neighbor Aluel Mariel, had mastered pottery. She processed cooking and frying pots, water pots, bowls, and many other products which she sold not only to locals but also to towns like Pachong and Rumbek. Her two sons were my friends, and we ate together, so I spent most of my time watching her work. Sometimes, she would ask us to accompany her to mine clay because she feared the wild animals if she went alone.

First, she collected the clay. Finding clay sources and mining it are not easy rituals. There are two places where clay is found: (1) Along the Naam River and its tributaries, and (2) from termite hills built in clay soil. After digging the clay with a hoe and carrying it home with a basket, she used a pestle to pound the clay and sieve it into fine powder. Stones and other foreign objects were picked out by hand. Then she broke an old pot and beat it down to make a temper. Sometimes, Aluel used chopped straw or goat or sheep dung instead of the old pot. The function of the temper is to prevent the pots from cracking by creating a space for the clay molecules to expand or contract. Both the temper and the clay were thoroughly mixed. Then water was added and left to soak for days.

To prevent it from picking up dirt, soil or debris, she placed it on a hide or mat. Then she continually rolled and kneaded the clay with her hands, adding either water when too thick or powder when too watery till she felt the right clay was formed.

After the clay was kneaded, Aluel built the base of the pot and placed it on a grass ring covered with soft clothes specifically designed for this purpose. She cut pieces of the clay and made long pieces which looked like sausages with her hands. When the base was built, she added the long pieces or sausages layer after layer. A clamp spoon was used to smooth the sides of the pot. To prevent the pot from collapsing, the pot was left to dry after a few layers were added. The process continued after this.

When thoroughly built, its back was decorated with patterns which helped when handling the pot. She used a wide variety of decorating tools, which she made herself, including twisted cord, woven fabric, sharp sticks, clamps, and thumbnails.

The pot's mouth was smoothed and decorated with a red smear made from red clay. The pot was first dried in the shade before taken to dry in the sun. If it was raining, the pots were placed in a dry hut or room near a fire to dry completely. Pots dried this way took a long time to try. Luckily for Aluel, there was always sunshine in our area. When thoroughly dried, the pots were ready to be burned.

Before firing, the surfaces of the pots were modified by various types of impressed ornamentation achieved by grooving, incising, and comb stamping. Cooking pots required the least decoration because the soot of the cooking fire quickly turned them black. Water carrying pots were mostly decorated because they were always seen on the way to the well and back.

Aluel began this process by placing a thick layer of burning materials on the ground on which the dried pot was laid out; sometimes when she was burning more pots, she would arrange them one on top of the other, with each layer separated by a layer of burning material. The burning material suitable for this job was usually palm tree branches. This was because they completely burned to ashes without even leaving ambers or charcoal behind. Palm tree branches were also light, so they could not break the pot when they were placed on top. Additionally, palm tree branches were plentiful and easy to get.

The whole heap was burned late in the afternoon, just before the sun went down. This was so the burning materials and the pots were completely dry. Also, the weather was calm without wind to disrupt the burning process. When the heap was completely burned, the pots were left to cool. The broken and defected were separated from the good ones; the good pots were taken to the market and the defected ones were reused as a temper in the next process.

In addition to different sizes, shapes, and functions, the pottery colors varied and included black, orange, pale brown, gray, and red. Sometimes, one pot had a combination of more than one color.

Gourds

In addition to clay, gourds are turned into a wide range of utensils. Liquid containers, dry goods containers, and serving bowls, cups, scoops, strainers, and many other utensils were (and still are) made from gourds. Traditionally, the Agaar people have used gourd utensils for generations. They are cheap and convenient. This is because you grow them in your own fields.

As they are tropical plants, gourds are seasonal and grown once a year, like any other crops. When the first rain falls in March or April, you plant the seeds, along with pumpkin seeds, and let them grow. You dig several holes, put two or three seeds in one, and cover it with the soil you just dug out. You leave them to grow. It takes up to six months to grow and harvest the gourds. While growing, the gourd will change colors from pale green to yellow and finally to brown.

When dry, the gourds are selected based on function. Then the fine flaky skin of the shell is scraped off with a clamp spoon. Sometimes, it is just dampened with water and it will peel right off. To make a bowl, the gourd is cut open with a hot knife; one gourd can make two bowls or scoops. The seeds and pulp are removed; the pulp is put in the field as fertilizer, and the seeds are stored for next season.

The remarkable number of shapes and sizes in which it grows has made it suitable for a variety of purposes ranging from the obvious to the ingenious. Simply opened and cleaned, the gourds are used for storage or for serving food or drink. Gourds are also used as ritual regalia. They are light, durable, portable, tractable, and watertight.

Lifestyle

Family Structure

The family is the foundation unit that plays a central role in the lives of the Agaar. As a collectivistic society, every individual in the family works for the interests of this institution. People avoid things that will tarnish the name or reputation of their family and do something that will alleviate or honor it. In other words, an individual's priority is the family, and decisions affecting one's personal life, such as education and marriage, are generally made in the consultation of one's family. A young person sent to school by his family must work hard to make his family proud. After he finishes school, he finds a job to support his family. When he grows, he marries a good wife, with the approval from his family. This wife will then bring more children into the family.

However, the Agaar people have a unique way of defining what constitutes the family. This definition bears little or no resemblance to the Western idea. The term *ruai*, which loosely means relationship or kinship, is the web of relationships woven by family and marriage. You can trace your kinship through your father, parents, grandparents and great grandparent. When you are marriage, the relationship extends to your spouse's parents, grandparents and the entire clan or even tribe. Therefore, the *ruai* is formed in two ways: birth (*dhiëth*) or marriage (*thiëk*).

Every young person has two genealogical connections of his family: maternal and paternal. Remember, the young person can recite names up to 20 generations back on each side to form his identity. When the young person gets married, his wife's maternal and paternal relatives also become his relatives, making a total of four genealogical connections. So, marriage is not considered as a relationship or union between two people (husband and wife), but a relationship between two families, two clans, two tribes, or even two ethnic groups. An Agaar who married from Rek or Bor will consider the entire tribe as his in-laws.

The interweaving of the genealogical (*dhiëth*) and affinity (*thiëk*) relationships live in a separate homestead, called *anïn* ("dwelling"). Each *anïn* or residence consists of both nuclear and extended families, including parents, grandparents, children, aunts, uncles, cousins, nieces, and in-laws. Traditionally, aunts and uncles are considered mothers or fathers in the absence of biological parents, and cousins and nieces are siblings. "Your aunt smells like you mother" and "your maternal uncle is your master alone" are phrases that reaffirm the importance of one's maternal relatives in the family.

This large multi-generational family acts as an economic unit. For example, a homestead may have four huts, acres of farmlands, cattle, and individuals from both genealogical and affinity relationships performing different tasks. The wisdom and expertise of grant parents are valued and appreciated in the family. The workforce that the cousins and nieces provide goes to the welfare of the homestead.

When polygamy occurs, the family unit is based on mothers. Each wife has her own house or homestead and property that are generally transferred to her children. The mother and children form the basis of family and kinship in such communities. Because polygamy is practiced, each man may have several wives, each with her separate homestead surrounded by farmlands. Large families are highly valued, due to subsistence strategies, such as farming and cattle-rearing, which demand many hands.

These families living in different homesteads form a village. In this extended-family system, society lives collectively or communally. The neighborhood, called *akeu-nhom*, dictates that a relative, neighbor, or a total stranger can ask for something that is needed and must be given willingly, without expectation of repayment. Families, relatives, friends, and neighbors act as an important social safety net in need. You help others and hope to get help in return when needed.

The *ruai* family units are fundamental to the success of the family. People generally have a close relationship with their aunts, uncles, cousins, in-laws, and friends. This bond enables people to live together and help each other in times of need with the understanding the help will be reciprocated in the future. Wealthy members, therefore, are obligated to help less fortunate relatives. It is common for relatives, even distant relatives, to show up at the family home for announced stay. The host must feed and house the visitor for the duration of the visit. In rural areas, the host usually pays for the return trip home. Remember, a very close relative is not considered a visitor; he or she is part of the family.

This *ruai* system does not work well in cities and towns. In Rumbek or Juba, you can find one house with up to 20 members living there, and the owner does not even have a job. Relatives in rural areas take their children to towns and cities and expect relatives to feed, shelter, and school them. For business people, their relatives from rural areas may come and expect to take goods in the store free of charge. When they return home, they expect return fees. This has put a strain on businesses in Rumbek. Subsequently, the modern economy is altering the traditional family structure in negative ways.

Gender Role

The Agaar, like any other Jieng group, is a male-oriented society. The male figure in the house does the decision-making in the family, and inheritances are passed down father to son. Both boys and girls are valued equally to some degree, but a father must have a son to carry on the family name. So the father who has all girls will continue to have children until he has a boy. If he does not have a boy, he may marry another wife or two if he can afford it.

Traditionally, gender roles were rigidly defined. Within the family, work was divided between men and women. This allowed each sex to have their privacy and specialize in skills that were often difficult to master. Men hunted, fished, or herded cattle. Women collected water, firewood, and cook. It was a taboo to send a little girl to fetch kitchen utensils, but not the boy. Men and boys didn't directly touch or even talk about cooking stick (*pïc*) and scoop (*abïny*). There was a story of a man who indirectly helped his wife to find a cooking stick.

Once, a man came home from a journey starving. His wife started to cook so her starving husband could eat. When the water boiled, the woman brought the floor to add to the boiling water to cook the *cuin*. But the stirring device or *pïc* was missing. She looked and looked for it, but she could not find it. The husband saw the cooking stick, but it was taboo for men to talk or point at the device. If he showed his wife where the stirring device was, his friends would laugh at him. So he found a smart way to indirectly show the pïc to his wife.

"I went hunting the other day," the husband said. "Man, I saw the animal standing at the distance where that cooking stick is, so I speared the animal."

His friends knew he was indirectly helping his wife find the cooking stick, and he was laughed at. So any boy who tried to hang around in the kitchen with women was warned not to be like the man who indirectly showed the cooking stick to his wife.

But in the absence of women, men usually cook. In fishing camps, for example, men usually cook. Even in the village, men normally roast meat or groundnuts in open fire. But they can't cook using pots or saucepans.

Specific jobs, such as farming, construction, and babysitting, were shared equally. For example, cultivation, weeding, and harvesting were done by both sexes. The same thing applied to the construction of houses. Men did heavy-duty jobs, such as cutting and carrying heavy poles. Women cut the grass for roofing. Another shared job was child-care. Although a newly born baby stayed with the mother at all times to breastfeed, any member of the family, including the father, could carry the baby, especially when the mother was busy. Even with jobs that were rigidly divided between men and women, rules were sometimes bent, but not broken, to accommodate certain situations. For example, in the absence of women, especially in the fishing camp, men usually cooked.

Since gender roles were divided, it was expected that boys followed their fathers' behavior and girls learned from their mothers. As soon as the children started to learn things, a mother often discouraged male children from the kitchen and encouraged female children to be involved. By the time the children were four or five years old, boys would attend sheep and goats, and girls would sweep, wash dishes, or collect water or firewood.

The same traditional family model, the ideology of separate gender roles, is still being practiced in cities and towns. Women primarily stay home to do chores such as cooking, cleaning, and caring for the babies. In contrast, men are mainly responsible for supporting the family financially and are considered the head of the family or families when they have two or more wives.

Recently, the South Sudan government declared that women should be 20 percent of the workforce, so a few women have jobs in education and are providing financial support for their families. But in general, tradition prevents women from promotion to higher positions in many occupations. So many women are forced to work informally as sidewalk vendors, selling farm produce. Others open their salons or restaurants or bars.

In the ideology of divided gender roles (the traditional family model), women are primarily responsible for the home, child-rearing, and the maintenance of good relationships. Men, in contrast, are mainly responsible for the financial support of the family.

Gender relations in South Sudan are complex: the roles and responsibilities of women, men, boys, and girls are delineated but can and do alter. Women and girls are responsible for farming, collecting water and firewood, cooking, cleaning, childcare, and brewing beer. Men and boys are responsible for the community and their families' decision-making, cattle, hunting, fishing, and charcoal making.

If there are financial constraints in a family, it is most likely that the boy will go to school. Girls often get married after completing high school.

Housing

Throughout history, people have built shelters that fit their surroundings. Access to tools, the availability of materials, and the type of climates are some factors that affect how people define the concept of home. In all regions—tropical, temperate, dry, polar, or cold—people build houses using readily available materials, such as wood, mud, snow, ice, grass, stone, leaves, branches, hides, or cow dung. Mother Nature provides for all, and if you are attached to her, you will have all you need in life, including a roof over your head.

But people in urban areas don't adapt to Mother Nature; they live separately from her. Instead of raw materials, urban dwellers build houses using processed materials such as concrete, steels, tiles, and marbles. But these expensive materials, in addition to the skill needed to build a house, are not accessible for all. People who can't afford them end up homeless—one consequence of living separately from Mother Nature.

Homelessness does not exist in the Agarland because individuals live a life in sync with nature. Like other African peoples, the Agaar developed their unique architectural traditions—a type of vernacular architecture passed down orally from generation to generation. Individuals build their traditional houses using locally available materials such as mud, wood, grass, vines, and ropes.

The art of building houses using raw materials is an ancient practice that has stood the test of time. The building method and architecture have evolved from their environment, the geology, topography, and climate of the region, and been influenced by the social and historical development of the Jieng people.

The Agaar traditional house, called ɣöt, uses a combination of mud, grass, wood, bamboo, vines, and ropes. It is always round in shape, with a muddy wall and a conical grass-thatched roof. Every house must have a round or oval door and two circular peepholes—no windows. The house may seem rudimentary and straightforward, but it is well built and perfectly suited to requirements.

The modern world calls houses built in this manner "primitive," but the wisdom behind the architecture is complex. Traditional Agaar builders construct roundhouses for sound reasons. First, the architecture reflects what they see in the surrounding nature, such as the earth, sun, and moon that are circular or oval. If you look at the oval shape of the door, it reminds you of an egg. The peaked roof looks precisely like anthills.

Second, the round buildings are more comfortable to build from a circular foundation with cheap, readily available raw materials like mud, grass, and wood. But the logic is not just in the architecture, it is mostly in the communalism and complementary nature of society. Because of this relaxed philosophy to shelter, the Agaar people are not enslaved by the acquisition of housing, as is often the case in the modern world, often causing homelessness. How can one be homeless when Mother Nature provides for all? That is insane!

Roundhouses are cozy and environmentally friendly because they required less material to build, unlike rectangular houses. Additionally, huts are suitable in any climate and are ideal shelters as they are warm in winter and cool in summer. This is because mud is a bad conductor of heat. During the summer, it is hotter outside cooler inside the mud house. In winter, it is colder outside and warmer inside the mud. It does not matter where the fire is lit; the heat swirls around, warming everyone in the house. In towns and cities, they build iron roofs and rectangular or square dwellings, but these houses are too hot in summer or too cold in winter.

Most importantly, there seems to be something inclusive about the round shape. At the dance grounds, Agaar dancers form a circle to clap, sing, and dance; spectators form another circle around the dancers to watch. During prayers and invocation, people don't only create a circle around the holy ground or sacrificial pegs, but walk in a circle clockwise or counterclockwise as they chant prayers. People sit around the plate or fire to eat or warm-up. In court, at meetings, and all other social gatherings, people sit in a similar round pattern. It is not, therefore, an accident that houses are also built in this manner. Circular shapes symbolize unity or communalism. Try to sit around a plate of food in a rectangle, triangle, or square; there will be people too far away from the plate. Stand in rows or lines in a social gathering, and others will be on the far side of the line. This generates advantages and disadvantages, haves and have-nots. Circular is the norm.

The roundhouses are designed to withstand natural disasters. The most common natural disasters in the Agarland are whirlwinds, which usually occur during the dry season. Whirlwind waves move naturally around, and the waves swirl about smoothly around a round building. In a rectangular structure, the waves of the whirlwind are caught at the corner, hence destroying the house. The circular wall and roof make it harder for the wind to build enough air to lift off the structure.

Traditionally, families live in two types of houses: *hön-nhial* (the sky-house) and *hön-piiny* (the ground-house). Typical homesteads usually have two or three houses, two sky-houses and one ground-house or vice versa.

The Ground House *(hön-piiny)*

As the name suggests, the ground house merges into the bare earth with a mud wall and a conical grass-thatched roof. Round, with one door and two small peepholes, it is constructed using a combination of grass, mud, bamboo, or thin poles secured with vines, ropes, hides, or sisal fibers.

Construction: The construction of the house begins by finding a location. After clearing the site, you need to draw a circle for the base of the wall. A rope of a certain length is pegged down in the center and rotated around the peg to draw a perfect circle.

The soil pit's site is identified with trials to make sure it does not have a lot of clay, sand, or silt content. When a suitable soil is identified, the top layer of the soil that is full of organic matter is removed because it is not ideal for construction. Remember, not all types of soil are suitable for contraction. Sometimes, three types of soil (sand, clay, and silt) can be combined to make a good mixture. The soil is dug to loosen it, and water is poured into the pit to soak it overnight. The moisture of the soil is critical, so remixing is done from time to time. You can cover the hole with grass or palm leaves so the water does not evaporate.

In the morning, people mix the mud with their feet. They add water, soil, and dry grass and continue mixing the mud—the thicker, the better. The dry grass helps hold the mud when it is dried. When thoroughly mixed, the moist mud is kneaded by hands into balls to make the base of a wall and allowed to dry; wet mud cannot bear its weight and would slump. Each course or layer is leveled correctly out on the top of another. An experienced architect takes care of this process. Each layer is built, set to dry, and then the next layer is built on top. More mud is added and allowed to dry to form successive layers until the wall is complete. Openings for windows and peepholes are noted and left during construction. Sometimes, the door is carved out after the wall is completed.

While the wall is being constructed, the roof is built separately. Typically, the roof is made on the ground and lifted onto the roof. Remember, the building and mending of houses takes place in the summer only, usually between January and March during the driest months of the year. The gathering of roof materials such as grass, poles, vines, and ropes starts in November or December after harvest. Once the building materials are gathered, they are left to dry.

The most important material is grass; not any grass, but the tall elephant grass of the savannah. The grass must be properly harvested and free of any loose materials. Poorly made and uncombed bundles of grass at harvesting contain loose materials and seed heads. The grass should also be acceptably straight. It must be thoroughly dry to ensure the nodes are tight. After the grass has been cut and loosely bundled, each bundle is shaken vigorously to dislodge all loose material. The bundles are then cleaned by passing a sickle through them, working from top to bottom. Grass bundles are around 100 mm in diameter. These bundles are tied with ropes or twines and packed in heaps to dry. No nails are needed, so vines, ropes, or hides are also gathered. During the roofing, the tying materials are soaked in water to avoid breaking when tied.

Three or four bamboo poles are tied at the ends when building a roof. Then they are stood vertically and spread on the base to form a conical shape. You must make sure the frame sits appropriately on the wall with the intended overlap. If the correct lengths of poles are not appropriately calculated, shortcuts will happen, such as dropping the height to accommodate short rafters or even redoing the whole thing. The frame must extend beyond the walls to create shade.

Many bamboo poles are added to the frame. These poles are secured by double rings (interior and exterior) made of thin poles or bamboo splits tied with ropes, vines, or hide. The rings form several layers on the skeleton roof. The outer ring will be used to secure the grass.

After the skeleton and conical roof is built, it's time to add the grass. Thatch valleys are formed by gradually orientating the thatched bundles in each layer from the standard vertical alignment direction to one that is parallel to the valley. Additional material is laid in the valley to provide extra thickness to prevent water penetration into the thatch layer and to provide a gradual sweep rather than a sharp bend. Care should be taken to ensure the full thickness of the thatch is maintained as it progresses around the arch of the lip of the roof. Loosely tied ropes will allow the layer of thatch to slide downward.

Thatching begins from the bottom of the roof, and the grass bundles are laid vertical against the parallel framework. The full thickness of the thatch should be maintained around the bend of the hip. Thatch must be correctly laid from the beginning, noting the distance from the binding to the butt ends. An incorrectly laid thatch will shorten the lifespan of the roof. The length of the thatched grass shouldn't be too short or too long. This detail should be carefully monitored throughout the thatching installation to ensure the maximum room life; longer ends can make the roof prone to wind damage. With proper maintenance at required intervals, a well-constructed thatch roof should have a long lifespan.

Once the fixings are exposed, rainwater can be channeled down through the thatch by running the stitching twine into the thatch layer and the building. Exposure of the fixings will result not only in the weathering of the twine stitching but also in the deterioration of the entire roof. Because thatch is a natural material, it will deteriorate at a given rate depending on the environmental conditions for that area.

When the roof is completed, the youths of the entire village lift the thatched roof onto the wall with care to make sure the roof does not tear. The huts are finally plastered internally and externally with silt soil. It is practical to put on only about half an inch of mud plaster at a time and, where a thick layer, each being allowed to dry for a day. The undercoats are left rough to hold the ext layer firmly in place. The last layer is finally given a smooth finish with the silt soil.

The Sky-House (*Hön-nhiaal* or *Aduël*)

The sky-house is raised over six feet above the ground on a platform supported by tree trunks. The house is designed to keep people safe from wild animals.

Construction: The building of the sky-house is exclusively a man's job. You gather long, short, and thin poles. The short poles must be thick with pronged forks to hold beams which support the platform. Sometimes, V-notches are cut at the end of the short poles to anchor the wooden frame you use to hold the roof. Pick the strongest poles because they have to support a considerable weight.

Next, you dig holes about a man's arm deep and several feet apart to receive the poles. The holes are six by five or so, depending on the intended size of the building. Poles are then placed in the holes, but not firmly backfilled; horizontal and vertical poles are first lodged at the pronged-fork poles to form a rectangular platform. When accuracy and height are achieved, the poles are firmly backfilled. Several long poles are placed to shorten the gap before short and thin poles are arranged on the platform in a horizontal, vertical, or crisscross pattern. The poles must be tied to stop mud falling through when the platform is being constructed.

While the platform is still soft, thin poles are planted in the mud in a circle and allowed to dry. When dried, mud is applied to form a wall. The remaining side of the platform will be a living area where people sit and cook at night. Then a roof is built on the ground and lifted to the rooftop. Finally, both the wall and the living area are plastered. Unlike the ground house whose doors are made from woven wood or vines, the sky-houses' doors are just grass doors called *athin*.

Traditional Courtship and Marriage

Traditionally, an Agaar man must pass on the family name to a new generation, who will carry on the lineage. The lineage connects one with the past and the future. To keep this lineage, one must get married to produce offspring. Marriage, therefore, is essential, and all men and women should get married and have children.

Having a family is the ultimate goal for Agaar traditional youths (both males and females). Children learn the idea of marrying (boys) or being married (girls), and there are even marriage games, where children pretend to have a marital life. Parents also talk openly with their children about this matter. For example, a father may say to his naughty boy, "Who will marry you a wife?" Fathers usually marry wives for their sons, so the naughty child may find it hard to marry when he grows up. Female children are also taught to live according to tradition, or else who will marry them?

Since the marriage concept is one of the ultimate goals in life, children have to build their reputation at a very young age. Young men and women should always be careful to maintain a favorable reputation by maintaining a respectful attitude with all people (family members, relatives, and strangers) and avoiding confrontation of any kind. Relatives will eventually contribute their required bride-prices when a young man is getting married. But the young man must earn this by ensuring his behavior toward relatives is unquestionable; otherwise, relatives may refuse to pay their share or even attend the marriage when they are not on proper terms with the groom. The young men must be charitable not only to relatives but total strangers. Strangers are considered potential in-laws. For example, if a young man runs into a stranger, he will give the stranger the valuable fish they caught to increase his reputation.

The courtship (*thuööt*) among the Agaar begins with a young man approaches a girl he admires and asks her name. There are many places where young men and women meet. In towns, young men and women meet in the markets, parties, schools, or churches. In rural areas, they meet at cattle camps, dancing grounds, and all other social gatherings. When a young man sees a girl he admires, he approaches her and asks for an introduction. The polite way to ask a girl for an introduction is, "Could we know each other?" Others are direct and forceful, and say, "Tell me your name." But whether the man is direct or polite, it's not always easy to get the girl's name.

Usually, Agaar girls, especially mature ones looking for marriage, don't introduce themselves to men on the street. So when you meet her on the road for an introduction, she will ask you to come to her homestead if you want to know her. "I'm not a street girl to introduce myself on the road," she may say. "Come to my house." She will even give directions on how to get to her house by giving you the name of the village and the description of her homestead, say several homes, etc. She plays hard to get by hiding her feelings, even if she likes the man. Appearing too easy to get may tip off the man, and playing hard to get will enable her to get to know a serious man with good intentions, who is not just playing around.

The young man will rally his friends and brothers to visit the girl's homestead with him at the appropriate time. Late in the afternoon or evening after dinner is the best time to call on a girl. If you visit at the wrong time, the girl could send you away saying she is busy. Experienced suitors know when to visit. They even inform the girl in advance that they will come on this day, so the girl does her chores in advance. The girls also may invite her friends to keep her company during the courtship.

When the suitors reach the girl's homestead, they stand at the edge of the courtyard until they are seen and welcomed. If they are not seen, they may do several tricks to make their presence known. They may snap their fingers, jingle their spears, or loudly clear their throats. The girl then sends her little sister to recognize them. If the girl wants to invite them inside, she will first ask permission from parents. If not, the suitor is rejected (*dhet*) and told to come tomorrow. When you are rejected several times without apparent reasons, the girl does not like you, and you should stop paying her a visit.

The courtship usually begins with an introduction; girls introduce themselves first before men, not the other way around. That is an appropriate protocol. The submission must be thorough to avoid incest. To introduce myself to a girl, for example, I would say: My name is Mayom Maker Majok. I'm from the Thiyith section and my clan is Palou people who are related to the bamboo. We are also related to *ruaal* tree. My mother is called Akur Chadak Dhiac, from the Kook section. Her clan is Pacuer, people who are related to the lion. The girl will also introduce herself in the same manner. Sharing the same clan means you are related and the courtship will discontinue. For example, if the couple is from the Pation clan, they cannot marry even if they are from different tribes.

After the introduction, the young man will declare his intention by saying, "*Yin aca lëk thuööt*," which means I have declared my courtship. The potential groom is present, but he talks less in this process and his friends do all the talking. Again, the girl will hide her feelings, and she may not say yes or no. Instead, she will say, "I need some time to think about this matter." There are two reasons why she delays. First, she wants to play hard to get. Accepting the courtship right away may give the guy the wrong impression that she is a woman who says yes to every man. No one wants to marry such a woman. Second, she wants to know how serious the guy is. Third, she wants to know if the suitor is eligible to marry. Brothers marry according to seniority. Meaning when there are five brothers, the oldest brother gets married first. After a couple of years, when enough cows are generated, the next brother in line will get a wife and son on. You can never jump the queue. If you are the youngest, you must wait your turn. And so the girl wants to know the status of the man before she accepts or rejects the courtship. If the suitor is the firstborn or the next in line to get married, she will accept the courtship if she likes the man. The phrase girls use is "*thuööt aca gam* (I've accepted the courtship)."

After the man has been accepted, he may want to approach female relatives, especially the mother of the girl, to introduce himself and show he is serious. The father or uncle of the man will later approach the father of the girl when things progress. In the meantime, the man will continue visiting the girl's home to court her. He may even come to spend the night at the girl's home. The act of spending the night at girl's house is called *köör/göör nïn*. The couple will talk all night, but there must be no physical connection or sexual activity. Again, if the man tries sexual advances, the girl must decline. If the girl gives out sex that easily, the man may think she sleeps with everyone, because girls can have multiple suitors at a time, and the man will not marry such an easy-to-get girl.

When things get serious, the two families will secretly investigate each other. The boy's family wants to know if the girl has good bones or gene; she is discrete, responsible and a hard worker. When the girl has these traits, then the investigation extends to the parents and the entire clan. Is the father a drunkard? Has the mother of the girl been accused of unfaithfulness or did she divorce? Has the family or clan been suspected of witchcraft? These are red flags that may end the courtship. On the other hand, the girl and her family look for the same traits. And they also want to know if the man has good manners, is brave, hard-working, charitable, and responsible. If he is not, the courtship will end.

The active involvement of relatives and friends of both the male and female in the courtship is to weed out unsuitable couples. The final verdict comes when the young man's father declares it is time for his son to get married. Since the girl has been in courtship for quite some time now, she welcomes the declaration of serious intention of marriage—provided her relatives have no serious objections. Even so, the marriage will not be finalized until the man's family provides enough cows for the hand of the woman.

The Brideprice

The common factor in all marriages is the payment of the bride-price by the groom's family to the bride's family. As mentioned earlier, without cows, or at least the promise to pay cows, the marriage is not legally binding. Even Agaar couple who live in Western countries such as Canada, the USA, Australia or the UK and wish to get married, must pay in money, and the rest are paid back home by the relatives of the groom to the relatives of the bride. If they have no close relatives back home, documents are signed with the promise to pay the cattle when they return to Rumbek. Bride-price payment, usually in cattle, is the crucial component of any marriage.

The average endowment is now around 75 cows. Taken into account are the beauty of the girl, her characteristics and her family background. For example, a tall girl with white teeth and dark gums who is a hard worker and hails from the right family can be very expensive. Usually, only rich men will compete for this type of girl. In 2018, a six foot tall 17-year-old girl named Nyalong Ngong Deng from Eastern Lakes State attracted wealthy suitors, mostly businessmen and politicians. The highest bidder was a wealthy businessman who paid the girl's relatives 500 cows, three luxury cars, and $10,000 as dowry to become Nyalong's husband.

In most cases, it is not possible to pay the expected price. You can pay half, three-quarters or less, and then you owe the rest, which will be paid slowly while living with your wife. If the groom does not keep his promise of paying the amount, the relatives may retrieve their daughter, especially if the groom didn't pay enough installments in the first place.

To outsiders, the payment of bride-price is considered as buying the girl. But to the Jieng, especially those who maintain traditional values, the amount of the endowment is far more complicated than that. To begin with, the bride-price is considered a sign of respect and gratitude the groom shows toward the bride's family—a thank you gesture for rearing this woman they are now giving to him as a wife. After all, no one wants to lose their child. So, the bride-price is something the parents and relatives of the bride can hold on to, to remember their daughter by. Bride-price, in a sense, is considered as "wiping away the tears" after losing their daughter.

The cattle paid as brideprice are usually divided by the bride's maternal and paternal relatives, respectively. Often, the paternal relatives of the bride take a more significant share. However, if the father of the bride did not pay a full bride-price when he married the mother of the girl who is now getting married, the maternal relatives may take all the cows, or at least the exact number. After the maternal and paternal relatives have taken their share, the rest of the cows will be given to the brother of the girl (bride), who will use the cattle to marry his wife with them.

For the groom, successfully paying the brideprice to get his wife is the highest achievement of his life. It means he will have children who will carry his name to the next generation, connecting the past and the future. Marriage is not an easy task, especially if you are not from a wealthy family. Even though relatives contribute to the brideprice, the groom must come up with his cows, and then relatives may add. This is known as "wash your front first, and then I will help you by washing your back." If you are a lazy bum who doesn't work hard, you won't get married until you die. If your father doesn't have cows and you don't have a sister to bring in a brideprice, your only option is to grow crops and fish and sell them to generate enough money to buy cows. When you have your cows, even if they are just ten, it means you have already washed your front, so your relatives will contribute or wash your back.

The relatives' contribution seems free, but it's not; it must be earned. When he is young, the potential groom must treat every person he meets with respect and courtesy. When sent to do something by a relative, the boy must skip to get it enthusiastically. Later on, when he grows up, an elder has the right to refuse to contribute his bride-price to a young person whom he perceives to be disrespectful. So, it is not uncommon for a child who is misbehaving to be warned by parents or relatives, "How will you marry?" implying that he can't get a wife without their contributions.

Additionally, the courtesy and respect mentioned above are also expanded to any adult, including those who are not related to you. This is because he does not know who will be his in-laws, so he treats everyone as his potential in-law. He must be willing to share without hesitation because people rarely give their daughters to a stingy man who doesn't share. And so for the young man to have a successful marriage, it means he is an Agaar gentleman (*adhëng*), who earns respect from both his relatives and in-laws.

Furthermore, another reason the bride-price is paid in cattle is for the naming of children. Agaar names are exclusively derived from cattle. These are not just cattle, but the brideprice the groom paid to the bride's family. If you have not paid cows, your children will bear only regular names such as Deng, Sebit, Yomjima, etc. If you have paid cows, you will name your children after the cows you spent to marry the mother of the children. For example, my name is Mayom. Mayom means a white bull with a redhead which was one of the beasts my father paid as a bride-price to marry my mother.

The bride does not benefit directly from the brideprice her husband paid to marry her. However, the pride and self-worthiness of having been married legitimately with many cows is prestigious. Every woman likes it when she is admired by men because of her beauty and character and loves it when men are competing for her and she ends up with the wealthy man who pays the most cows. Additionally, a woman who has been legitimately married with many cows does not entertain nonsense from both in-laws, including her husband and her relatives. To her in-laws, including the husband, she always argues when mistreated, "You didn't just pick me up on the street, you found me in our house, so don't treat me like a street girl, because I'm not." She is highly respected by her relatives, who have directly benefited from her brideprice. So, whenever she visits her maternal or paternal relatives, she speaks with her head up and gets away with it, and she is allowed to grab anything she wants such as food or utensils, without objection. But a girl who didn't bring wealth into the family is not respected.

Recently, moderate women, especially the educated ones, have spoken up against the payment of brideprice. They said the payment of brideprice is like purchasing of a woman. Even though this claim is supported by outsiders, the traditionalists dismiss this argument as insanity. For them, it is an abomination to take someone's daughter as a wife without a brideprice. It is an insult when someone says, "You got your woman free." It implies that you are so poor you got someone's daughter free of charge. Because of these strong attitudes, the dowry payment is here to stay for awhile.

Wedding

The crucial part of the marriage is when both families engage in lengthy bargaining sessions to finalize the amount of the cattle payment. These negotiations of the bride's wealth are the most challenging part of the marriage. It is usually a prolonged discussion that may take months or even a year—each side trying to get the best deal. The bride's side wants the groom's family to pay as much as possible, while the groom's family wants to pay the least amount possible.

After the couple has been dating for a while, the marriage process begins with the groom's relatives meeting the bride's father and other male relatives. This is when the real negotiations for brideprice begin. The bride's family puts forward a proposal, which is countered by the groom's relatives. For example, if the bride's family wants 150 cows, the groom's family says they have only 100 cattle.

When there are many suitors, the bride's family may wait for other suitors to see how many cows they will offer. If the bride's family thinks they have a better deal, the next step is to go to the cattle camp to inspect the cattle offered. Age, size, color, and the overall health of the animals are considered. If some cows are inferior, the bride's family may argue that the cows should be replaced. In this part of the negotiation, the marriage is hanging on by a thread, and any wrong move could jeopardize the marriage.

Most often, the women's preference is not considered. To avoid being viewed as a bad girl, the girls always marry a husband accepted by her parents and relatives. But in some cases, if she does not like the man, she may elope with the man she loves.

After scrutinizing the cattle, the two families settle under a tree, each family on one side. In the center is the *agamlong* (repeater of the word), whose functions are to repeat every word loudly and clearly so everyone can hear. The groom's family usually provides food and beer for the occasion. The bride's family, especially the women, taunt the groom's family through songs and insults to be fed very well:

Which one is the groom?
There he is the black one with the belching tummy in the middle.
Hahaha, I'm retrieving my daughter today (if I'm not fed).

When the bride's family accepts the offer, a moment usually met with jubilation, the preparation of the wedding starts. The agreed amount of cattle, or some of it, will be delivered to the bride's family. The groom's female relatives will rush to the bride's family's house to get their wife. The celebration will continue for days as young men and women will "dance the bride into her house." The Agaar traditional wedding is complete, and the marriage is legally binding.

Polygamy

The number of wives a man can marry is determined by how wealthy he is. Wealth is measured by the herds of cattle one has or, more recently, by the amount of money one has to buy the cows. As mentioned earlier, the more cattle one has, the more wives he can marry. The main reason people marry many wives is to have many children and carry forward the name of the clan—connecting the past and the future. Because lineage is traced in the male line, a man must have a male child or children. Daughters are welcomed and valued because they bring wealth in the family, but a man who has only daughters will marry another wife or two, if he can afford it, to find a male child to carry the name of the family forward. This contributes to the polygamy.

Another factor which contributes to polygamy is a deceased wife or wives. Dying without a male child to preserve the lineage and carry it forward is unacceptable. If a man marries and dies, a close relative of the deceased will take the widow as a wife, and any children born of this union will be raised in the dead man's name. So even if you have one wife, chances are you may inherit your deceased brother's wife or marry a wife to unmarried deceased brother. The act of taking a dead man's wife is known as *lo-hot*, meaning "entering the dead man's house." If a man dies before he marries again, a relative will marry a wife in the name of the deceased. This is called *kööc ë nhom*, literally meaning "standing of the head".

There are rules to follow when performing the *lo-hot* and *kööc ë nhom*. For example, when a father dies, one of his sons, usually the oldest son, who is mature enough, will inherit all his father's wives, except his mother. The children the son has with his father's wives will be called his younger brothers, not his children. But a father cannot inherit his son's wife. If a son dies, his wife will be given to a younger brother or nephew. Also, a younger brother can inherit an elder's brother's wife, but not vice versa.

This inheriting can be very complicated to strangers. Let me try to explain it using my example: My name is Mayom Maker. But Maker was not my biological father. He was my uncle, the youngest brother of my father, who died as a child. My mother was married to Malei. After Malei and my mother gave birth to three of my two older brothers and sisters, he died. As a result, his younger brother, Mathou Majok, inherited my mother, and I was born in that union. Mathou, therefore, was my biological father, but he raised me as the child of his brother, Malei. So I became known as Mayom Malei, and so did all my brothers and sisters.

Now it gets even more complicated. Mathou, the only living child of Majok, had two wives and three wives he inherited from his deceased brothers, including my mother. Maker, the youngest brother of my father, who died as a child, needed a wife. But Mathou, the only living member, was utterly overwhelmed with five wives and their children to care of, and he had no cattle to marry a wife to Maker. Subsequently, Mathou took me from Malei and named me after Maker. From then on, I became known as Mayom Maker. That way Maker's does not vanish utterly on face of this earth. You are considered to be truly dead when you have no one to carry your name forward.

The standing of the head is not for men only; women who have no children can marry if they can afford it. An infertile woman can marry another woman as her wife. The infertile woman then finds a male relative to sleep with the wife and the children belong to the infertile woman. One of these women was Ager Gum. Ager Gum devoted her time to the liberation struggle, fighting in both wars (Anya-nya One and the SPLA). By the time she came to settle down to have children, it was too late. So Ager Gum married several wives for herself and she gave these wives to male relatives to bear children in her name. Though she died after the independence of South Sudan, Ager Gum wives and children are still in Rumbek. These sophisticated arrangements promote polygamy in the Jing society and make them the largest population in the country.

Divorce

Even though it is common in cities and towns, divorce is extremely rare in rural areas. Given that marriage creates extended kinship ties, divorce means not just the separation of a couple, but the dissolution of bonds between extended kin—a very drastic state of affairs. Apart from breaking the tie of kinship, the retrieval of the bride-wealth is also the most drastic affair of all. The groom must retrieve all his cattle from the bride's family. If the bride's family members have already used the cattle to marry their wives, they have to retrieve them, which can be impossible.

Because of this agony, both families and tribal elders will seek to deal with marital problems without resorting to divorce. If the husband and wife have problems in their marriage, the extended family and village elders will meet together to resolve the issue. When the wrongdoer is detected, say the wife is not fulfilling her wifely duties; her family will pay one or two cows to the husband of their daughter for their daughter's pain and suffering. The bride's family will advise or beg their daughter to remain in the marriage to not relinquish part of their wealth.

If separating becomes their only option, either partner may seek divorce. The most common factors that cause divorce include drunkenness, adultery, and infertility. If this is the case, the couple can go to court for a divorce. Under customary law, the brideprice must be returned to the husband and his family will finalize the divorce. The amount of the bride price to be returned depends on the number of children the woman has borne during the marriage; the more children, the lower the amount recovered. Children remain with the father or his family, as they are considered part of his lineage. If the father did not pay the brideprice, the children belong to the bride's family.

Therefore, culturally, brideprice plays a significant role in guaranteeing the correct and good behavior of both the wife and husband in the future. The wife knows that incorrect behavior can lead to the dissolution of the marriage with the obligation of returning the brideprice. Similarly, the husband must treat his wife well, knowing that if she leaves, he loses his brideprice.

Life Cycle

Pregnancy and Birth

EVEN THOUGH MANY OF AGAAR'S TRADITIONAL RITES associated with pregnancy, childbirth, milestones, and death have disappeared, pregnancy and birth are still considered the most significant events. These two events indicate the beginning of a new life; the parents are reproduced through their offspring. To society at large, birth is not just the arrival of a new member, but also the continuation of the lineage, growth of the population, and reproduction of future generations.

Pregnancy and birth are also seen as way men and women prove their masculinity and femininity. Childless couples are frowned upon. An infertile man (*buɔc*) and woman (*rol*) suffer from social and psychological problems, as they are ridiculed or insulted by peers and families. If a man cannot produce children because he is infertile, he gives his wife to his brother to produce children on his behalf—the "entering of the house" (*lɔγôt*) mentioned earlier. Infertile women and men are psychologically on the bottom of the social ladder because they are not able to fulfill their obligations: the contribution to the continued existence of humankind. For these reasons, pregnancy and birth are crucial for husbands and wives.

Even though pregnancy and birth are vital, they are acknowledged but not openly celebrated. The mortality rate is high in rural areas because of a lack of modern medicines, so new parents are always uncertain about their babies. But death, abortion, and miscarriage are attributed to the overall unhappiness of gods and ancestors who either kill the baby or don't protect it from evil or witches. Parents are discreet about pregnancy and birth, so they do not invite the anger of the gods and their ancestors, who could curse the pregnant mother and the unborn child with death, Illness, or bad luck. Parents do not want to attract witches and evil spirits capable of interfering with or even stealing the pregnancy. Therefore, pregnancy and childbirth are marked by a myriad of beliefs and practices meant to preserve both the pregnant woman and the baby.

Before the fetus develops into a baby, the woman is said to have "bloods in her body" (*anɔŋ guôp rim*). And after the baby fully develops in the womb, she is said to have "a bad body" (*arac guöp*). This is because the Agaar believe a pregnant woman oscillates between life and death. Hence, Agaar management models are put in place to protect the mother and ensure the child's safe delivery.

The family members, especially the husband, will make sure the pregnant mother is protected and well-rested. Other female members of the family will carry out heavy duties such as carrying loads or pounding the grain. But a pregnant woman is expected to continue with her regular tasks such as cooking, cleaning, and caring for other children. This renders a woman fit and healthy during pregnancy, enabling the unborn baby to grow into the right size for the mother to give birth.

For her dietary and behavioral precautions, a pregnant Agaar woman is expected to follow a rich and healthy diet for her well-being and that of the fetus. In the entire gestation period, the woman is familiarized with the appropriate diet to follow during pregnancy and the breast-feeding period. The conventional diet during pregnancy includes *cuin* served with meat, fresh vegetables. The common and seasonal green vegetables are the pumpkin, okra, tiam akuor, and other varieties of leafy green vegetables such as amok-bek, amok-ding, and amok-tiok.

In some instances, a woman delivers her first child at her parents' home, where she benefits from her mother's experience and care. But in most cases, a woman typically delivers in her husband's house, where the mother of her husband and other female relatives assist in the delivery. Men, including the father of the child, are not allowed in the delivery room. The father is encouraged to leave home when the child is born. The delivery is done by women, especially older women and traditional midwives.

For several weeks after giving birth, the woman stays inside the house with her newborn baby to avoid meeting people. Only female relatives are allowed to go in and out, and provide food. Male relatives, even the father, do not see the baby for several days or even weeks. This seclusion protects the mother and her baby from infection and disease.

After birth, a length of dry *dura* cane or grass, taken from the roof of the hut, is split in half. Its edge is razor-sharp, and with this, the umbilical cord is severed, leaving a length of about 10 cm of cord on the baby. Shea butter is used to treat the remaining umbilical cord, which falls off after a couple of days. The placenta and cord are buried.

A goat, sheep, or cow is slaughtered at this time. The skin is treated and sewn into a calfskin sling, called *kôndôk*, for carrying the baby. The meat is boiled so the new mother will have fresh soup or broth from the animal to prepare her for lactation. They want to make sure the mother is healthy and "fattening up" to breastfeed. Food and drinks are provided so that the mother and her baby don't leave the room, allowing the mother and her newborn baby to enjoy a sacred bonding moment. This postnatal care is known as *nyup ë thok* ("burning of the mouth").

Before being brought out to be seen, the baby wears beads adorned with cowry shells that protect the baby from witches and evil eyes. After a month, the newborn baby is brought out, and every family member sees it. The mother will be ready to cover the baby or take it inside when strangers and neighbors who are not trusted arrive. Approaching a newborn baby in Agaar traditions is a fascinating matter. Whether you are a relative or stranger, don't ever take an interest in the baby or use complimentary phrases such as, "This is a beautiful baby." Doing so implies you are there for ill-intentions. To compliment children, you call them "bad things," just as the pregnant mothers are said to have "a bad body" to prevent them from attracting witches and evil spirits. But the safest thing a visitor can do is not to pay too much attention to the newborn baby.

During breastfeeding, the mother refrains from sexual activities as sex is considered unhealthy for the baby. She must wean the baby before engaging in sexual activities with her husband. Not engaging sex during the breastfeeding is the only family planning in Agaar culture.

Milestones

The Agaar people have major initiation rites fundamental to their growth and development as a distinguished people. Their ancestors initially established these rites while they lived to link the individuals to the community and the community to their ancestors. These rites are critical because they guide individuals to become responsible and community-oriented in their life cycle from birth to death.

The Agaar people, especially those in rural areas, do not keep track of ages and birthdates; there are no birthday celebrations. Reaching adulthood is not associated with a certain age; rather, it is seen as a gradual process.

The growing stages of life differ between men and women. In the old days, when a girl received her first menstruation, a typical, festive party was held by women only—men were not allowed. The women performed a *Dany* dance with a song composed explicitly for this function. The girl wore a rope made from bark. The girl abstained from drinking fresh milk for a week. She might drink sour milk when an alternate was not available. The girl did not leave the house, and only women could visit her. Grandmothers and other older women in the community advised the young woman the entire time. It was women's talk, and men, including the father, were not supposed to know.

Currently, in cities and towns, parents throw a big party when their daughter receives her first menstruation. In this party, the girl is exposed to potential suitors. There is no set age for marriage in rural areas, but a girl can get married three or four years after her first period.

For men, on the other hand, there are major initiation rites they go through when starting a new phase or beginning of life. These rites are essential components of the Agaar as they help guide the individuals from one stage in life into the next stage of one's life and development, from birth to death.

The essential rites include extraction of the six lower teeth and scarification marks in the forehead. The removal of teeth distinguishes children from small boys, and the scarification separates men from boys. Some taboos come along with every initiation to guide people into responsible people in the community. After the teeth extraction initiation, the initiated refrains from eating raw groundnuts. It is believed that eating uncooked peanuts makes people "dumb." It is not that people get dumb; instead, it's because you have reached a new phase in life and are looking forward, not backward, to the next phase. So reaching the next stage in life and still doing things you are not suppose to do, like eating raw groundnut, makes you stupid.

Similarly, the bearer of the scarification marks must be a positive example to the community; he should not be a thief, drunkard, or evil person. Such traits prevent someone from being a respected elder in the society. He must be an elder—a reservoir of knowledge and wisdom. Without wisdom, culture, and righteousness, you are just an older person, not a respected elder.

The rite of eldership is another major initiation rite. It is a crucial component of the initiation system because it is the elders who represent the tradition and wisdom of the past. In Agaar culture, there is a fundamental distinction that has to be made between an old person and an elder. An elder is someone who has mastered all the components of *cieng*—the accumulated lessons from ancestors— and teaches them to the next generations. An old person is someone who grows up without mastering Agaar way of life.

In the old days, stages of development were marked accordingly. Ages zero to five were babies. From babies, they became boys. Boys were grouped into three categories. Those aged between five and 10 years were called the Red Ants (*Anyiny Luat*). Those aged between 10 and 15 were the Black Ants (*Anyiny Col*). And ages 15 and above were known as the *Amujung* (the biggest black ants).

From *Amujung*, they received scarification marks to become full warriors (*apäräpuôôl*). These warriors were known as the Wasps (*Apiin Manyiël*).There were two types of *Manyiels*: the Small Wasps (*Manyiel-thii*), who were recently initiated young warriors aged below 20. The Big Wasps (*Manyiël-dït*) were aged 20 and above—full warriors who protected their communities and were ready to die if needed. After the Big Wasps was the middle age group called *Arolkou* (ages between 40 and 50), and ages 50 and above were considered elderly persons (*rôrdït*).

To transition from childhood to adulthood, there was a ritual that one must go through. The first stage was the extraction of the six lower teeth. Like any other Jieng peoples, the Agaar must remove their lower teeth. To them, a grownup with lower teeth looks extremely ugly. Some people even remove an additional two upper canines to give the other teeth remove to grow with spaces between them. The Agaar people like it when their teeth have spaces between them. The extraction of the teeth usually occurs at age 10 when teeth have not grown fully yet. Both boys and girl go through this initiation. And the initiated can no longer eat uncooked groundnut. That is the most important taboo which distinguishes the Agaar from the rest of the Jieng: Agaar grownups do not eat raw groundnut.

To transition from boyhood to manhood, you must go through scarification. Scarification is a sign of strength, courage, and bravery. This procedure is understandably painful and takes a long time to heal, so going through it without howling is a brave thing, and crying embarrasses yourself and your family.

For Jieng tribal groups, girls receive scars at puberty to demonstrate that they are mature and ready to be married, and that they are strong and courageous, and most importantly, members of the Jieng people. The scars are seen as beautiful to touch and to look at.

Every Agaar looks forward to the day he will be initiated to adulthood. The initiation usually takes places once a year, between September and December, when food is plentiful. At this time of the year, adolescents would be initiated to manhood and become *apäräpuööl*, when six scarification marks were cut bone deep into their forehead to mark them as permanent members of the Agaar people.

Before the initiation season arrives, each boy asks permission for his parents. And when he is too young, the parents usually tell the boy to wait for a year or two. Sometimes, a boy will escape home and go for initiation when his parents disapprove. No boy wants to remain a boy when his age-mates are initiated to become *apäräpuööl*. If you are not initiated, you can no longer socialize with the initiated individuals even if they are your age-mates or friends, because they are *apäräpuööl* and you are just a boy.

The night before the initiation, village boys get together in the house near where the village initiator (*amëgɔ̈ɔ̈r*) lived. Their heads have been shaved by their mothers. First thing in the morning, they will go to the field where one each will dig a hole where his blood will flow into. Parents, relatives, and onlookers gather to watch. The boys sit in one line, each looking straight and fierce to show bravery. You can't even blink to show you are scared. The shame will be too great for your relatives and the entire clan. Your father or uncle has the right to spear you to death when you scream during the initiation.

Soon, the initiator will come and inspect the boys. Sometime, he throws the knife right in front of the boys and goes to fetch fire for his tobacco. He does this to intimidate those who are not ready to return home. When the time is right, the initiator grabs the knife with his right hand and holds the boy's head with the left hand as he cuts six scars one by one from ear to ear. The boy looks straight and fierce, staring into distance; not blinking, or sighing, and certainly not screaming. Some will shout out their boasting phrases as the marks are cut, to show bravery. The boy's father or uncle will also shout boasting called *many* or *nyöl*, which the others, including the initiated, will recite. "*Lou maguäät,*" a totem name of the Palou clan (people of the bamboo); "*Wën anyuɔn,*" son of the grass" for a clan whose emblem is the grass. These are the phrase the boys recite during the scarification. The boy's female relatives, including the mother, will thrill and utter their boasting phrases.

When done, the initiator moves on to another boy until all the boys have received their scarification marks. Every boy digs a hole where the blood will flow into. When the bleeding stops, each boy closes the hole with soil; the boyhood has been buried. After the initiation, each boy ties a broad *raap* leaf on their head to cover the scar wounds from flies. After a couple of days, the *raap* leaf is replaced with a *taar (sisal)* leaf. The sap from the *sisal* leaf helps prevent the wound from tetanus and impedes the healing process. When the wounds have healed, the *sisal* leaf is removed to reveal the six parallel scars running from ear to ear. This shows he has just become an Agaar warrior. He stops doing boys' activities or chores, including milking cows; hence *apälräk* or *apäräpuöl* (one who has stopped milking).

From the warrior, he becomes a middle-aged man before turning into an elder. It's crucial to note that there is a different between an old person and an elder. Being an elder meant having gone through all stages of life and accumulated all the vital components of *cieng*. Having not mastered *cieng* and its components implied that you were just an older person. The elders were highly regarded as a living model that the entire society emulated. Innocent infants and wise elderly persons, therefore, were the highest respected because they were the closest groups to the spiritual world. The child was a gift from Nhialic God and the ancestors, and the elder would soon die to join the ancestors and Nhialic God to complete the life cycle.

Death

Death is the final passage in a long chain of transition from the world of the living to the world of the dead. After death, a deceased person lives in a spirit world as an ancestor and as God's agent with the capacity to move about as an ancestor.

In the Agaar traditions, deaths are usually attributed to spiritual elements (witchcraft, and offending one's ancestors or the gods) regardless of the real cause of death. In 2017, my nephew, who was a soldier, was killed by armed Gelwong youth. My 90-year-old mother believed that her daughter, the deceased mother, wanted her son.

"I have nothing to say," she cried, "if my daughter, Yar, has taken her own son away from me."

The implication was that Yar, who was now God's agent could protect her son from any harm, but she let him die because she wanted him to join her in the spiritual world.

In many Jieng societies, especially in towns and cities, after the body is buried, the family has two elaborate funerals. The first one is called "picking of the sheets". Mats, sheets, and blankets are spread on the floor, so mourners can sit on them. At the end of the funeral, people pray and eat before they disperse, leaving the relatives to pick up their sheets and put them away. The second and more elaborate funeral is done forty days after the first burial. This culture is borrowed from the Arabs.

In urban areas, people are buried in cemeteries. But in traditional villages, families bury their loved ones in the courtyard near the family houses. Since the dead person is becoming an ancestor and agent of God after death, he or she is given a proper burial after death; an improper burial or anyone buried too far away from the family may turn into a wandering ghost who could cause harm to those who are still alive.

The bereaved family members and relatives of a deceased person perform particular rites and rituals that are respected and reinforced prescriptions of culture. A woman who has lost her husband will wear dark clothes and a string, called *acuöth* (**plural,** *acuth*), a rope made from the bark of a tree.

As time progresses, the deceased person will become an ancestor who is also the messenger of God. The living people send their requests to the deceased who takes them to God. In this way, the deceased is still part of the family, even though he or she is in the spiritual world.

Lightning Source UK Ltd.
Milton Keynes UK
UKHW010633260722
406393UK00001B/61